TOWARD THE FUTURE

Studies in
Judaism and Christianity

Exploration of Issues in the
Contemporary Dialogue between
Christians and Jews

Editors
Michael McGarry, CSP
Mark-David Janus, CSP
Yehezkel Landau, D.Min.
Peter Pettit, Ph.D.
Elena Procario-Foley, Ph.D.
Rabbi Stephen Wylen
Rena Potok

A STIMULUS BOOK

Toward the Future

*Essays on Catholic-Jewish Relations in
Memory of Rabbi León Klenicki*

**Edited by Celia M. Deutsch,
Eugene J. Fisher, and James Rudin**

A STIMULUS BOOK
PAULIST PRESS ♦ NEW YORK ♦ MAHWAH, NJ

Photo of León Klenicki, p. viii, courtesy of his family
The Scripture quotations contained herein are from the New Revised Standard Version:
Catholic Edition, Copyright © 1989 and 1993, by the Division of Christian Education of
the National Council of the Churches of Christ in the United States of America. Used by
permission. All rights reserved.

Cover image by gregor/Shutterstock.com
Cover design by Sharyn Banks
Book design by Lynn Else

Library of Congress Cataloging-in-Publication Data

Toward the future : essays on Catholic-Jewish relations in memory of Rabbi León
Klenicki / edited by Celia M. Deutsch, NDS, Eugene J. Fisher, and James Rudin.
    pages cm. — (A Stimulus book)
    Includes bibliographical references and index.
    ISBN 978-0-8091-4841-7 (alk. paper) — ISBN 978-1-58768-292-6
    1. Judaism—Relations—Catholic Church. 2. Catholic Church—Relations—Judaism.
I. Klenicki, León. II. Deutsch, Celia, editor of compilation. III. Fisher, Eugene J., editor
of compilation. IV. Rudin, A. James (Arnold James), 1934– editor of compilation.
    BM535.T595 2013
    261.2`6—dc23

                                                                              2013022733

ISBN 978-0-8091-4841-7 (paperback)
ISBN 978-1-58768-292-6 (e-book)

Published by Paulist Press
997 Macarthur Boulevard
Mahwah, New Jersey 07430

www.paulistpress.com

Printed and bound in the
United States of America

Contents

IV. Theology

V. Spirituality: Liturgy

VI. Spirituality: Spiritual Practice and Mysticism

VII. New Frontiers

VIII. Conclusions

Contents

In honor of León Klenicki (1930–2009), of blessed memory

Beloved husband and father,
rabbi, friend, and companion in dialogue,
in gratitude for a life that continues to inspire us
with courage, light, and grace.

Acknowledgments

Toward the Future is the result of friendship and dialogue between León Klenicki and the editors of this book. Our journey together has also been the consequence of decades of conversation representing the transformation of relations between two peoples, Jews and Christians. This is evident in the articles, both the texts and the reference notes. It is also the result of particular conversations, between León Klenicki and participants in this project, between ourselves and our communities, and between the editors and authors in the process of creating *Toward the Future*.

We, the editors, have been privileged to collaborate in this process. Many have helped us in what has been, and continues to be, an intellectual and spiritual journey. We are especially grateful to Myra Cohn Klenicki and León's children Ruth Finkelstein and Daniel Klenicki, and his grandson Ely Finkelstein for their unwavering support and generosity. Our families have born with our distraction and preoccupation. We especially thank Catherine and Sarah Fisher (for whom Rabbi Klenicki was simply "Tío León"); Marcia; Rabbi Eve Rudin and Jennifer Rudin; Paula, Jeffrey, Hank Deutsch, and Lynn Davis-Deutsch; Joan Wilson; and Peter Stone. Celia expresses deep gratitude to the Sisters of Our Lady of Sion, her religious community.

Our professional communities are a constant source of challenge and support. We express our appreciation to the American Jewish Committee; the Anti-Defamation League; the Center for Catholic-Jewish Studies at Saint Leo University, Florida; the Council of Centers for Jewish-Christian Relations; Barnard College/Columbia University (New York City); and colleagues in the Catholic Biblical Association, Catholic Historical Association, Society of Biblical Literature, and the American Academy of Religion.

Many conversation partners have challenged us to new awareness of the ways in which Catholic-Jewish relations is being transformed, both through the maturing of the dialogue(s) and by global population shifts. We are grateful to our students and to audience members, to parish and synagogue congregants, and all those others who raise interesting and sometimes difficult questions, impelling us to continue reflecting in new ways on what it means to be Catholics and Jews journeying *Toward the Future*.

We wish to express our gratitude to those individuals, institutions, and other groups who have made it possible to bring this work to completion: Ely Finkelstein; Abraham Foxman, National Director, Anti-Defamation League; Eric Greenberg, Director, Department of Interfaith Affairs, Anti-Defamation League; Burton L. Visotzky, Director of the Milstein Center for Interreligious Dialogue, The Jewish Theological Seminary of America (New York City); Ruth Langer, Chairperson of the Board of Directors, Council of Centers for Jewish-Christian Relations and associate director of the Center for Christian-Jewish Learning at Boston College (Chestnut Hill, MA); Philip A. Cunningham, Director of the Institute for Jewish-Catholic Relations at Saint Joseph's University (Philadelphia); and the Sisters of Our Lady of Sion. Finally, we thank Donna Crilly and Diane Flynn at Paulist Press, who guided us so diligently in the process of editing *Toward the Future*.

Introduction

Rabbi León Klenicki (1930–2009) died on January 25, 2009, after a long and courageous struggle with multiple myeloma. He had spent most of his professional life working in the field of Jewish-Christian relations, particularly Jewish-Catholic relations, most of that time as Director of Interfaith Affairs for the Anti-Defamation League.

León Klenicki, then, was a professional in the area of interfaith dialogue. But for him, dialogue was far more than a profession. In his words, it was a vocation. In 2005, toward the end of his life, Klenicki reflected:

> Dialogue is the acceptance of the other as the other, the other in God, a particular being. Dialogue is a meeting with another person with its [sic] own rights and its [sic] own commitments....It is a process of the heart: from disdain to recognition, from alienation to creative proximity, an evolution from confrontation to a challenging relationship of equals. This is in essence the mystery and summons to the Christian-Jewish encounter of faith. It is a reality that requires a theological dimension....The dialogue encounter involves a meeting of persons of flesh and blood, but also continents of faith, the presence of God in different religious covenantal vocations. This experience of recognizing the other as a person of God, entails a consideration, the theological consideration of religious matters, because God is our common ground and sense. This is essentially the nature and the end of a theological discussion in the dialogue relationship: sharing the sacredness of God's presence, the tradition of all respective faith commitments, and the consideration of the past, a reckoning of the soul, and a discussion of present questions facing both faith commitments.[1]

León Klenicki had a working vocabulary that he used to articulate his understanding of his vocation, and the relationship between Christians and Jews as persons of God: vocation, encounter, dialogue, the other, covenant. The words *theology* and *spirituality* occurred repeatedly. Klenicki lived his vocation, on the one hand, in the long shadow of the Shoah, which he characterized as exile. He also lived and worked in the hope yielded by the rebirth of the state of Israel and his experience of the radical transformation of Jewish-Christian relations on the other hand.

León Klenicki's intellectual and spiritual life was shaped by biblical and classical Jewish sources, but there were other influences, as well: Martin Buber and Franz Rosenzweig, Hans Jonas, Elijah Benamozeg, Joseph Soloveitchik, and Emmanuel Levinas. The list included Jacques Maritain, a Roman Catholic philosopher. His B.A. thesis was on the Spanish Roman Catholic mystic, John of the Cross, and his M.A. thesis was on the *Biblia de Alba*; both works reflected the commitment to Christian-Jewish relations that first came to life in Klenicki's reading of Maritain during his secondary school days in Argentina. From his early years as a student, then, León Klenicki was involved in a theological reflection on Christian-Jewish relations and engaged with Christians as interlocutors and friends, as well as—on occasion—hostile "others."

While Klenicki was involved in dialogue with Christians from many traditions, perhaps he was most preoccupied with his relationship with Roman Catholics. In part, he felt a certain kinship with Roman Catholicism; it was the form of Christianity that dominated the society of his early years in Argentina. The position of Catholicism in Argentina, with its complicated relationship of civil government and institutional Church, marked León's early experience with a profound ambivalence. Nonetheless, it was Catholicism that was also the faith of so many of his friends and of the occasionally inspired teacher, as well as the authors of books he continued to cite throughout his long life. It is also true that the massive size of the institution itself, and the public nature of both the positive developments and crises that have occurred periodically since Vatican II, resulted in a perhaps disproportionate claim on León's attention.

Much of León's professional life in dialogue coincided with the papacy of John Paul II (1978–2005). John Paul's tenure was marked, to be sure, by tensions and controversies, such as those concerning his receiving Kurt Waldheim in 1987, the canonization of Edith Stein in 1998, and the ongoing debate about the role of Pope Pius XII during World War II and lack of full access to the complete documentation in the Vatican Archives for his papacy. But John Paul's long tenure was even more noteworthy for his close ties to the Jewish community and for the ways in which he developed the teaching, first presented in *Nostra Aetate*, on the relationship of the Church and the Jewish People. León's last book, co-edited with Eugene Fisher, is the definitive collection of John Paul's documents on Catholic-Jewish relations. His introduction to the volume represented his final publication.[2]

Toward the end of his life, León Klenicki grew increasingly concerned that frequent crises in the institutional relationships between the Roman Catholic Church and the Jewish community had left Catholics and Jews preoccupied with the problems, such as those exemplified by the controversy over the Good Friday prayer for the Jews.[3] Klenicki had addressed the question of the future of Catholic-Jewish relations as early as 2003, when he contributed an article to the journal *Théologiques*. The issue was titled "Juifs et chrétiens; le dialogue théologique a-t-il un avenir?" ("Jews and Christians: Does the Theological Dialogue Have a Future?"). Klenicki's response was a resounding "yes," and he summarized some of the questions explored and laid out issues that he believed needed further attention.[4]

But for all his hope, León Klenicki remained concerned about the future of Christian-Jewish relations, especially the dialogue between Jews and Roman Catholics. He feared that scholars and institutional leaders alike, might be distracted by frequent crises in institutional relations, from common exploration of the great questions about history, theology, and spirituality, and from sharing with one another the experience of the God of Israel, whom he called "our common ground and sense." While recognizing fully the dominating significance of the Shoah—much of his extended family had died in the camps—and the rebirth of the state of Israel in contemporary Jewish history, Klenicki also feared that preoccupation with those realities might foreshorten the theological reflection he felt essential to the dialogue. A few months before his death, León Klenicki asked that friends and colleagues might produce a festschrift in honor of his eightieth birthday. At his request, it was not to focus on his work, but rather on the future of Catholic-Jewish relations. Moreover, it was to focus on questions of theology and spirituality.

We have tried to honor León's request. The outline of the book reflects some of the issues of theology and spirituality involved in Christian-Jewish relations in a post-Shoah, post–Vatican II world. The authors bring to their work a breadth of ethnic, linguistic, and cultural perspectives that seems particularly fitting in a volume honoring a man from an eastern European family who was himself a Latino immigrant to the United States. The international perspective of these articles means that Mexico, Central and South America, the Caribbean, and Asia are present in focus or as backdrop for our consideration of questions of Jewish-Catholic relations. This outlook reflects ways in which the center of the Christian world has shifted, and continues to shift from North America and Europe to Asia, Africa, and Latin America. Our authors' perspectives also reflect ways in which the reality of immigration has already brought the global south to the global north, and the east to the west. The work of Catholic-Jewish relations in this new context thus occurs at the convergence of the global north and west, home to most of the world's Jews, and the global south and east where most Catholics live.

The articles gathered in this volume focus on questions of theology and spirituality. However, our authors frequently remind us implicitly as well as explicitly that these questions have broader contexts. This is not surprising. The 1991 document "Dialogue and Proclamation" speaks of four forms of dialogue:

a) The dialogue of life, where people strive to live in an open and neighborly spirit, sharing their joys and sorrows, their human problems and preoccupations.

b) The dialogue of action, in which Christians and others collaborate for the integral development and liberation of people.

c) The dialogue of theological exchange, where specialists seek to deepen their understanding of their respective religious heritages, and to appreciate each other's spiritual values.

d) The dialogue of religious experience, where persons, rooted in their own religious traditions, share their spiritual riches, for instance, with regard to prayer and contemplation, faith and ways of searching for God or the Absolute.[5]

The articles in *Toward the Future* reflect ways in which these various forms and aspects of ecumenical, interfaith, and interreligious dialogue, converge and intersect, providing a matrix for conversation.

A note of friendship and personal relationship occurs throughout the volume. Many of the authors knew León Klenicki. Others did not. But all, authors and editors alike, understand Catholic-Jewish relations as relationship. Tensions are not ignored—indicated by the references to controversies, such as those surrounding the Good Friday prayer, and the document "Covenant and Mission." But the authors do not allow tension and controversy to have the final word.

As fitting a volume about relationships between two peoples, *Toward the Future* begins with statements of appreciation by people who knew and worked with León Klenicki: Jews and Christians from various institutional perspectives. The book has been divided into themes in theology and spirituality, with most sections having articles by a Jew and a Catholic. These articles do not necessarily correspond to each other, for the relationship between Catholics and Jews is asymmetrical. For example, in the section on "God," Hans Herman Henrix has written on Christology and Adam Gregerman on theodicy in light of the Shoah. Nonetheless, the authors' contributions reflect the decades of conversation between Jews and Christians, sometimes between the contributors themselves.

The first section following the "Introduction" and "Tributes" focuses on Sacred Scripture, a common ground for the conversation between Catholics and Jews. Tamara Cohn Eskenazi writes on "Biblical Resources for Interfaith Dialogue." Acknowledging differences in canon and interpretation, and the ways in which sacred texts have been employed to divide our communities, Eskenazi yet looks to the Hebrew Bible as a primary resource to deepen Jewish-Christian relations.

Eskenazi demonstrates the possibilities of biblical texts as inspiration for interfaith dialogue by examining passages that reflect the complicated ways in which Israelite and Jewish authors understood those other than themselves. She turns her attention to texts that do not treat "otherness" in exclusionary ways, but hold commitment to the God of Israel in tension with positions that do not attempt to convert or otherwise dominate the "other." Eskenazi examines Ezra-Nehemiah and Isaiah 56–66. But she also looks at Leviticus 19, where one finds commands both to "love your neighbor as yourself" (19:18) and "love the stranger as yourself" (19:34), the story of Moses and Jethro the Midianite (Exod 18), and the account of David and Ittai the Gittite (2 Sam 15:19–23).

These texts present the "other" "as a culturally, religiously 'other' who remains 'other,' and who works jointly with Israelite protagonists for a better world." Eskenazi observes that the Hebrew Bible offers resources for understanding ways to complicate the matter of boundaries, whether religious or cultural. She uses the work of the Jewish feminist theologian Rachel Adler who understands boundaries, not only as barriers, but as "loci of interaction."[6] Eskenazi turns to Levinas to help us understand the importance of maintaining the "otherness" of the "other," and resisting the urge to control, dominate, or assimilate the "other."

In their article "Dialogue in the Margins: the *Biblia de Alba* and the Future of Catholic-Jewish Understanding," Carmen M. Nanko-Fernández and Jean-Pierre Ruiz engage in a multivalent conversation with the *Biblia de Alba*, an early fifteenth-century translation from Hebrew into Castilian Spanish by Rabbi Moses Arragel of Maqueda. Their work affords the authors—and us, the readers—an opportunity to encounter Rabbi Moses; Luis de Guzmán, the Master of Calatrava who commissioned the translation; and León Klenicki, who wrote his master's thesis on that work. This new encounter takes place in the context of the twenty-first century in which religious, national, and cultural boundaries are being reconfigured in ways that evoke the boundary crossings displayed in the margins of Arragel's translation.

The commission by Luis de Guzmán, Master of Calatrava, specified that Arragel's translation include glosses explicating problematic texts. Those glosses include material, not only from Jewish commentators, but from Christian ones as well. They are actually "dialogues along the edges," in the words of Nanko-Fernández and Ruiz. Those "dialogues along the edges" reflect the conversation between Arragel and the biblical text, between Arragel and commentators (Christian as well as Jewish), and between Arragel and Guzmán. One perceives the attempt by all parties to maintain religious and intellectual integrity. This is enacted in an atmosphere of fear and tension engendered by the power dynamics prevalent in

fifteenth-century Spain. Despite the inequality of those power structures and subsequent tragedy, the *Biblia de Alba* offers hope for new
ways of relating across boundaries.

The section on Sacred Scripture is followed by two articles on
"Identity." In "Jewish Identity," Shira Lander considers the perenni-
ally fluid understandings of Jewish identity. She notes the varied def-
initions of "Israel" as used historically by Jews and Christians,
beginning with ancient sources. Lander acknowledges that some contemporary Jews claim Jewish identity without Jewish belief or practice. Nonetheless, she indicates the overwhelming evidence of a wide
variety of sources, from the rabbinic period to the modern, suggesting that the weight of evidence is in favor of at least a theological
component in the articulation of Jewish identity.

As she reflects on the "complexity and dynamism of Jewish
belief," and of the understandings of Jewish identity, Lander reiterates some of the conclusions from *Dabru Emet* concerning what it is
that Catholics and Jews share. While lauding the achievement of
mutual understanding between members of both communities,
Lander also notes the tensions that continue to arise. This is exemplified in the controversy that arose around the document "Reflections
on Covenant and Mission,"[7] and the response in 2009 by the United
States Conference of Catholic Bishops titled "A Note on Ambiguities
Contained in Covenant and Mission."[8] While the final version of the
"Note" eliminated the reference to invitation to baptism implicit or
explicit in the context of dialogue between Jews and Christians in
paragraph 7 of the earlier text, it failed to address concerns about the
bishops' teaching regarding the ongoing validity of the Mosaic
covenant between God and the Jewish people.[9]

Lander notes that this controversy in Catholic-Jewish dialogue
also reflected internal Roman Catholic tensions, signaling the intimacy
of the relationship between Catholics and Jews. She observes the dam-
age to trust engendered in the controversy, calling into question as it
did, the ongoing validity of the Mosaic covenant between God and the
Jewish people and, thus, Jewish self-identity. Lander ends with a word
on the "interpersonal dimension of this relationship" that parallels the
memories of León with which she began her article.

Elizabeth Groppe similarly frames her article "Toward the
Future as People of God and Partners in the Covenant" with a reflection on the interpersonal nature of Catholic-Jewish relations. She

opens with an account of two siblings, one a colleague's biological child and the other her Haitian adopted sister. Groppe uses both the closeness and the sibling rivalry to begin her reflection on the relationship of Church and synagogue.

Groppe turns from the often-supersessionist understandings of traditional Roman Catholic ecclesiology that reach back to the earliest centuries of Christian history, to the understanding of the Church as people of God, rediscovered in the *ressourcement* that prepared the way for the Second Vatican Council, and articulated in *Nostra Aetate* and *Lumen Gentium*. The concept of "people of God" was problematic, vulnerable to certain forms of typology. However, Groppe notes that postconciliar developments "invite us to find our Christian identity as the people of God in a true partnership with the Jewish people."

Jews and Christians alike, Groppe observes, share a "vision of all people of the earth united in right worship of God." She calls for Jews and Christians to express in "visible and social form" the solidarity that is the eschatological hope of both communities. She looks for inspiration to the "Christian theologies of humans as persons-in-communion and the relational philosophies of Jewish scholars such as Martin Buber and Emmanuel Levinas." Such communion is embodied in the concrete, in collaboration between Christians and Jews, such as that which made possible the adoption of her colleague's Haitian children.

The section on "Identity" is followed by two articles on perspectives on Christian and Jewish understandings about God. Adam Gregerman turns to the question of theodicy in his article "The Dreadful Past, the Jewish Future: Post-Shoah Reflections on David Hartman's Theologies of Suffering." As the title suggests, Gregerman engages in conversation with Hartman and his work *A Living Covenant: The Innovative Spirit in Traditional Judaism*. In the exchange, he reflects on the intractable questions about God's relationship to the people Israel in the context of the "dreadful" reality of the Shoah.

Gregerman engages in a dialogue with the biblical and rabbinic texts chosen by Hartman to illuminate the problem. While Gregerman appreciates Hartman's desire to encourage a practical Judaism, he also believes that Hartman fails to acknowledge the "nearly unbridgeable" distance "between expectations and reality in the Shoah."

Hartman's work, Gregerman notes, raises questions ranging from the nature of God's presence in Israel's history to the granting of free will to human beings. Ultimately, Gregerman acknowledges his own disappointment in God, and concomitant desire for others, in our day, to join him in "contemplating the abyss of the Shoah."

The tension remains between living an observant life and the questions about God's power and fidelity in the context of the Shoah and its aftermath. Ultimately, Gregerman turns to Gregor Maria Hoff and Terrence Tilley, Roman Catholic theologians whose work on other questions regarding Jewish-Christian relations leads them to acknowledge that there are "unavoidable limits to our speech about God." Gregerman then turns to the nature of paradox as holding possibilities for maintaining that tension.

Hans Hermann Henrix believes the most difficult theological question in Jewish-Christian relations to be the issue of the Incarnation, the Christian belief that God has become present to humankind through the Incarnation, the embodiment of the Son in the man Jesus. In his article, "God's Presence in Israel and Incarnation: Christological Reflections in Dialogue," Henrix enters into conversation with Michael Wyschogrod, who reflects as an Orthodox Jew on ways in which Judaism itself is incarnational. Henrix chooses another dialogue partner, Emmanuel Levinas, who considers Christian belief in the Incarnation to be "too much for divine poverty" and "too little for God's glory." Henrix brings these reflections to bear in a new consideration of the ancient teaching of Chalcedon. Unlike earlier articulations of that teaching, he emphasizes that the Incarnation is in relation to the particularity of Jesus as a Jew. He concludes by raising the question "whether the most profound difference in the understanding of God does not also include an element of proximity and of unity, even of something that Jews and Christians have in common."

In the next section, authors explore issues of "Spirituality," understood here as the intersection of tradition and experience, both collective and personal. The section is subdivided into articles on "Liturgy" as the public expression of that intersection, and "Spiritual Practice and Mysticism" as referring to the personal. Relationships between the two peoples, Jewish and Christian, are reflected in liturgy, or ritual, the public worship of the respective communities. Using space and objects, the cycle of festivals, and the public reading of sacred texts, our communities—as do those of other traditions—

embody myth, sacred story, and the values that define their collective identities.[10]

In ritual, communities "experience the event" enacted in the celebration and internalize the values of the liturgical moment.[11] Communities construct memory, and are constructed by them. They also engage in the practice of erasure of memory, as Ruth Langer tells us in her "Constructing Memory in Jewish Liturgy." Langer begins by focusing on the festival of Purim and the preceding Shabbat, which is called *Shabbat Zakhor* ("Remember" Sabbath), so named for the reading from Deuteronomy 25:17–19. That reading commands Israel both to "Remember what Amalek did to you" and to "blot out the remembrance of Amalek from under heaven." She notes the tension in "Jewish liturgical memory"—memory and the blotting out of memory—and the risk implicit in this aspect of Jewish ritual. Langer asserts that "in our world where Jews are no longer powerless, 'blotting out the memory' can go beyond the figurative and become simply an indiscriminate 'blotting out.'"

Langer notes that the realities of the Holocaust and the State of Israel require the Jewish community, as it engages in worship, to construct new memories, including memories that give "new presence to the 'other.'" Constructing such memories, and the liturgical expression that will enact them, will account for the "other's" repentance, and allow for new relationships.

Roman Catholic liturgy was marked by the supersessionism that characterized so much of preconciliar theology. Thus, Catholic ritual both enacted those attitudes and reinscribed them in the Church's self-understanding. Catholic ritual, however, contained the resources, for expressing and embodying a new experience of relationship between Catholics and Jews. There was, of course, the use of the Hebrew Bible, essential to Christian ritual since earliest times.[12] Another resource was found in the cycle of feasts, including the Feast of the Circumcision.

Philip Cunningham's article "Reviving the Catholic Observance of the Feast of the Circumcision of Jesus" notes the irony in the removal of this ancient festival from the Church's calendar in the years following the promulgation of *Nostra Aetate*. He writes an imaginative proposal that the feast be restored as a way to express the Church's new awareness of Jesus' Jewishness. Cunningham acknowledges the difficult questions of gender, as well as the controversial nature of circumcision in broader political discourse. Nonetheless, he invites us to consider what the celebration of this feast might say about Jesus' Jewish identity in light of traditional Christian sources, as well as recent Church teaching. He proposes lections for a restored liturgy and comments on them. Cunningham's reflections draw the reader's attention to Jesus' initiation into the life of the Covenant through the ritual, as well as the ongoing fidelity to covenantal relationship embodied in observance of Torah, by both Jesus and his family.

While "Spiritual Practice and Mysticism" refer to personal experience, they are not set apart from the collective by our authors. Arthur Green grounds his article "Toward a Theology of Empathy" in a reflection on the *Shema' Yisra'el*, the call to hear that God, Being, is One, followed immediately by the command to love God with one's whole being. It is central to Jewish belief and ritual practice, and implies that because God as Being is One, then all of being is one and that the transcendent dwells in the immanent. God's oneness and our love of God and of neighbor are thus bound inextricably.

Green suggests that empathy is at the heart of the human quest and challenge. He offers "a theology where otherness is not quite absolute. Ultimately, we are all of the One, embodiments of the same divine presence. Behind the mask of the other lies the oneness of the Maker reflected in the deed. Empathy means both embracing each of us in our diversity and seeing through to our oneness." Green acknowledges the temptation to exclusivism common to people of all traditions; that tendency acquires a particular quality among Jews in the shadow of the Holocaust. Mindful of the this, Green recalls to his readers that the heritage of Israel's prophets demands that all of us, Jew and Christian alike, work together to face the great challenges that include "the endless lure of selfish materialism, fostered by unchecked capitalism and the great injustices it engenders, and the very preservation of our planet itself...."

For Green, the encounter with Being as One implies encounter with all beings in the One. Finding the transcendent in the immanent takes people beyond their immediate circles to join with others in responding to the prophetic demand to attend to the vulnerable and to the planet that is home to all of us.

Michael Barnes addresses questions of personal religious experience in the context of community in "The Turn to the Self: Spiritu-

ality across Religious Borders." Barnes notes the quest of interiority
that has become such a prominent part of the cultural landscape in
some western countries. He also notes the fact that "religion" is often
seen in opposition to "spirituality." Rather than focusing on individual experience or spiritual practice as distinct from "religion," however, Barnes wishes to think about the great religious traditions as
"schools of faith"[13] where people can learn ever anew the wisdom that
is communal as well as personal. Schools of faith teach prayer and
meditation. They provide a space for communal study and worship,
and they provide the inspiration and structure that "leads to and motivates engagement with 'the world' at large."

Barnes turns to Heschel and Levinas for intellectual tools that
will help to reintegrate "religion" and "spirituality." He believes that
the very fact that he, as a Christian, learns from Jewish thinkers suggests the possibility of a "school of schools in which Jewish and
Christian learning and spiritual practice reinforce, challenge and
transform each other." Barnes emphasizes Levinas' resistance to con-
ceiving of God the Other as an "object" of personal experience, such
as to become a focus in an individual quest for interiority. Barnes
notes that Lévinas is "both entranced by and suspicious of the power
of language...." And he "insists on the absolute demand for justice in
the face of blind self-absorption...." Barnes notes that such "[h]olis-
tic, comprehensive visions need a broader inter-personal base than
interiorized pursuits allow." His conclusions imply that interreligious
dialogue "can open up new relationships and retrieve old ones in a
spirit of respect and understanding," and, thus, facilitate the process
of bridging the gap between religion and spirituality in relation to
broader society.

The profound transformation of the global context of Catholic-
Jewish relations since the promulgation of *Nostra Aetate* is illustrated
by developments in the United States. A Church that was, for the
most part, white and of European descent, is now increasingly com-
prised of Latinos/as and other immigrant groups from Africa, Asia,
and the Caribbean. And so, we turn to the section "New Frontiers"
and the question of Latino/a Catholic-Jewish relations, a matter of
particular significance as we honor the Latino immigrant, León,
whose love for Spanish, his mother language, was a lifelong joy.

In "Latino/a and Catholic-Jewish Relations in the United
States," Hillel Cohn comments on relationships between Jews and

Latino/a Catholics in the United States. He speaks of the difficulties inherent in situations often marked by socioeconomic and linguistic disparities, and unequal power relationships. He notes candidly that Jews and Latino/a Catholics are often not aware of each other's concerns. Preoccupation with questions of anti-Semitism and the concern for Israel's well-being, on the one hand, and racism and the problems surrounding immigration on the other, often present obstacles to fruitful engagement among these communities.

Nonetheless, Cohn is able to point to signs of hope for new ways in which Jews and Latino/a Catholics have already begun to relate to one another. He notes developments on university and college campuses, whether among scholars and professionals, or students. He reports on efforts in parishes and synagogues, on collaboration in interreligious and interfaith congregational networks for political and social action. Cohn speaks of groups coming together to share a variety of cultural experiences, and he ends with a prayer of blessing that looks ahead to the work yet to be done.

In "Latina/o and Catholic-Jewish Relations in the Americas," Jacqueline Hidalgo considers relationships between Latino/a Catholics and Jews in the Americas, and observes the complicated, often non-innocent, nature of those relationships, extending back through the colonization of the Americas to Spain itself, the land both of *convivencia* and expulsion. She remarks on a history characterized as much by power and domination as by conversation, and she notes the ways that history continues to complicate the ongoing processes of religious experience and practice and the reworking of cultural memory. Hidalgo's work moves from Spain to colonial Latin America and "the relationships between Roman Catholics and *anusim/conversos*/crypto-Jews." She then examines the reality of *mestizaje* (mixture) created in colonial Latin America. Finally, Hidalgo shifts her attention to the Latino/a reality in the United States, and the complicated ways in which those earlier narratives are reworked, sometimes unconsciously.

Hidalgo exemplifies her theoretical work through three case histories that "signal the importance of work done to retrieve and negotiate historical memory." That work will allow Catholics and Jews to "learn from each other's distinct histories while recognizing that these histories are also shared." Thus, she tells us of Manuel, whose family's engagement in crypto-Jewish practices led him to examine their history and then to integrate his identity, not only for himself but for his children. Michael's Jewish history is that of Argentine Jewish grandparents who converted to Christianity. His journey led him to convert to Judaism as his cultural and religious "home." And finally there is Daniel, who learned as an adult of the Jewish identity of his maternal grandfather. Exploration of his family's history exemplified ways in which Latino/a Catholics and immigrant Jews from Europe often shared the same neighborhoods and occasionally married.

Hidalgo offers these case histories as examples of the fraught, non-innocent history as well as ways of interacting positively that frames relations between U.S. Jews and Roman Catholics. She believes that uncovering such history will allow for deepened theological reflection and common action.

The volume's last essay, "Catholics and Jews: Looking Ahead," is co-authored by David Gordis and Peter Phan, a Jew and a Catholic. Both note the progress of recent decades that allows such collaborative projects. At the same time, they chart directions for further work. They note the ongoing challenge to move interreligious conversation beyond elite circles and into the broader communities, both Catholic and Jewish. Phan and Gordis observe the ambivalent nature of language, of words and policies, with their potential both to ennoble and to enflame. They call for a "new mode of discourse" that will reflect the transformative nature of interfaith and interreligious conversation.

Such a mode of discourse occurs in the humble mindfulness of the power of language. Understandings of chosenness, for example, have the potential to allow the speaker(s) to devalue the other all the while claiming a universalist position. Looking to the painful example of the 2009 decision concerning the bishops of the Society of St. Pius X, Phan and Gordis suggest that the discourse of dialogue, relationship, and conversation become actualized in the ways in which our communities make decisions that affect each other. New modes of discourse imply that Jews and Christians alike are not threatened by the "'otherness' of the other" and that they allow one another to join in healing a shattered world.

The Epilogue gathers the themes reflected in the book, both overt and implied. It foregrounds questions of global interreligious dialogue, population shift, and the quest for spiritual experience as matters to be integrated into new and deeper understandings between Jews and Catholics, as we celebrate the coming fiftieth anniversary of *Nostra Aetate* in 2015 and look "toward the future."

Finally, there are two bibliographies. The first is a selected bibliography of León Klenicki's work in Spanish and English. Choices have been made from a massive body of work, including scholarly articles and books, as well as edited volumes, monographs, pamphlets, and liturgical services directed at a broad congregational audience. We have tried to include some of his most significant work. Both sections, Spanish and English, are arranged chronologically beginning with his latest contribution.

The second is a selected bibliography for further reading. We have included some of the references signaled in the notes. More often, we have attempted to offer suggestions for pursuing further the questions raised by our authors, as well as by León himself. These bibliography entries are arranged according to topics and include relevant work on interreligious as well as interfaith relations. It is our hope that a broad spectrum of readers, from specialized to the more general, will find material that will help them pursue their interests.

NOTES

1. "Eccleasia [*sic*] et Synagoga; Judaism and Christian, a Reflection toward the Future," *CCAR Journal* 52 (Spring 2005): 22–23.

2. *The Saint for Shalom; How Pope John Paul II Transformed Catholic-Jewish Relations: His Complete Texts on Jews, Judaism and the State of Israel 1979–2005*, ed. and with commentary by Dr. Eugene J. Fisher and Rabbi León Klenicki; presented by the Anti-Defamation League (New York: Crossroad; a Crossroad Herder Book, 2011).

3. See http://www.catholicnews.com/data/stories/cns/0800689.htm (accessed Oct. 17, 2012).

4. León Klenicki, "*Dabru Emet*: une appréciation personnelle," *Théologiques*, 11.1–2 (2003), 171–86. See http:id.erudit.org/iderudit/00953ar.

5. See http://www.vatican.va/roman_curia/pontifical_councils/interelg/documents/rc_pc_interelg_doc_19051991_dialogue-and-proclamatio_en.html Here, in #42, "Dialogue and Proclamation"

recalls the 1984 document "The Attitude of the Church towards the Followers of Other Religions: Reflections and Orientations on Dialogue and Mission" (DM 28–35). See http://www.cimer.org.au/documents/DialogueandMission1984.pdf Accessed September 1, 2012.

6. Rachel Adler, "The Question of Boundaries: Towards a Jewish Feminist Theology of Self and Others," in M. Lerner, ed., *Tikkun Anthology* (Oakland/Jerusalem: Tikkun Books, 1992), 465.

7. See http://www.jcrelations.net/en/?id=966.

8. See http://www.ccjr.us/dialogika-resources/documents-and-statements/roman-catholic/us-conference-of-catholic-bishops/578-usccb-09june18.

9. This, however, was addressed in the accompanying USCCB "Statement of Principles for Catholic-Jewish Dialogue." See http://www.ccjr.us/dialogika-resources/documents-and-statements/roman-catholic/us-conference-of-catholic-bishops/584-usccbdialogue 09oct2.

10. On ritual and its relationship to "embodied knowing," see Catherine Bell, *Ritual: Perspectives and Dimensions* (New York and Oxford: Oxford University Press, 1997), 107. Bell, moreover, notes the potential for refashioning and transformation of the "schemes from the shared culture," 116.

11. See S. J. Tambiah, "A Performative Approach to Ritual," *Proceedings of the British Academy* 65 (1979): 119.

12. Note Justin's reference to the use of Hebrew Scripture in *1 Apol.* 67.

13. As Barnes acknowledges, the expression is that of Nicholas Lash, *The Beginning and End of "Religion"* (Cambridge: Cambridge University Press, 1996), 21; see Barnes' reflection on the theme in his earlier *Theology and the Dialogue of Religions* (Cambridge UK: Cambridge University Press, 2002), 182–204.

I
TRIBUTES

1

Honoring León Klenicki

Abraham H. Foxman

ADL [the Jewish Anti-Defamation League] was truly fortunate and blessed to have had Rabbi León Klenicki represent us as our Interfaith Affairs Director for a quarter of a century. He brought unique gifts, experiences, and interests to ADL.

León understood what it was like for Jews living in a country where anti-Semitism was rife and where the Church was a source of that anti-Semitism. That is because he grew up in Argentina. Because León was a congregational rabbi in Buenos Aires, he could relate to the individual happiness and pain that people in our community experience. For him it was never simply an abstract endeavor, but a human experience.

León could talk to Jews and Christians with equal facility. It was amazing to witness the depth of respect Catholic leaders showed Rabbi Klenicki. This was because he was honest with them, ready to criticize when necessary, to praise when appropriate, and always to be constructive in the relationship.

León was an intellectual with a sharp sense of humor. You could always count on him to inject some of his wit into very serious discussions and, in the process, not diminish the seriousness one bit. Rather, León's humor brought new perspective. He personified ADL in that he believed in the need to speak out in the face of Christian anti-Semitism and in his equally strong conviction in the need to educate Christian leaders for the long run. His favorite work, I believe, was his interpretation of the Gospels for Christians, showing that it was not inevitable that churchgoers be exposed to anti-Jewish renditions of Christian Scripture. This was always a priority for León because he understood the long-term impact of the ways in which biblical texts are interpreted.

In October 1973, León accepted ADL's invitation to become head of the Jewish-Catholic Relations Department. In 1984, he became Director of ADL's Department of Interfaith Affairs and ADL's Co-Liaison to the Vatican. He held this position until his retirement in January of 2001.

León met with Pope John Paul II on many occasions, in Rome and in the United States, and held him in high regard. He spoke of meeting Pope Benedict XVI when he was Cardinal Ratzinger, and he told the then-cardinal about ADL's (really León's) educational programs on early Christianity and rabbinic Judaism, and the presentation of Jews and Judaism that have sometimes been misunderstood and misused to promote anti-Semitism. León also spoke of other meetings with Cardinal Ratzinger in which they focused on the need for Catholics and Jews to reflect together on the theological meaning of the Holocaust.

The United States Conference of Catholic Bishops recommended that all U.S. bishops and cardinals observe Holocaust Day by using as a liturgy the service prepared by Rabbi Klenicki and Dr. Eugene J. Fisher called "From Desolation to Hope: An Interreligious Holocaust Memorial Service."

In 2008, Pope Benedict XVI honored León with the highest award that can be given to a non-Catholic by the pope—the Knighthood of St. Gregory. He is one of only a handful of Jews to be so honored. We are extremely proud that Rabbi Klenicki's decades of work to help reconcile the Catholic and Jewish faiths was recognized by Pope Benedict XVI. We can think of no better person to deserve this honor.

It is very fitting that we, Catholics and Jews, come together to celebrate Rabbi Klenicki in this way and I am honored to be part of it.

2

León Is Everywhere!

Eric J. Greenberg

On my workdesk, smothered with multicolored file folders and news reports, there is a stack of reference books that are essential to my job. Glancing at the books titles, a clear pattern emerges. *Toward a Theological Encounter,* edited by Rabbi León Klenicki. *In Our Time,* co-edited by Rabbi León Klenicki. *A Dictionary of the Jewish Christian Dialogue,* co-edited by Rabbi León Klenicki. *Biblical Studies: Meeting Ground of Jews and Christians,* co-edited by Boadt, Kroner, and, oh yes, Klenicki.

You get the picture.

Like Elvis, in my office, León is everywhere.

And that is a good thing.

I was privileged to know León in several capacities. He was a news source, confidante, and, most importantly, a mentor and friend. I first met León when I was a newspaper reporter covering religion, first at the *New York Daily News* and later at the *Jewish Week,* where I was a reporter and columnist. León and I quickly developed a rapport and trusting relationship. I soon found myself calling León for background information on a variety of religious issues. I looked forward to these calls, not only for their educational value, but to hear León's honest, off-the-record assessment of topics and personalities and, equally as important, his sharp sense of humor.

When I launched what became the first regular interfaith newspaper column in the country, León was happy to help, sharing ideas and discussing with me the difficult theological issues that were part of the evolving Catholic-Jewish dialogue. He was a patient and thorough teacher.

As the director of ADL's Interfaith Affairs Department for a quarter of a century, León was instrumental in nurturing the new and positive relationship between the Catholic Church and the Jewish people after nearly two thousand years of tragedy. He was greatly influenced by such important Catholic thinkers as Jacques Maritain. It is worth noting that León and Pope John Paul II both wrote their theses on the same religious figure, St. John of the Cross.

León embodied our agency's dedication to interfaith relations. While deeply immersed in Judaism, León recognized the sacredness of other paths to God. He viewed believing Christians not as "others," but as fellow subjects of faith. One key part of his job was to help Christians understand their Jewish roots and to acknowledge that for Jews, the covenant God made with Moses at Mount Sinai is eternal and irrevocable. But León also helped educate the Jewish community about Christians. He sought to deepen our understanding and highlight our commonalities, while acknowledging our differences.

Two catch phrases best explain León's approach. One was "tea and sympathy." As León was quoted by a newspaper in 2006: "For many years we engaged in what I call 'tea and sympathy.' We got together and smiled and complained about the past." Instead León believed the dialogue needed to dig deeper and address the tough issues, such as worldwide anti-Semitism and the historical "use and abuse" of traditional texts by Catholics to persecute Jews.

The other Leónism was "Let us have mercy upon words," which he would proclaim when interfaith religious conversations became overly heated or personal. León's call for civility in dialogue was indeed prophetic, especially considering today's political and religious climate.

Several years ago, when I was trying to decide whether to leave the newspaper business so that instead of writing about interfaith relations, I could actually do it, I sought León's counsel. His sage advice and words of encouragement will always be with me.

In 2008, I had the honor of being among a small group of Catholic and Jewish leaders who witnessed León receiving the highest award that can be given to a non-Catholic by a pope, the Knighthood of St. Gregory. León's closing remarks at this historic ceremony summed up his profoundly optimistic future perspective on a historically tragic relationship. He said, "Through our dialogue with each other, people of faith, as equals we can overcome the historical domain to enter into a dominion of sacredness. Let us build on this sacred relationship of Catholic to Jew and Jew to Catholic that God may light the world with understanding and blessing."

Shortly after León's death in January of 2009, it was my honor to plan a memorial tribute for him. In the Jewish tradition, there is a custom to hold a gathering in honor of the deceased on the thirtieth day after burial and learn Torah together in order to bring merit to the departed.

It was decided to hold the memorial at the Pope John Paul II Center in Washington, DC, quite an appropriate setting for this pioneer of Catholic-Jewish relations. Attending were national leaders of Catholic-Jewish relations, including noted rabbis and cardinals, professors, and theologians, gathered from around the country to pay respects to their beloved colleague. Cardinal William Keeler, Archbishop Emeritus of Baltimore and longtime Moderator of Catholic-Jewish Affairs for the United States Conference of Catholic Bishops, had this to say on León's passing:

> This faithful son of Torah leaves behind more than thirty
> years of scholarship and leadership in interfaith relations.
> For the Catholic Church in the United States and Latin
> America, León was a pioneer in the promotion of a vision
> of Catholic-Jewish relations that drew inspiration from the
> Second Vatican Council and the vital streams of contem-
> porary Jewish thought.

Nearly four years after his passing, León still is everywhere in my office. There is the bulging green folder containing the plans to publish his last book, co-edited with longtime collaborator Gene Fisher, about Pope John Paul II. Then there is the red folder concerning a proposed university archives project for León.

I am proud and honored to carry on the work of our beloved teacher, colleague, and friend, Rabbi León Klenicki, z"l. May his memory be for a blessing.

3

Remembering León Klenicki

Judith Banki

I believe I first met León when he came to work for the Anti-Defamation League, but his name was known to me before then, because of the work he had done to promote dialogue and understanding of Jews and Judaism in Latin America.

León made an immediate and lasting impression: his unique personality combined an exasperated impatience of inaccuracies or sloppy thinking with the most gentlemanly, cultivated, old-world manners. He might disagree vehemently with your position or with your approach to an issue, but he would always kiss your hand first.

I must confess that when we first met, I was a bit intimidated by him. His frequent and passionate insistence that "only scholars" could carry on the work of Jewish-Christian relations stirred all my insecurities, because I was neither an academic nor a rabbi (there *were* no female rabbis when I began working in interreligious affairs) and was a woman in a field dominated by male academics and patriarchal traditions. However, as we worked together—perhaps side-by-side is more appropriate—over the years, I came to realize that León's impatience was directed toward the cynics who regarded the dialogue as a power game in which the winner scored the most points against the "other." It was also directed at those who, out of innocence or ignorance, minimized differences and overlooked particularities in a search for superficial unity. Where there were commonalities and shared spirituality, he was first to recognize and teach about them—he resonated deeply with Catholic spirituality—and his writings in this area, together with Eugene Fisher and other scholars, constitute an enduring legacy in the field. But he also strongly believed that Jewish-Christian understanding and mutual respect could not be achieved by ignoring past history.

8

We were at a Lutheran conference in Hungary when the World Trade Center was attacked on September 11, 2001. We were participating in small-group discussions in a rural conference center when someone ran in to announce that the Twin Towers had been demolished. We rushed into the main building and assembled in the one room that had a TV set carrying CNN. It was León's room, and it became our place of mourning. The conference ended abruptly that night with a memorial service for the fallen victims. All of us there, but particularly colleagues who had worked together to advance understanding and peace among religious communities, bonded together in affection and despair. One doesn't forget such moments. Shortly afterward, my husband suffered a major stroke, and I lost track of colleagues. I heard that León was ill, but only realized how seriously ill he was when he failed to show up for Eugene Fisher's retirement dinner. Sick as he was, he sent a beautiful message.

León was, above all, an educator. He relished teaching and the opportunity it gave him to share the depth of his profound knowledge about his own faith with others—both Christians and Jews. I suspect he enjoyed his teaching engagements at Cambridge, at Graymoor, and at Leuven University as much as anything else in his professional career.

He was blessed in his talents and in his loving, mutually supportive marriage to Myra Cohen. He married the boss's daughter and became a giant in his field, with a long, productive career. Not many of us could ask for more. May his memory be for a blessing.

4

Remembrance and Appreciation

Peter Stravinskas

As many know and as the Rebbe was fond of pointing out, he and I met for the first time as combatants since our respective jobs had us on opposite sides of important issues. With the passage of time, we became honest brokers for our communities and eventually collaborators on many fronts, which called for a common voice and witness, writing articles and books together as well as sponsoring symposia. Our professional relationship developed into a personal one, evolving into a deep and lasting friendship.

As Rabbi Klenicki and I conversed both "on the job" and off, several positions or approaches of his endeared him to me more and more. I note them here because I believe them to be important as Jews and Catholics look "toward the future," as this volume desires.

First, he abhorred a masquerade of false unity, papering over differences as though they did not exist. With disdain, he referred to such encounters as "tea and sympathy." No, he insisted that differences be acknowledged, honestly and respectfully. Only then, he asserted, could true dialogue begin.

Second, he had no time for any form of religious syncretism, adopting Hegelian modes of operation, whereby a thesis and its antithesis forged a synthesis. Of course, the problem would be that the "synthesis" would not be faithful to either tradition.

Third, his interest in the first century after Christ drew me in. He maintained that that first century saw not only the beginnings of Christianity but also a new beginning for Judaism and, on that score, a propitious starting point for interfaith study.

Fourth, he insisted on exhibiting respect for sacred texts. The way to handle potentially problematic passages was not to ignore them and surely not to rewrite them; it was to understand them in their historical context and then make a contemporary application. Not for him treating the Gospel of John as one, long anti-Jewish screed.

Fifth, he had adopted a personal policy of maintaining what I have dubbed "a prudent and even holy silence" on Pope Pius XII's wartime record until all the historical data was available.

Those were his professional stances that I deem his legacy to the Jewish-Catholic dialogue. What impressed me personally about Rabbi Klenicki was that he was the quintessential man of God and man of prayer; he knew the God of his fathers. And how could one consider the personal dimension of the man without discussing his devoted and loving wife, Myra, the exemplar of that ideal wife praised in the Book of Proverbs? Indeed, "when one finds a worthy wife, her value is beyond pearls. / Her husband, entrusting his heart to her, has an unfailing prize" (Prov 31:10–11). Needless to say, we Catholics were all delighted that Pope Benedict XVI conferred on the rabbi the extraordinary honor of papal knighthood. Truth be told, no one was more delighted than León himself! He took it to be a kind of Catholic "Good Housekeeping" seal of approval on all his years of work to foster mutual understanding between our communities.

In the twilight of his life, as he and I prayed and shared reflections on the life to come, it was my great privilege to be able to pray our own prayers for the dying for him and to bless him on his journey into eternity. The lovely and moving *In Paradisum*, which concludes every Catholic funeral Mass, is still my prayer and hope for dear León:

> *May the Angels lead you into Paradise;*
> *may the Martyrs come to welcome you on your way*
> *and lead you into the holy city, Jerusalem.*
> *May the choirs of Angels receive you*
> *and, with Lazarus who once was poor,*
> *may you have eternal rest.*

5

On León Klenicki

William Cardinal Keeler

León Klenicki, with his Polish name and Argentinean back-
ground, was a person of many parts. I met him in Rome in 1987,
when he sat at the table with us as a representative of the Anti-
Defamation League at an extraordinary meeting of the International
Liaison Committee, composed of the Holy See's Commission for
Religious Relations with the Jewish People and the International
Jewish Committee for Interreligious Consultations.

The meeting was extraordinary in two senses: it had not been
planned, and the pope himself was going to participate. Before we met
at Castel Gandalfo, we were together for a day in Rome. I can recall
telling the meeting about the people who, with tears in their eyes,
would relate to us the suffering in families of people whom the Nazis
wished to eliminate because they were reputedly feebleminded and
how hurt these family members were by *Holocaust*, a show on television that spoke only of the Jewish suffering. They had spoken to me on
Sundays after Mass at St. Lawrence Church in Harrisburg.

Also, one of the Jewish people present in Rome told me pri-
vately that, at a meeting in Chicago, there were a number of Jewish
and Catholic people of Polish extraction participating. The meeting
had begun with much shouting at one another. When the Jewish
people began to reflect on their escape from the concentration camps,
they saw quickly that, in each instance, a Catholic was the guide who
got them to safety. The tone of the meeting changed radically.

The Polish pope was an unknown factor in Catholic-Jewish
relations at that time. Earlier, in June, he had received Kurt Waldheim,
the President of Austria, and was blindsided by the information that
Waldheim's election as President was opposed by the World Jewish
Congress.

12

Pope John Paul II spoke at the meeting. He said that he had gone back to his hometown of Wadowice, and found no people of Jewish origin there. That meant that the Nazis had killed the Jewish people or sent them away, to a fate other than death, and perhaps worse than death. He mentioned that he had been meditating on the Exodus, and saw the new Jewish state of Israel as something special, and that he could understand how the people of Jewish origin could see that there was a place for them there.

Only later did it come out that the pope's best friend at the time was Jewish and that he had come to Rome by a circuitous route. Jerzey Kluger was his name and, frequently, he would spend Sunday afternoons with Pope John Paul II.

At Rabbi Klenicki's funeral, I recalled how only two of us were praying the psalms on the plane home from Rome, he and I—I from the Roman breviary, and he from the Hebrew Scriptures. His wife, Myra, said that León's practice of reciting the psalms gave her great confidence in traveling with him.

Rabbi Klenicki helped enormously in getting the message out that the Second Vatican Council had changed the course of the Catholic Church in its relationship with the Jewish people. We Catholics should be grateful to him for the efforts he made and for his passion to communicate this word to all.

II
SACRED SCRIPTURE

6

Biblical Resources for Interfaith Dialogue

Tamara Cohn Eskenazi

In 1967, a year after his ordination, Rabbi León Klenicki told Latin American Catholic and Jewish leaders who gathered in Bogotá, "Two thousand years of history made the discussion difficult." He then added, "The time of hope has arrived. The task is hard, but not impossible."[1]

Rabbi Klenicki's own efforts in the following years helped to make the hope a reality. It is rewarding to know that he lived to see the extent to which the conversation between Catholics and Jews has progressed. This volume is both a testimony to his success and a link in a tradition of continuing dialogues across a divide, whether between Jews and Catholics or among other communities of faith.[2] The Hebrew Bible/Old Testament continues to provide common ground in Jewish-Christian dialogue. Although biblical texts may be subject to different interpretations, they offer a shared vocabulary and shared narrative with which to examine our roots and the potential for revitalizing them in response to new circumstances. And yet, as history has shown, the Bible also functions as a divisive force. Ancient and modern interpreters point to many examples in the Bible (both the Hebrew Bible and the New Testament) in which the "outsiders" (however defined) are deemed not God's people (with "God" defined as exclusive and excluding on different grounds) and, therefore, vilified.[3]

Do we then have sufficient resources in the Bible to foster interfaith dialogue? Can we find in the Bible examples of encounters that sustain authentic commitment to one's own faith or culture yet respect those of another, without attempting either to convert, control, or assimilate the other? This paper seeks to show that the answer is

"Yes." In order to contextualize such examples, I first review briefly
the range of attitudes toward "the other" in the Hebrew Bible and
place these attitudes in their historical contexts. This is followed by
examples from the Bible of texts that illustrate positive engagements
with the other who remains an "other" across religious or cultural
boundaries. Finally, I look briefly at some contemporary discussions
about "the other."

AN OVERVIEW OF ATTITUDES TOWARD
"THE OTHER" IN THE HEBREW BIBLE

Much of the Hebrew Bible is written and/or redacted from the
perspective of a community that has lost its political status, and has
suffered destruction and exile.[4] That is, most of the Bible took definitive form in the aftermath of the destruction of 587/6 BCE by the
Babylonians, and in the exile and restoration periods that followed.
The formation of the Bible was an essential component of the reconstruction that began after the tides had turned and the period of
Persian imperial rule had began.[5]

According to the Bible (Ezra 1:1–16), exiles were encouraged
to return and rebuild their lives and community in Jerusalem and
Judah, in an era now called the postexilic (or Persian) period (beginning in 538 BCE). In that period, Jews lived as a minority, some living in Judah others scattered in Diaspora (especially Babylon, Persia,
and Egypt). The hallmark of the community at that point was its
smallness and fragility. Referring to an even earlier period, Deuteronomy tells us that the Israelites, from the very beginning, were a
small and vulnerable people, the smallest according to Deuteronomy
7:7: "It was not because you were more numerous than any other
people that the LORD set his heart on you and chose you—for you
were the fewest of all peoples." This is the rationale for the opposition in 7:1–5 to the seven powerful nations that inhabit the land.
Other texts, depicting specifically the postexilic situation, speak of
the community as but a weak remnant (see, for example, Ezra 9:8,
referring to the fifth century BCE).

The issue of maintaining a distinctive identity in the midst of
diversity became particularly significant in the postexilic era, given
that previous unifying structures such as geographical boundaries,

native monarchy, and other defining characteristics had been shattered. Now the remnant of ancient Israel and Judah lived under Persian imperial rule in the midst of other ethnicities, with differing religious and social practices and different histories. These dramatic changes required redefining boundaries and establishing a basic core or criteria for membership, as well as articulating binding values.

In its emphasis on forming a cohesive community, the Hebrew Bible wrestles with the tension that results from seeking to incorporate a variety of voices in the face of internal and external pressures to blend in with surrounding cultures. The biblical canon, in its multivoiced perspective, is, then, an embodiment of both commonality and differences, the latter evident in the diverse, at times also seemingly contradictory, perspectives on a number of important issues.[6] This diversity leaps off the page, so to speak, already in the first two chapters of the Bible, with two different stories of creation (Gen 1:1—2:3 and Gen 2:4–24);[7] it continues as the theologies of Deuteronomy are challenged by Job or Ecclesiastes,[8] and as Chronicles retells with a difference the entire history of the Israelites.[9]

Extant writings from this postexilic or Persian period show a lively debate about how to rebuild the nation under its radically altered circumstances. This includes diverse views about membership in the community and different attitudes toward those who are outsiders. A particularly sharp debate seems to revolve around inclusion and exclusion, with books like Ezra-Nehemiah, Ruth, and the latter part of Isaiah reflecting different positions.[10]

We learn from Ezra-Nehemiah that in the fifth century BCE, returning exiles had married "foreign" women from the people(s) of the land(s). The authors of Ezra-Nehemiah object to such unions, claiming that such actions endanger the survival of the newly restored community. According to Ezra the priest, these marriages violate God's earlier teachings; therefore, the community must separate itself from such people (Ezra 9:10–15). According to Nehemiah, the governor of Judah under Persian rule, foreign women diverted King Solomon from God and caused him to sin; therefore, Israelite men must not marry foreign women such as Moabites or Ammonites. Nehemiah then compels men to vow to prevent future intermarriage (Neh 13:23–27). On the other side of the spectrum, the Book of Ruth (most likely written in roughly the same period) depicts the journey of a Moabite woman who enters the community in Judah first by binding herself to her mother-in-law Naomi and next by marrying a prominent Judean man, Boaz.[11] Ruth articulates her commitment in the well-remembered, eloquent vow addressed to her mother-in-law: "Wherever you go, I will go..." (Ruth 1:16). Her great grandchild is David, Israel's most illustrious king.

The story of Ruth is particularly important because of its departure from the teachings in Deuteronomy that specifically exclude Moabites from joining the community. According to Deuteronomy 23:3: "No Ammonite or Moabite shall be admitted to the assembly of the LORD. Even to the tenth generation, none of their descendants shall be admitted to the assembly of the LORD." One must note that Deuteronomy does not object to all foreigners. It states that other groups like the Edomites or Egyptians can be included over time (see Deut 23:7–8). But Ezra 9:1–2 objects to Egyptians as well as Moabites and other groups.

The Book of Isaiah includes messages dated to the postexilic community and offers yet another perspective on membership in the community. The prophet announces in God's name that those previously excluded are now welcomed by God when they adhere to the covenant.

Happy is the mortal who does this,
   the one who holds it fast,
who keeps the sabbath, not profaning it,
and refrains from doing any evil.

Do not let the foreigner joined to the LORD say,
"The LORD will surely separate me from his people";
and do not let the eunuch say,
   "I am just a dry tree."
For thus says the LORD:
To the eunuchs who keep my sabbaths,
   who choose the things that please me
   and hold fast my covenant,
I will give, in my house and within my walls,
   a monument and a name
   better than sons and daughters;
I will give them an everlasting name
   that shall not be cut off.

And the foreigners who join themselves to the LORD,
  to minister to him, to love the name of the LORD,
  and to be his servants,
all who keep the sabbath, and do not profane it,
  and hold fast my covenant—
these I will bring to my holy mountain,
  and make them joyful in my house of prayer;
their burnt offerings and their sacrifices
  will be accepted on my altar;
for my house shall be called a house of prayer
  for all peoples. (Isa 56:2–7)

These different, even contradicting, positions are made normative by being included in the Bible. They reflect an ongoing debate generated by specific circumstances and by the constant social, political, and economic changes, which required adaptation in a variety of ways. By including diverse opinions, the Hebrew Bible allows future generations to draw relevant conclusions for their own times and needs. In this sense, the Bible can be regarded as a complex cultural and religious DNA, capable of developing new lifelines along many and diverse paths as the need arises.

The restrictions in Ezra-Nehemiah reflect the measures that some in the community advocate. In reestablishing themselves anew in the midst of more numerous, more secure, and more prosperous neighbors, the returning Judeans needed to redefine themselves. Ezra-Nehemiah articulates the view that strong social and religious boundaries are necessary in order to protect the Judeans from being absorbed into the surrounding cultures. It should be noted that this position does not entail an opposition to foreigners per se. It is only when introduced as members that foreigners are deemed to pose a danger to community. Other contacts with foreigners are not subject to such censure.[12]

This backdrop is important when aiming to foster interfaith understanding. It helps readers understand how and why the Bible, in certain circumstances, rigorously defends communal boundaries against what it claims to be "outside influences" and why, at other times, it interacts amicably with others.

Interpreters frequently explore the variety of attitudes in the Bible toward "the other." Most contemporary readers laud the welcome extended to Ruth the Moabite or to the foreigners in Isaiah 56. The position of Ezra-Nehemiah is more often criticized even though it continues to have its defenders. Lawrence M. Wills effectively explores the biblical attitudes toward outsiders.[13] Examining both the Jewish and the Christian Bibles, he identifies some of the common features that account for animosity toward outsiders, including those within the community who refuse to toe the line.

Addressing the other end of the spectrum, Anna L. Grant-Henderson highlights other texts from the same period. She examines a variety of texts in which the other is welcomed into the community, looking at passages such as Isaiah 56:2–7, as well as Ruth.[14]

The important work of Grant-Henderson and Wills, and others like them, offers a vivid antidote to the perception that the Hebrew Bible (or the Old Testament) is overarchingly inimical to non-Israelites/non-Jews, or that it values only those who belong by virtue of their birth. These books help us understand the biblical foundations of the variety of attitudes toward the other and the conditions that engendered them. However, these texts and interpretations they highlight do not suffice because, finally, neither inclusion nor exclusion offers a paradigm for an interfaith dialogue. Welcoming the outsider who seeks to join the community is different from respecting and valorizing the outsider who wishes to interact meaningfully, yet remain an outsider. For this reason, we examine other texts in order to discern biblical resources for interfaith dialogue.

SPECIFIC EXAMPLES THAT SUPPORT
INTERFAITH DIALOGUE

An interfaith dialogue aspires for a relationship with those who, in their encounter with us, neither seek to join us nor aim to influence us to join their faith community or society. Several important texts offer a solid basis in the Bible for such conversation. Some of these portray encounters that result in mutual enhancement without leading to absorption or control of the other.

Love the Stranger as Yourself

The most obvious starting point in thinking about "the other" in terms that safeguard difference is the command in Leviticus and

Deuteronomy to love the stranger (Lev 19:33–34; Deut 10:19). In Leviticus, at the very heart of the Pentateuch, and in a book that largely occupies itself with the distinctive practices of the Israelites that are to make the Israelites holy (see the repeated instructions in Leviticus 19: "You shall be holy"), we read that one must love the neighbor as oneself (Lev 19:18). But we read as well that one must also love the stranger (Lev 19:33–34). The rationale for such love of the stranger is the experience in Egypt: having been oppressed, the Israelites must not perpetuate the abuse of the stranger that was inflicted upon them; on the contrary, they must protect the stranger or (as translated in the NRSV) the alien: "When an alien resides with you in your land, you shall not oppress the alien. The alien who resides with you shall be to you as the citizen among you; you shall love the alien as yourself, for you were aliens in the land of Egypt: I am the LORD your God" (Lev 19:33–34).

Who counts as a "stranger" to be loved? The Hebrew term is *ger*. Later rabbinic teachings use this term to refer to a proselyte, one who joined or is in the process of joining the community as a member. But the biblical context makes clear that this is not what Leviticus has in mind. The Israelites in Egypt are the paradigm for who the *ger* is: one who does not wish to be absorbed by the surrounding culture but, rather, retain a distinct identity. The NRSV specifies in translating Leviticus 19:33–34 that the *ger* is "the alien who resides with you." In other words, the reference is to an individual or a group living as a minority.

It is significant that this instruction appears also in Deuteronomy (10:19), a book that includes some of the most severe restrictions on contact with other groups (see Deut 7:1–10 and 23:4–7). The injunction is a clear indication that Deuteronomy is not a blanketed opposition to "the other," but a book that raises selective objections to some who seem to pose a threat, even as it protects a relationship or intermingling with others (Edomites and Egyptians, for example, as in Deut 23:8–9).

Love in these biblical books does not simply refer to a feeling but to loyalty.[15] Deuteronomy repeatedly uses the term *love* to define how one must approach God ("You shall love the LORD your God with all your heart..." Deut 6:4). It now extends the same attitude toward the stranger or resident alien. In both Leviticus 19 and Deuteronomy 10, love entails a commitment to persons living as a minority within the Israelite community. Such persons' rights have to be safeguarded. Underlying this extraordinary teaching is an awareness of the vulnerability of the other and the demand that those in power not take advantage of it. At first glance, it is striking that this command to love the stranger appears in two biblical books that also include some of the most restrictive requirements.[16] Yet this conjunction of restriction and openness ought not to be viewed as a paradox. On the contrary, the constructive attitude toward the stranger is an extension of having clear boundaries for the self. We will return to this point later.

The commitment to the well-being of the vulnerable other that Leviticus and Deuteronomy enjoin is a necessary starting point when encountering another in interfaith dialogue. This teaching, to love the stranger, sets a firm foundation for contemporary societies where so many individuals or communities constitute a minority within the larger cultural matrix. Yet, in itself, it does not suffice for a mutually enhancing dialogue because of its presumed hierarchies (the resident alien is dependent on the host society and does not have the same legal rights; see, for example, Leviticus 25:39–43 and 25:44–48). An important goal in interfaith dialogue is the opportunity to interact also as peers, as two "subjects" with equal stakes, without first privileging one group. For this reason, it is useful to examine additional examples of biblical encounters.

Biblical "Interfaith" or "Inter-cultural" Dialogues

The collaboration between Moses' sister and mother on the one hand, and Pharaoh's daughter on the other, is a pertinent example for our inquiry (Exod 2:1–10). The three women work together and cross boundaries established by religion, culture, and class. Jointly (and in defiance of the murderous law of the land) they save Moses' life. Neither side seeks to change the other and all parties benefit from their collaboration.

The more developed story of Jethro likewise offers an excellent example of what we might call, somewhat anachronistically, an "interfaith dialogue." Jethro is a Midianite priest and Moses' father-in-law. The stories about their relationship exemplify an appreciation of another person's religion, an offer of help, and a parting with respect that is free of any conditions. Both participants walk away as beneficiaries of this encounter; each retains his community and his "religion." In the episode in Exodus 18, Jethro comes to see Moses after Moses has successfully led the Israelites out of slavery in Egypt. The reunion between the two men is affectionate and enthusiastic. After they greet and kiss one another, Moses recounts all that has happened to him and the people. We then read the following:

> Jethro rejoiced for all the good that the LORD had done to Israel, in delivering them from the Egyptians. Jethro said, "Blessed be the LORD, who has delivered you from the Egyptians and from Pharaoh. Now I know that the LORD is greater than all gods [ha-elohim], because he delivered the people from the Egyptians, when they dealt arrogantly with them." (Exod 18:9–11)

There are several noteworthy elements in this declaration and in what ensues. First, we note Jethro's initial response. He blesses Israel's distinctive God, using that God's unique name (Y-H-W-H, translated here as "the LORD"). Second, he praises Israel's God as superior to others. In the following verses, we learn that he then joins Moses as they offer sacrifices and eat together with other Israelite leaders. However, Jethro's acknowledgement does not lead him to join the Israelites and their God on their journey and become a member of their community. We do learn next that "And Jethro, Moses' father-in-law, brought a burnt offering and sacrifices to God [elohim]; and Aaron came with all the elders of Israel to eat bread with Moses' father-in-law in the presence of God [elohim]" (Exod 18:12). But eventually, the joint sacrifice and meal will be followed by a separation.

It is probably significant that the narrator uses in this verse the Hebrew word ha-elohim to designate what in English is translated as "God." The word is a plural noun that can be used as a reference to Israel's God and, therefore, is translated in certain instances as "God" (as translated above in Exod 18:12), or it can be rendered as "gods," referring to divinities in general (as translated above in Exod 18:11).[17] Does the narrator imply that they offer sacrifices to one deity or each to his own? In the biblical text itself, the matter remains allusive.

What is nonetheless clear in this episode is that Jethro does not join the Israelite community. The next day, Jethro helps Moses manage communal affairs more effectively by offering indispensable guidance. He cautions Moses against trying to do everything himself and urges him to delegate judiciary roles to others and, thereby, create an infrastructure. Moses follows the advice (Exod 18:24), presumably to good effect, and after their farewell, Jethro returns to his own land (Exod 18:27).

The perspective illuminated by this episode, and by others in which Jethro appears, shows an amicable, respectful relationship of mutual trust and readiness to be of help.[18] In this case, the "other" is a Midianite priest who presumably remains a Midianite priest, but who is both welcomed and heeded even as Moses remains a leader of a different kind of community. Each of the two dialogue partners gives and receives something of value and each then continues on his own distinctive path, enriched by the encounter.

The Jethro episode is more detailed than some others in which we find cordial, mutually supportive exchanges between Israelites and "the other" in the Hebrew Bible, but it is not unique. The meeting of King Solomon and the Queen of Sheba is another colorful example in which an Israelite meets "the other" in mutuality and to good effect (1 Kgs 10:1–10). Other exchanges can be added to this list. One may consider the touching case of Ittai the Gittite. Presumably a man from the town of Gath, a Philistine city, Ittai offers his support out of loyalty to King David when the king is escaping Jerusalem. Although David discourages Ittai from risking himself and his men for David's cause, Ittai vows loyalty and remains. His oath echoes the words of Ruth the Moabite when she vows loyalty to Naomi.

> Then the king said to Ittai the Gittite, "Why are you also coming with us? Go back, and stay with the king; for you are a foreigner....Go back, and take your kinsfolk with you; and may the LORD show steadfast love and faithfulness to you."
> But Ittai answered the king, "As the LORD lives, and as my lord the king lives, wherever my lord the king may be, whether for death or for life, there also your servant will be." (2 Sam 15:19–21)

When Ittai joins forces with David, he does not cease to be a Gittite; rather, he becomes a supporting partner, acting out of a commitment to David's safety. The rapport between the two men is especially striking when one recalls that Philistines are frequent enemies of Israel in the Bible, especially in stories about David. Note, for example, that Goliath, who challenges the Israelites and whom David slays, also comes from Gath, the same town as Ittai (1 Sam 17:4).

SOME CONTEMPORARY REFLECTIONS ON THE OTHER IN THE BIBLE

David Perlstein devotes a monograph to the subject of God's "others."[19] As Perlstein makes evident, the Hebrew Bible recognizes and even celebrates those non-Israelites who act on God's behalf (Rahab in Josh 2, Jael in Judg 4–5, King Cyrus in Isa 45 and Ezra 1). In the present paper, I have focused on the "other" who is not presented necessarily as God's instrument but as a culturally, religious "other" who remains "other," and who works jointly with Israelite protagonists for a better world.

Such biblical texts, illustrating how "the other" remains an "other" even as partnership and mutual support are offered, help us think outside the box of the categories of exclusivist versus universal messages in the Bible. The Hebrew Bible does enjoin fervently certain beliefs and practices.[20] But it also offers examples of working with those who do not share and do not intend to share the biblical perspective. In such instances, the other remains an "other," honored and valued as such—at times protected, as is the case with the "stranger who lives among you"; at other times, appreciated for the support or recognition that the other offers (Jethro, Rahab, Ittai).

As noted earlier, the Hebrew Bible shows that establishing strong boundaries does not conflict with care and concern for those outside those boundaries. Indeed, a case can be made for the necessity of clear boundaries in order to secure interfaith dialogue. The theologian Rachel Adler can help us rethink models for contemporary interfaith engagements. In her groundbreaking article, "The Question of Boundaries: Towards a Jewish Feminist Theology of Self and Others," Adler reflects on the notion of boundaries and charts a model of an interactive self.[21] Although she focuses on persons and specifically in terms of gender, her insights are illuminating for the light they shed on communal interactions as well.

Adler contrasts the polarizing and alienating notions of self that

dominate Western tradition by objectifying the other (466). She invites
a different way of thinking about the subject of boundaries. "Some
boundaries are barricades—chain-link fences guarded by Dobermans.
Others are not primarily barriers but loci of interaction" (465). Using
the cell membrane as an analogue, she describes the boundaries as the
perimeter at which the cell conducts its life-enhancing interaction with
other cells; the flowing in and out helps maintain its life within its
environment. The Bible, she rightly argues, likewise offers us a
model of self and other that can enhance "a social matrix that allows
all human beings to flourish" (466). Adler highlights ways in which
the core of Judaism is an implicit challenge to alienating dualism
(467) in its insistence on justice as well as the connectedness of all
human beings. Her examples frequently come from the Bible.

Perhaps the most relevant example is her reflection on Genesis
1: "The creation proceeds not by polarization but by differentiation
within wholeness" (469). The varieties of humans as male and female
in God's image "embody diversity within similarity. Equally human,
they share equally in the responsibilities and benefits of the natural
world" (ibid.). While Adler focuses on gender issues in the text, the
process she depicts applies as well to the broader sense of creating the
world and human communities.

Adler considers the creation of humanity in Genesis 2 a divisive
alternative, one in which fusion replaces recognition of diversity. But
let me propose a different interpretation of Genesis 2 and show how
this story also can buttress our endeavors to strengthen meaningful
interfaith dialogue. Genesis 2:18 records that God, who repeatedly
saw how the created world was "good" (see Gen 1:4, 10, 12, 18, 21,
25, 31), now notes for the first time that something is not good: "It is
not good for the *adam* to be alone" (Gen 2:18). Although it used to be
translated as "man," the word *adam* means "a human being," perhaps
best rendered as "earth creature" given the connection to earth
(*adama*; see especially Gen 2:7).[22] God decides to create a helper. The
word *helper (ezer)* in Genesis 2:18 has conjured up images of an
assistant or a comforter to ease loneliness. But the language that God
uses suggests something else. God says, "Let me make an *ezer
kenegdo*" (Gen 2:18), a helper opposite him.[23] We can conclude on the
basis of this decision that what is harmful is the absence of a suitable
other. It is obviously uncertain what kind of an "other," since God
experiments, unsuccessfully at first, before producing the right kind

of an "other." Having failed in these attempts (Gen 2:19–20), God determines to subject the first human being to surgery, the result of which produces woman and man (2:21–24).

Let us linger a moment longer on the manner in which the intended solution is expressed, with the word *kenegdo* in Gen 2:18. The Hebrew word *neged* means in the Bible "opposite" or "in front of," as when the Psalmist says, "I keep the LORD always before me (*negdi*; Ps 16:8). The French translation of the expression catches the meaning best: vis-à-vis, a kind of "face-to-face." The gender of the help in Genesis 2:18 is unspecified (the noun *ezer* is a masculine noun). It is not gender but being opposite to or in front of the created *adam* that constitutes the intended help. The division of the *adam* into a woman and a man is one concretization of this larger goal.

Genesis 2 suggests, at the very foundational level of human beginnings, the valorization of another who is different yet related. Without such a counterpart, "it is not good" (2:18). We can draw from this initial impetus in the creation of the human community insights to bolster our appreciation of interfaith encounters. It is not good for a human being to be alone and it is not good for a religious tradition or a religious community to be alone. It too requires an *ezerkenegdo*. We help one another by facing one another.

The Jewish French philosopher Emmanuel Levinas helps us see the broader and deeper implications of a relationship to the other.[24] His work repeatedly illumines the incomparable significance of the relationship to the other in which the integrity of the other is protected. For Levinas, facing the other as other is constitutive of the ethical self and essential for any becoming. The other intrudes upon the self and elicits the responsibility that makes us human. The face of the other is a command to responsibility. As Richard Cohen puts it, "'otherness' of the other person arises precisely as a moral imperative that pierces the self with moral obligation, with service to the other."[25] This approach to the other is to be contrasted with the powerful tendency to seek to assimilate or be assimilated that has dominated not only personal relationships but communal ones.

Like Levinas's work in general, his insight about persons can also apply to communities in general and to interfaith dialogue in particular. The perspective of Genesis 2:18, which, like Levinas, posits the worth of another as constitutive of our fundamental humanity, can be seen as an instantiation of Levinas's more developed insight into the subject. It urges us to recognize interfaith dialogue across boundaries as essential to each community, not merely a luxury.[26]

CONCLUSION

It would be a misrepresentation to claim that the Bible overtly advocates interfaith dialogue. Such a claim at best would be anachronistic and essentially inaccurate. However, in portraying encounters that resemble attempts at interfaith dialogue today, the Hebrew Bible affirms continuity between contemporary goals and biblical foundations. The covenantal bond that the Hebrew Bible establishes does not preclude responsibility for and amity with those outside the covenant. The particularity in the Hebrew Bible is intimately linked to a universal perspective with support and care for the broader realms of God's created world. We can, therefore, sum up how the Bible can serve as a resource for approaching the task with integrity. First, the core premise about humankind acknowledges the importance of difference as well as commonality. Second, the Hebrew Bible exemplifies cases in which dialogues across religious, ethnic, class, and other boundaries are mutually sustaining. Third, the Bible does not have a categorical objection to such dialogue. Instead, it illustrates the ways attitudes toward the other are contingent upon the community's experience of itself in the face of internal and external pressures. A climate of mutual respect and commitment to honor the other as other can set such dialogue on a footing that would be consistent with biblical teachings and examples.

NOTES

1. Dennis Hevesi, "Writing on Rabbi Klenicki," *New York Times*, January 31, 2009, New York edition, A22.

2. The long list of publications by León Klenicki exemplifies the vibrant dialogue that developed and that he sustained. It is best expressed perhaps in the title of the 1991 book *In Our Time: The Flowering of Jewish-Catholic Dialogue* (Studies in Judaism and Christianity), which he edited with Eugene Fisher. One also notes important statements by Jewish and Christian representatives, such as "*Dabru Emet*: A Jewish Statement about Christianity" (2000) and the Pontifical Biblical Commission publication *The Jewish People*

and Their Sacred Scriptures in the Christian Bible (2001). Other important contributions include James Aitken and Edward Kessler, eds., *Challenges in Jewish-Christian Relations* (New York and Mahwah, NJ: Paulist Press/ Stimulus Books, 2006); Michael Barnes, *Theology and the Dialogue of Religions* (Cambridge: Cambridge University Press, 2002), esp. chap. 2 ("Remembering the Covenant," pp. 29–64) and chap. 3 ("Facing the Other," pp. 65–96); Helga Croner, ed., *Stepping Stones to Further Jewish-Christian Relations: An Unabridged Collection of Christian Documents* (London and New York: Stimulus Books, 1977), and *More Stepping Stones to Jewish-Christian Relations an Unabridged Collection of Christian Documents 1975–1983* (New York and Mahwah, NJ: Paulist Press/Stimulus, 1985); Philip A. Cunningham et al., eds., *Christ Jesus and the Jewish People Today: New Explorations of Theological Interrelationships* (Grand Rapids, MI, and Cambridge, UK: William B. Eerdmans, 2011); Tikva Frymer-Kensky et al., eds., *Christianity in Jewish Terms* (Boulder, CO: Westview Press, 2000); Irving Greenberg, *For the Sake of Heaven and Earth: The New Encounter between Judaism and Christianity* (Philadelphia: Jewish Publication Society, 2004); Edward Kessler, John Pawlikowski, and Judith Banki, eds., *Jews and Christians in Conversation: Crossing Cultures and Generations* (Cambridge, UK: Orchard Academic, 2002); M. Moyaert and D. Pollefeyt, eds., *Never Revoked: "Nostra Aetate" as Ongoing Challenge for Jewish-Christian Dialogue* (Louvain: Peeters, 2010); David Novak, *Jewish-Christian Dialogue: A Jewish Justification* (Oxford: Oxford University Press, 1989), and *Talking with Christians: Musings of a Jewish Theologian* (Grand Rapids, MI, and Cambridge, UK: William Eerdmans, 2005); Peter C. Phan, *Being Religious Interreligiously; Asian Perspectives on Interfaith Dialogue* (Maryknoll, NY: Orbis Books, 2004), esp. chap. 10 ("Jews and Judaism in Light of the *Catechism of the Catholic Church*: On the Way to Reconciliation," pp. 147–60), and chap. 11 ("The Holocaust: Reflections from the Perspective of Asian Liberation Theology," pp. 161–85); Franklin Sherman, ed., *Bridges: Documents of the Christian-Jewish Dialogue,* vol. 1, *The Road to Reconciliation* (New York and Mahwah, NJ: Paulist Press/Stimulus, 2011).

3. In the Hebrew Bible, see, for example, Exodus 23:23–33; Deuteronomy 7:1–5; Malachi 1:2–4. In the New Testament, see, for example, Matthew 11:20–24; John 8:23–24; 2 Corinthians 1 1:2–15. For a recent, thorough exploration of both Jewish and Christian Scriptures, see esp. Lawrence M. Wills, *Not God's People: Insiders and Outsiders in the Biblical World* (Lanham, MD: Rowman and Littlefield, 2008). Other relevant books include Robert L. Cohn and Laurence J. Silberstein, eds., *The Other in Jewish Thought and History: Constructions of Jewish Culture and Jewish Identity* (New York: New York University Press, 1994); Paula Fredriksen and Adele Reinhartz, eds., *Jesus, Judaism, and Christian Anti-Judaism: Reading the New Testament after*

the Holocaust (Louisville, KY: Westminster/John Knox, 2002); Jack T. Sanders, *Schismatics, Sectarians, Dissidents, Deviants: The First One Hundred Years of Jewish-Christian Relations* (Valley Forge, PA: Trinity Press International, 1993); Kenton L. Sparks, *Ethnicity and Identity in Ancient Israel: Prolegomena to the Study of Ethnic Sentiments and Their Expression in the Hebrew Bible* (Winona Lake, IN: Eisenbrauns, 1998).

4. On the role of defeat in the formation of the Bible, see Jacob L. Wright, "The Commemoration of Defeat and the Formation of a Nation in the Hebrew Bible," *Prooftexts* 29 (2009): 433–73.

5. For a recent discussion of the subject, see David M. Carr, *The Formation of the Hebrew Bible: A New Reconstruction* (Oxford: Oxford University Press, 2011). See also Gary N. Knoppers and Bernard M. Levinson, eds., *The Pentateuch as Torah: New Models for Understanding Its Promulgation and Acceptance* (Winona Lake, IN: Eisenbrauns, 2007), as well as Gary N. Knoppers, Lester L. Grabbe, and Deirdre N. Fulton, *Exile and Restoration Revisited: Essays on the Babylonian and Persian Periods in Memory of Peter R. Ackroyd* (New York and London: T & T Clark, 2009).

6. The biblical writers engage in frequent polemics against surrounding traditions. Yet the Hebrew Bible is shaped by such traditions and incorporates elements from them. For details, see, for example, Rainer Albertz, *A History of Israelite Religion in the Old Testament* (Louisville, KY: Westminster/John Knox, 1994).

7. Note some of the contradictions between the two accounts. In Genesis 1:26–30, humankind is created last, as male and female, after the animals. In Genesis 2, the human being is created first (2:7), with animals created next as potential partners (2:19–20), and finally the human being is divided into woman and man (2:21–22).

8. Deuteronomy explicitly develops a theory in which certain actions yield certain predictable results: obedience to God's teachings ensures safety and fertility and disobedience ensures disaster (see, for example, Deut 28). Job, however, repeatedly denies the claim that the righteous are rewarded and the wicked are punished (see, for example, 9:22–24). Ecclesiastes likewise denies that just reward and punishment operate in the perceptible world (see, for example, Eccl 9:11). See, for example, Leo G. Perdue, *Wisdom in Revolt: Metaphorical Theology in the Book of Job* (Sheffield, UK: Almond Press, 1991).

9. Chronicles reworks the history of Israel by, for example, casting a very different King David. In Chronicles' retelling, David's affair with Bathsheba and the murder of her husband Uriah, as well as the fratricide that plagues David's household in 2 Samuel 11–19, are all lacking. Instead, David's most ardent efforts in Chronicles are devoted to preparations for the Temple and its personnel (1 Chr 21:18—29:30).

10. On this subject, see, for example, Mark C. Brett, ed., *Ethnicity and the Bible* (Leiden/New York and Cologne: E. J. Brill, 1996), esp. Daniel L. Smith-Christopher, "Between Ezra and Isaiah: Exclusion, Transformation and Inclusion of the "Foreigner" in Post-exilic Biblical Theology," 117–42.

11. On the date of the Book of Ruth, see F. Bush, *Ruth/Esther,* (Dallas: Word Books, 1996), 18–30; and Tamara C. Eskenazi and Tikva Frymer-Kensky, *The JPS Bible Commentary: Ruth* (Philadelphia: Jewish Publication Society, 2011), xvi–xxi.

12. The returned exiles contact Tyre and Sidon for provisions for rebuilding the Temple (Ezra 3:7); Nehemiah himself provides for non-Judeans at his table (Neh 5:17) and allows merchants from Tyre to conduct business in Jerusalem as long as they do not do so on the Sabbath (Neh 13:16–21).

13. Lawrence M. Wills, *Not God's People: Insiders and Outsiders in the Biblical World* (Lanham, MD: Rowman and Littlefield, 2002).

14. Anna L. Grant-Henderson, *Inclusive Voices in Post-Exilic Judah* (Collegeville, MN: Liturgical Press, 2002).

15. On love as a covenant term in the Bible, see, for example, Susan Ackerman, "The Personal is Political: Covenantal and Affectionate Love in the Hebrew Bible," *Vetus Testamentum* 52 (2002): 437–58. See also William L. Moran, "The Ancient Near Eastern Background of the Love of God in Deuteronomy," *Catholic Biblical Quarterly* 25 (1963): 77–87.

16. Whereas Deuteronomy erects social and political boundaries, Leviticus focuses on cultic boundaries, instituting demanding purity laws (see, for example, Lev 12–15). For a comparison between the two perspectives, see Mary Douglas, *Leviticus as Literature* (Oxford: Oxford University Press, 1999).

17. For example, the NJPS translates *elohim* as "God" here but as "divine beings" in Genesis 3:5 and Job 1:6; NRSV renders it likewise as "God" here but also in Genesis 3:6, and uses "heavenly beings" in Job 1:6.

18. Jethro appears with this name or as Moses' father-in-law also in Exodus 2:16–21, and Numbers 10:29–32. The latter case complicates the picture of Jethro. This may account for the rabbinic view of Jethro as a proselyte (see, for example, *Sifre* Num 78–80).

19. David Perlstein, *God's Others: Non-Israelites' Encounters with God in the Hebrew Bible* (New York and Bloomington, IN: iUniverse.com, 2010).

20. See, for example, Deuteronomy 18:9–22 for examples of identity and boundary formation vis-à-vis another population.

21. In M. Lerner, ed., *Tikkun Anthology* (Oakland, CA, and Jerusalem: Tikkun Books, 1992), 465–71. The article first appeared in *Tikkun*, May/June 1991, 43–46, 87.

22. See Phyllis Trible, *God and the Rhetoric of Sexuality*, Overtures to Biblical Theology (Philadelphia: Fortress Press, 1978): 78.

23. The third person, masculine suffix.

24. See, in particular, *Totality and Infinity* (Duquesne University Press, 1969) and Levinas's numerous other works on the subject, including some concise summaries of his key ideas in Levinas's *Ethics and Infinity: Conversations with Philippe Nemo* (Duquesne University Press, 1985).

25. Introduction, in Levinas, *Humanism of the Other* (University of Illinois Press, 2003), xxvii.

26. On Levinas and the Bible, see, for example, Tamara C. Eskenazi, Gary A. Phillips, and David Jobling, eds., *Levinas and Biblical Studies* (Brill, 2006). About interpreting Genesis 2:18 from a Levinas perspective, see also Eskenazi, "Re-Reading the Bible with Levinas," in *Responsibility, God and Society: Theological Ethics in Dialogue; Festschrift Roger Burggraeve*, Johan de Tavernier et al., eds., 69–82 (Leuven and Dudley, MA: Peeters, 2008).

7

Dialogues in the Margins

The *Biblia de Alba* and the
Future of Catholic-Jewish Understanding

Jean-Pierre Ruiz
Carmen M. Nanko-Fernández

INTRODUCTION: READING TOWARD *CONVIVENCIA*

In 1967, just two years after the promulgation of *Nostra Aetate* set Catholic-Jewish relations on a new and promising trajectory, León Klenicki submitted to Hebrew Union College–Jewish Institute of Religion in Cincinnati, a thesis for the degree of master of arts in Hebrew letters and rabbinical ordination titled "The *Biblia de Alba*. The Examination of the Method and Sources of a Translation of a 15th Century Illuminated Spanish Bible Translation."[1] While, to the best of our knowledge, Rabbi Klenicki never revisited this topic in his many published contributions to the body of scholarship on Catholic-Jewish issues, in many ways this modest, unpublished typescript set in motion a career that was deeply devoted to advancing interreligious understanding at every level.[2] More than just a work of erudition on an obscure medieval manuscript that was even less familiar then than it is now, Klenicki's study of the *Biblia de Alba* underscores the wisdom of a saying attributed to the Baal Shem Tov, the founder of Hasidism: "Forgetfulness leads to exile while remembrance is the secret of redemption."[3] Decades later, Klenicki's unpublished thesis remains one of relatively few English language treatments of the medieval masterpiece that he suggests "may have been one of the last intellectual 'dialogues' between a Christian and a Jew before the Expulsion," that is, the expulsion of the Jews from Spain in 1492.[4]

35

Before proceeding, a word is in order about the process by which we worked together to write this chapter, and about what led us to focus our attention on Rabbi Klenicki's work on the *Biblia de Alba*. One of us a Latino biblical scholar and the other a Latina theologian, we are both deeply committed to the practice of *teología de conjunto*, that is, of doing theology in the first person plural. In fact,

> ...there isn't really a convenient and succinct translation that captures the genius of the expression or the wisdom of what underlies the expression. As we see it, the work of theology—of faithful reflection on the workings of God's grace in our lives and the lives of those around us—is not a task at which an individual can succeed. It is a task and a responsibility and a grace to be shared. So too did the Jewish sages teach, by the way, in the Mishnah tractate *Pirqe Aboth* where Joshua ben Perahyah urges those who would study Torah to do so with a teacher and with a fellow disciple. (*m. Aboth* 1.6)[5]

For *teología de conjunto*, the "goal is *convivencia*, a living together as community that is predicated upon analysis of the complexity of that living with the hopes of living together justly and well."[6] We refer to *convivencia* not as a romantic reminiscence, not as a utopian ideal, and not as an eschatological desideratum, but with deliberate and realistic sensitivity to its challenges. We do so with full awareness of the complexities of the centuries of medieval Iberian *convivencia* among Jews, Christians, and Muslims as *tiempos mixtos* of extraordinary opportunities and of equally significant tensions.[7] To engage in *teología en conjunto* is to work toward *convivencia*. Yet "Engagement accomplished *en conjunto*—that is, together, within community—recognizes the need to cross borders while respecting the integrity of boundaries. Fruitful relationships grow in contexts of gracious hospitality that appreciates that when we are in each other's company we are on sacred ground."[8]

The experience we share that provides the background for this appreciation of Rabbi Klenicki's work and what it says about the place of the Bible and its interpretation among Jews and Christians also includes our work as organizers and faculty members for *Comunidades y Convivencia*, a June 2007 seminar that was co-sponsored by the

Bernardin Center for Theology and Ministry of the Catholic Theological Union and the American Jewish Committee. The seminar brought Jews together with a group of Latino/a Catholics who are involved in ministry and theological studies with the aim of broadening mutual understanding between Catholics and Jews and advancing Latino/a Catholic-Jewish relations. What the participants—Catholic and Jewish alike—learned from a week spent together studying and singing, sharing meals and sitting down to serious discussion and debate—was that *comunidad* is not just "a Latino thing" and that *havrutah* is not just "a Jewish thing." In effect, *havrutah*, the time-tested traditional practice of study, discussion, and debate with a partner, is a matter of learning *en conjunto*. What Rabbi Klenicki's study of the *Biblia de Alba* teaches us is that such study among Christians and Jews is nothing new, and so in the twenty-first century, we can learn from study partners whose fifteenth-century footprints we follow in its pages.

With all that in mind, what follows is divided into two sections. In the first section, we will examine the *Biblia de Alba* less as an artifact of medieval artistry and scholarship than as a document that preserves a complex and lively interreligious give-and-take. In the following section, we will then turn to consider some of the many lessons that this fifteenth-century manuscript offers twenty-first-century Christians and Jews, not only for reading the Bible together, but for conjoining our efforts and energies in the construction of authentic *convivencia*. It must be said that this modest study offers only the beginning of a work of *ressourcement* that calls for meticulous and sustained attention. We are convinced that Rabbi Klenicki would urge us to move forward with all diligence in this direction, and we are grateful for his own pioneering first steps in this important project of remembering in the service of recommitment to *convivencia* between Christians and Jews.

READING THE *BIBLIA DE ALBA* EN CONJUNTO

On April 22, 1422, Don Luis de Guzmán, Grand Master of the Military Order of Calatrava, commissioned Rabbi Moses Arragel of Maqueda (c. 1385–1456) to produce "*una biblia en rromançe, glosadae ystoriada*," a Bible in Spanish with glosses and illustrations, to be prepared under the supervision of Don Vasco de Guzmán, the Archdeacon of Toledo, of Franciscan Friar Arias de Ençinas, and the Dominican Friar Johan de Zamora.[9] The Master of Calatrava wrote:

> We, the Maestro de Calatrava, send regards to Rabbi Moses Arragel, our servant in our village of Maqueda, whom we wish honor and good luck. We have been informed that you are a wise man, who knows the law of the Jews, and that you recently moved here. Rabbi Moses: let it be known to you that we need a Bible in Castilian, with glosses and illustrations. We believe that you are capable of this task. Two motives move us to demand this from you: one, the fact that the language of the actual Bible is very corrupt; and secondly, that we are in great need of the glosses for the understanding of the obscure passages. For God knows that in these few moments left to us after battling the evil Moors, the enemies the Holy Catholic Faith, and the service of our Lord the King and the honor of his kingdom, it is convenient for our Order to listen attentively to the Bible. This should be done in order to contemplate God, rather than hunting or reading novels or hearing poets, or playing chess or similar games. It is evident that by reading the Bible, one may reach beatitude and happiness, and this is because it is the Law of God.[10]

Nine days later, Rabbi Moses (of whom little else is known) answered Guzmán in a long letter (preserved in the prologue of the *Biblia de Alba*) in which he proffers countless reasons for declining the commission. He claims, for example, "If I would translate into Spanish in a different fashion from the Latin version and St. Jerome the Master would find the translation quite corrupt, and if I would follow them...there are already others who have done better than I can do."[11] Reluctant to challenge the authority of the Vulgate, Rabbi Moses attempts to sidestep the project by suggesting that by comparison with the translation into Latin, a Christian reader would be likely to judge his own work inferior. Addressing the delicate situation in which Rabbi Moses found himself, A. A. Sicroff explains:

In making his case for not complying with the Grand Master's request, he reminded him that Jews and Christians disagreed on the authenticity of their respective editions of the Bible. While Jews held St. Jerome's Vulgate erroneous because it was translated from the faulty Greek Septuagint, observed Rabbi Mosé, Christians claimed the Jewish Hebrew version was corrupt since the authentic original text had been lost, according to them, during Israel's Babylonian captivity. Thus any translation into Castilian from the Hebrew would necessarily differ from the Latin Vulgate. Christians would therefore condemn it as corrupt—and, we may add, it would only provide them with still another confirmation of Jewish "perversity" in rejecting Jesus as the Messiah who had been promised them.[12]

A further objection on the part of Rabbi Moses has to do with Guzmán's desire for a translation of the *Tanakh* that included illustrations. Rabbi Moses protests: "Once again, O most Noble Sire, another problem arises because of your demand [of illustrating the Bible] that restrains me to accept [the task]. It is important to mention to you that the Ten Commandments commands us not to make images…and it is a great danger to give form to the image of God, for God is incorporeal, with no form comprehensible to us or to any angelical nature."[13] Guzmán dealt with this objection by commissioning others to paint the illustrations, with Rabbi Moses offering the artists his advice.[14] In the end, Guzmán prevailed over Rabbi Moses' objections and the work of translation moved forward. It should be emphasized, I think that Arragel, as a Jew, really had no choice in the matter. In 1433, eleven years later, the project was completed, a manuscript volume of 513 pages, including Arragel's translation and glosses (more than 6,000 of them), with 324 illustrations, as well as a glossary of important terms and an extensive prologue that includes extensive documentation of the give-and-take between patron and translator.

The *Biblia de Alba* (so called because the manuscript is now among the holdings of the Duke of Alba) is an exceptional example of Jewish-Christian engagement in fifteenth-century Spain.[15] Klenicki explains that "the original text was adorned in the margins or in between lines with comments on obscure words or expressions. The glosses written by Arragel are a running commentary to the books of

the Bible. The translator gives the Jewish opinion and sometimes
only the Catholic....Many times in the same paragraph the two opinions are given...."[16]

The inclusion of the correspondence among the principals in the
extended (the first twenty-five folios of the book, fifty manuscript
pages) prologue of the *Biblia de Alba* also enhances the sense of dialogue in the very pages of the volume inasmuch as it "prepares the
reader to encounter the commentaries as a debate between equals."[17]
The exegetical and theological conversation that takes place around
the edges of the pages and in the prologue reflects the content of the
deeper discussions carried out among the principals in their written
correspondences as well as the inevitable results of the censorship
process. The tension between translator and censors finds expression,
for example, in the handling of Genesis 1:26. For example, Arragel
translates Genesis 1:26 as *Dixo el Señor: fagamos omne a nuestra
ymagen e nuestra semeianca*, ("*Let* us make the human in our own
image and likeness"). Klenicki explains the translator's gloss:

> It starts denying the fact that the words "Let us make man
> in our image" means that God sought the advice of the
> angels when he planned to create man. The midrash relates
> that the angels, at least some of them, reacted violently to
> this idea of God and resented that so much of divine love
> should be lavished on a new creature. This is the Jewish
> explanation as found in the classical sources, and it is evi-
> dent that Arragel wanted to include it but the censors con-
> sidered the Catholic version more important. The fact that
> the comment starts with a negation of the Jewish point of
> view is evidence of the strict control upon Arragel's work.
> The Catholic opinion included in the text says that the
> verb in the plural "naase" means that God had the cooper-
> ation of His Son, Jesus Christ, who advised God in the cre-
> ation of man. The verb is proof of the trinity.[18]

The glosses often demonstrate integrity with respect to each
religious tradition as well as interdisciplinary engagement with a
range of contemporary and ancient sources, including those not
explicitly related to either faith community. Also visible in these dialogues along the edges is a cautious but daring venture into interreli-

gious cooperation that remains marginalized in the greater web of celebrated interreligious initiatives. According to Sonia Fellous, a preeminent scholar of this manuscript, the *Biblia de Alba* represents an attempt to deal with doctrinal divergence in a manner whereby the resulting translation with its glosses "became a work of comparative doctrine, a duality marking its imagery as well as its text. This deviant text resembles no other; it follows no known model; it is faithful to the original Hebrew while using Jerome's vocabulary; often its translation is completely original."[19]

This manuscript and the process and relationships that brought this translation into being should not be romanticized, for it bears all the marks of the tense and conflicted times in which it was produced. This is visually evident, for example, in the handful of caricatures of Jews found in the illustrations.[20] Fellous postulates several motivations for what she describes as this "unusual collaboration." First, the patron's "explicit impulse was scholarly: to have an accurate translation into good Castilian, and to provide himself and other learned ecclesiastics with an explanation of obscure passages."[21] She also suggests that the "point was to establish an official text of Hebrew scripture in the vernacular, as the terrain, if not of agreement, at least of serene discussion between Christians and Jews who might be converted more easily with an ecumenical version of the Bible."[22] The overt agenda for Christian conversion of Jews also appears in a letter from Fray Arias to Rabbi Arragel:

> ...let me tell you my dear friend rabbi that it would be better if you should recognize the Holy Trinity and the Roman Faith, and in this manner illumine with truth your soul and avoid hell, and know the real savior the king Messiah, Jesus Christ. But perhaps in your hardness you want to continue your heritage, and you want to be like that individual who used to eat bad food, and was asked the reason, and answered that he was so accustomed because his father did the same.[23]

The power dimensions in this medieval instance of *teología en conjunto* cannot be ignored, nor should the Rabbi Arragel's fear of the reprisals that might arise from misunderstandings of his work be easily dismissed.[24] Scholars of the *Biblia de Alba* note that, not only might this

have affected Arragel himself, but also that his family and the greater
Jewish community lived their daily lives in a vulnerable condition that
oscillated between precarious ambivalence and destructive violence.[25]
This reality may have contributed to Arragel's inclusion of a glossary
(that included explanations of such terms as *antichrist, apostle, son of
God*, and *theology*), as well as the care with which the prologue provides readers with clarifying instructions or a disclaimer. Anthony Pym
submits that these moves may signify a "self-protection program,
designed to keep the translator well out of the ring of any disputation
and to absolve him of any complaints that might ensue."[26] However, it
is Klenicki and his intimacy with the Spanish language as a native
speaker who recognizes in Arragel's strategy a creative subversion necessary for survival: "His use of the subjunctive verb is so subtle that it
allows him to say many of the things that his heart was hiding, without
incurring the wrath of the Maestro. The style shows the rich personality of the man, not only in knowledge but also in human wisdom and
the art of politics."[27] For "apostle," Arragel explains:

> In many places of this gloss apostles of God will be men-
> tioned. Also in this are Latins and Hebrews divided. For
> the Latins the word comes to mean the apostles that
> [preached] the faith of Jesus Christ and with them they
> sent letters to the provinces and kingdoms. And the Jews
> consider the apostles of God the holy fathers Abraham,
> Isaac, and Jacob, and the holy prophets, all of them carried
> the divine message and so this name of apostle can be con-
> sidered by two nations, and not only by one of them.[28]

Placing the two readings of "apostle" one after the next so that
neither denigrates or obscures the validity of the other, Arragel's deft
deployment of the arts of resistance make it possible for him to speak
his truth to his powerful patron while maintaining every appearance
of deferential submission to the Maestro. There are other occasions
where Rabbi Moses is more direct in underscoring the differences
between Christian and Jewish perspective. In the definition of "theology," for example, he tells his patron:

> It is important to note here, Maestro, that there are deep
> differences between Latins and Hebrews concerning the

definition and teaching of theology. As the Jews do not believe in the trinity of God, they say that this science is the only one that gives knowledge of God...but the Christians believe the Trinity of this science, and through it they believe in all the things that the Roman Church believes. Consequently, when in this work it is said in many places: holy theology, the Jew does not think [of] the trinity, but in one Divinity, and they call this science that we name holy theology, the science of Elahuth; but the Christians believe what we said before. At this point, each one should keep his law and his principles.[29]

Retrieving the complicated and non-innocent history of the *Biblia de Alba en conjunto* with León Klenicki opens spaces for new conversations around the margins of our biblical texts today, new conversations between Christians and Jews about texts that have been both common ground and bitterly contested space for our communities. Insights that can offer valuable guidance for productive interreligious engagement echo across the centuries. At the same time, the tragic memory of the deterioration of Jewish-Christian relations in fifteenth-century Spain serves as sobering reminder of the painful legacy of harsh words and the hostile actions that such words provoke. The words of the Baal Shem Tov surely ring true: "Forgetfulness leads to exile while remembrance is the secret of redemption." Yet remembering for its own sake is not necessarily either generative or salutary.

FUTURING OUR PAST[30]

On the 25th of September 1492, some Bibles written in Spanish, more than twenty volumes, were condemned in the city of Salamanca as heretic [*sic*], and also for contradicting our tradition. They were translated after the fashion of Hebrew texts, that they (the Jews) have already corrected and in many places are far from the truth, and specially in those passages referring to Christ the Saviour. For this reason, they were burned.[31]

The *Biblia de Alba* is one of a very few vernacular Bibles to sur-
vive the expulsion of the Jews from Spain, and to avoid the flames
that reduced to ashes so much of the hard work of Iberian Jewish
translators. Sadly, even this important manuscript has remained relatively unknown beyond a very limited readership.[32] Pym traces the
manuscript's journey from its original patron, the Grand Master of
Calatrava, through its two centuries of incarceration in the Holy
Office of the Inquisition and its 1624 return to a Guzmán family
descendant "in recognition of the 'generous amount' his ancestor had
spent commissioning the translation."[33] With the manuscript ultimately inherited by the House of Alba, Pym concludes that, "In a
sense, this is the profound symbiosis manifested not only in an illustrated Jewish bible but also in Jewish intellectual content being long
held, like a prize of battle, in very selected Christian hands. That long
historical conquest, that active sequestering, should adequately jus-
tify the text being described as a Christian trophy."[34]

Only two modern editions of the *Biblia de Alba* have ever been
published. The first appeared in two volumes (1920 and 1922) in a
limited edition of some 200 copies. A second lavish facsimile edition
was published in 1992, with only 500 copies produced. It is the
1920–22 edition that Rabbi Klenicki consulted in preparing his thesis. That edition, Klenicki explains, was published by the Duke of
Berwick and Alba to satisfy the requirements for his membership in
the Roxburghe Club, which proudly identifies itself—on the
Internet—as "the oldest society of bibliophiles in the world," with its
membership limited to 40, "chosen from among those with distinguished libraries or collections, or with a scholarly interest in books."
The club stipulates that "each member is expected to produce a book
at his or her own expense for presentation to the other members."[35]

Of his own contribution to the Roxburghe Club's editions, the
Duke of Berwick and Alba explains: "It was the purpose of the House
of Alba since the days of my deceased mother to publish this Bible
known as the Bible of the House of Alba; but the task was delayed by
the printing of other books. The rule of the Roxburghe Club of
London, to which I belong, is that each member should publish a
manuscript of his library, and this condition has hastened the decision
of the present edition."[36]

The only available facsimile edition of the *Biblia de Alba* was
published in 1992 under the aegis of the *Fundación Amigos de*

Sefarad and produced by Facsimile Editions.[37] Accompanied by a commentary volume edited by Jeremy Schonfield, the 1992 facsimile is priced at U.S. $49,950, putting it well out of reach of individual researchers and of all but a very few research libraries.[38] Tragically, the work that Rabbi Moses Arragel hoped would satisfy the wise and the ignorant has become a coffee table book for billionaires!

Fortunately, in our time, it is no longer unusual for Jews to be teaching Christians about the Bible, and even challenging mistaken Christian readings of the Bible—including the New Testament. In October of 2008, Shear-Yashuv Cohen, the Grand Rabbi of Haifa, addressed the Twelfth General Assembly of the Synod of Bishops as they convened around the theme of "The Word of God in the Life and Mission of the Church."[39] Jewish and Christian biblical scholars and theologians regularly engage in academic conversations about the Bible and its place in the life of their communities.[40] Amy-Jill Levine, a New Testament scholar whose Vanderbilt University Divinity School biography refers to her as a "self-described 'Yankee Jewish feminist who teaches in a predominantly Christian divinity school in the buckle of the Bible Belt,'" is an active member of the Catholic Biblical Association of America who serves as New Testament Book Review Editor for the Association's prestigious journal, the *Catholic Biblical Quarterly*.[41]

For his part, Michael J. Cook, Professor at Hebrew Union College–Jewish Institute of Religion, has taken up the task of addressing Jewish audiences to invite them to acquaint themselves with the New Testament. In so doing, he answers an urgent need. He writes: "As a result of not knowing how to engage the New Testament, Jews have allowed problems that began after the mid-first century not only to recur frequently, but also to intensify and fester. These problems have persisted into modern times, continuing to destabilize Jews' well-being on a communal as well as an individual basis."[42] It is not by any means Cook's intention to convert Jews to Christianity by inviting them to engage the New Testament, yet, his purposes are not merely academic. As the title of his book suggests, his agenda is a matter of enhancing Jewish well-being in a Christian environment—an environment over which the shadow of the Holocaust still looms large and menacing.

Among the lasting lessons from the fifteenth century that Rabbi Moses Arragel offers to Christian and Jewish readers of the Bible in the twenty-first century is that we can—and should—talk differently about the Bible. León Klenicki observed that "behind some of Arragel's comments there is the feeling of the great differences between both faiths, and the importance of certain concepts, vital importance, for each of them."[43] As Arragel explained to the Maestro de Calatrava,

> It was not intended for the Christian, and less the Jew, to commit a mistake in his faith, where the Christian feels that some point or gloss is contrary to the articles of his faith, he finds them in relation to the point of view of the Hebrews, and not because of a spirit of polemics. The same concerns the Jew....In this manner, if the Christians and the Jews accept this schema, he will not fall into error, and will not say that he finds heresies or contradictory opinions. And each one, Christian or Jew, should not forsake the articles of his faith because of the opinions found here, but should believe these credos firmly because in this work the different opinions are detailed, to relate without determining or affirming a disputation. For I am a Jew, I believe in the Jewish opinions, as the Christian believes in his....[44]

Learning from Arragel's thoughtful words to his patron, we discover that crafting *convivencia* does not call for imposing conformity in reading practices, in religious beliefs, or in the everyday exigencies of life.

As we approach the 600th anniversary of its commissioning, and in the light of nearly half a century of active Jewish-Catholic dialogue, perhaps we find ourselves at an appropriate moment to revisit the *Biblia de Alba* with fresh understanding. In the United States, the changing demographics of the Catholic Church bring a Latino/a plurality to the grassroots, as well as innovative ways of thinking and acting theologically. As Christians and Jews future our past *en conjunto*, the retrieval of a medieval Iberian text expands the parameters of what constitute the resources for our ongoing dialogue and challenges the myopia that confines interreligious dialogue to particular circles, academic or otherwise. From the conversations that take place in the margins, with and about texts and contexts that matter deeply to us, perhaps *convivencia* can be re-imagined and even sustained, so that, rich and confident in our diversity, we will be able to "live together, listening to the word of God; it is a river of true theology coming out of paradise."[45]

NOTES

1. We are very grateful to Frances Hankins, interlibrary loan supervisor at the Bechtold Library of the Catholic Theological Union, Chicago, IL, for her assistance in obtaining a copy of León Klenicki's thesis for the master's degree in Hebrew letters and rabbinical ordination. We are also grateful to the staff of the New York Public Library's Dorot Jewish division for providing us with access to their copy of the edition of the *Biblia de Alba* that León Klenicki consulted and also to their copy of the 1992 facsimile edition.

2. Rabbi Klenicki clearly recognized the vital importance of the Bible both as common and contested ground for Jews and Christians. This is evident based on his collaboration as co-editor of volumes that focus on this dimension of the ongoing dialogue. See, for example, *Biblical Studies: Meeting Ground of Jews and Christians*, ed. Lawrence Boadt, Helga Croner, and León Klenicki (New York and Ramsey, NJ: Paulist Press, 1980); and *Within Context: Essays on Jews and Judaism in the New Testament*, ed. David Efroymsen, Eugene J. Fisher, and León Klenicki (Collegeville, MN: Liturgical Press, 1993).

3. Frequently attributed to the Baal Shem Tov, the original source of this saying is elusive. It is cited, for example, in Lesli Koppelman Ross, "The Importance of Remembering," *My Jewish Learning*, http://www.my jewishlearning.com/holidays/Jewish_Holidays/Modern_Holidays/Yom_Has hoah/Importance_of_Remembering. shtml.

4. León Klenicki, "The Biblia de Alba: The Examination of the Method and Sources of a Translation of a 15th Century Illuminated Spanish Bible Translation" (master's thesis in Hebrew letters and ordination, Hebrew Union College–Jewish Institute of Religion, Cincinnati, OH, 1967), 25. Klenicki quotes Margherita Morreale, who observes, "It is a strange fact that despite the importance and quantity of the Spanish Bibles, so little has been studied. And today that the revelations between Christians and Jews are widely discussed it is difficult to understand that the precise documentation offered by the medieval versions is not the object of more research" (Margherita Morreale, "Apuntes bibliograficos para la iniciación al estudio de las traducciones biblicas medievales en Castellano," *Sefarad* 20 [1960]: 72, as cited and translated in Klenicki, "The Biblia de Alba," 60). Sadly, what Morreale observed half a century ago remains the case today.

5. Jean-Pierre Ruiz, "Beginning a Conversation: Unlikely Hermanos: Jews and Latinos/as in the United States," *Apuntes* 29 (2009): 47.

6. Carmen Nanko-Fernández, *Theologizing en Espanglish: Context, Community, and Ministry* (Maryknoll, NY: Orbis, 2010), xviii.

7. See Jean-Pierre Ruiz, "From Disputation to Dialogue: Jews and Latinos/as towards a New Convivencia," *New Theology Review* 22 (2009): 36–48.

8. Nanko-Fernández, *Theologizing en Espanglish*, 86.

9. Sonia Fellous, "Cultural Subversion: Text and Image in the Alba Bible, 1422–33," *Exemplaria* 12 (2000): 206. In 1414, Luis de Guzmán was elected twenty-fifth Master of the Military Order of Calatrava. This order, Klenicki explains, was founded in Castile during the twelfth century, with its rule approved by Pope Gregory VIII in 1187. Considered a military branch of the Cistercian order, and established to participate in the Christian *reconquista* against Muslim-controlled portions of the Iberian peninsula, its members were bound to "rules of silence in the refectory, dormitory, and oratory; of abstinence on four days a week, besides several fast days during the year; they were also obliged to recite a fixed number of paternosters for each daily hour they held office; [and] to sleep in their armour" (Klenicki, "The Biblia de Alba," 28). In his thesis, Klenicki makes use of the text (and offers translations from portions of) an edition of this Bible published in 1920 (vol. 1) and 1922 (vol. 2), Antonio Paz y Melía, ed., *Biblia de Alba (Antiguo Testamento). Traducida del Hebreo al Castellano por Rabi Mose Arragel de Guadalfajara (1422–1433?) y publicada por el Duque de Berwick y de Alba* (Madrid: Imprenta Artistica, 1920–22). Also see Sonia Fellous, "Les Rois et la Royauté dans la Biblia de Alba," *Jewish History* 21 (2007): 69–95.

10. *Biblia de Alba*, 1–2, trans. Klenicki, "The Biblia de Alba," 36.

11. Ibid., 10, trans. Klenicki, "The Biblia de Alba," 43.

12. A. A. Sicroff, "The Arragel Bible: A Fifteenth Century Rabbi Translates and Glosses the Bible for His Christian Master," in *Américo Castro: The Impact of His Thought. Essays to Mark the Centenary of His Birth*, ed. Ronald E. Surtz, Jamie Ferrán, and Daniel P. Testa (Madison, WI: Hispanic Seminary of Medieval Studies, 1988), 175–76. Sicroff cites page 10 of Rabbi Moses' prologue in the *Biblia de Alba*.

13. *Biblia de Alba*, 10–11, trans. Klenicki, "The Biblia de Alba," 44.

14. See Sonia Fellous-Rozenblat, "The Artists of the Biblia de Alba," in *La Biblia de Alba: An Illustrated Manuscript Bible in Castilian with Translation and Commentaries by Rabbi Moses Arragel Commissioned in 1422 by Don Luis de Guzmán and now in the Library of the Palacio de Liria, Madrid. The Companion Volume*, ed. Jeremy Schonfield (Madrid: Fundación Amigos de Sefarad, 1992), 65–77.

15. Two modern printed editions of the *Biblia de Alba* exist, although both are quite rare. One is the edition mentioned in note 9 above. Not a facsimile, this two-volume edition is a transcript of the original manuscript. In this edition, prepared by Antonio Paz y Melía and Julián Paz, the text of the translation of each book of the Bible is followed by the glosses, with numbers that correspond to the place of each gloss in the manuscript. Antonio Paz y Melía provides an introduction (vii–xxi), and the edition includes a number of color plates of the Bible's magnificent images. More recently, a lavish facsimile edition was published: Jeremy Schonfield, ed., *La Biblia de Alba: An Illustrated Manuscript Bible in Castilian* (Madrid: Fundación Amigos de Sefarad, 1992). That edition is accompanied by a companion volume with essays by leading scholars on the *Biblia de Alba*. See http://www.facsimile-editions.com/en/ab/. In an essay that appears in the companion volume of the 1992 facsimile, Moshe Lazar characterizes Paz y Melía's edition in the following terms: "While representing a major scholarly achievement in his generation, his transcription suffers from serious shortcomings which make his edition un-reliable for serious scholarly investigation" ("Moses Arragel as Translator and Commentator," in Schonfield, *La Biblia de Alba*, 158). Although Lazar mentions that a critical edition of the *Biblia de Alba* was in progress at the time of his essay, it is regrettable that (as of 2012) that publication has not yet appeared.

16. Klenicki, "The *Biblia de Alba*," 73.

17. Fellous, "Cultural Subversion," 210.

18. Klenicki, "The *Biblia de Alba*," 74–75.

19. Fellous, "Cultural Subversion," 207–8.

20. Fellous notes less than ten of the 324 miniatures include caricatures, that is, "the representation of the Jew according to Christian polemic: humpbacked, hook-nosed, with moneybag hanging from his belt" (ibid., 217).

21. Ibid., 208.

22. Ibid. Also see Emily C. Francomano, "Castilian Vernacular Bibles in Iberia, c. 1250–1500," in *The Practice of the Bible in the Middle Ages: Production, Reception, and Performance in Western Christianity*, ed. Susan Boynton and Diane J. Reilly (New York: Columbia University Press, 2011), 315–37.

23. Letter of Arias to Arragel April 25, 1422, trans. Klenicki, "The *Biblia de Alba*," 50.

24. See Carlos Sainz de la Maza, "Poderpolítico y poder doctrinal en la creación de la Biblia de Alba," *e-Spania* (June 3, 2007), http://e-spania.revues.org/116.

25. In "The *Biblia de Alba* and Its Times," Sonia Fellous-Rozenblat writes: "The evidence would suggest that the status of the Jews in thirteenth-century Spain was better than elsewhere in Europe. Nevertheless, they had

to live with insecurity and constant friction, due to the religious and nationalist tensions which might, at any moment, erupt and degenerate into persecution. Factional struggles among the nobility, was abroad or turbulence [*sic*] stirred up by the Church inevitably led people to search for a scapegoat and unleashed religious hatred against the enemies of God—the role all-too-easily assigned to Jews." This condition persisted throughout the fourteenth and fifteenth centuries. The massacres of 1391 are an especially vivid example: "Rioting began on 6 June at Seville and on 20 June at Toledo. A wave of violence swept the country, creating a climate of terror which lasted several months. Most Jewish communities, vulnerable to looting, murder, or forced baptism, were partially or totally destroyed" (Sonia Fellous-Rozenblat, "The *Biblia de Alba* and Its Times," in *La Biblia de Alba: An Illustrated Manuscript Bible in Castilian with Translation and Commentaries by Rabbi Moses Arragel Commissioned in 1422 by Don Luis de Guzmán and now in the Library of the Palacio de Liria, Madrid. The Companion Volume,* ed. Jeremy Schonfield [Madrid: Fundación Amigos de Sefarad, 1992], 38, 42).

26. Anthony Pym, "Negotiating the Frontier: A Christian's Rabbinic Bible" (unpublished work in progress, 1999), http://usuaris.tinet.cat/apym/on-line/intercultures/studies/alba.html.

27. Klenicki, "The Biblia de Alba," 68.

28. *Biblia de Alba*, 23, trans. Klenicki, "Biblia de Alba," 69–70.

29. *Biblia de Alba*, 27, trans. Klenicki, "Biblia de Alba," 70–71.

30. The expression is taken from the title of *Futuring Our Past: Explorations in the Theology of Tradition*, ed. Orlando O. Espin and Gary Macy (Maryknoll, NY: Orbis Books, 2006).

31. P. José Llamas, *Biblias Medieval es Romanceadas. Biblia medieval romanceada judio-cristiana* (Madrid: Instituto Francisco Suarez, 1950), 1:xvi, as cited and translated by Klenicki, "The Biblia de Alba," 58.

32. For an explanation of what became of the manuscript, see Sicroff, "The Arragel Bible," 180–81, note 1.

33. Pym, "Negotiating the Frontier." Also see Fellous, "Cultural Subversion," 229.

34. Pym, "Negotiating the Frontier."

35. See http://www.roxburgheclub.org.uk/.

36. *Biblia de Alba*, v, as cited in Klenicki, "The Biblia de Alba," 34. Also see Eleazar Gutwirth, "The Transmission of Rabbi Moses Arragel: Maqueda, Paris, London," *Sefarad* 63 (2003): 80.

37. Jeremy Schonfield, ed. *La Biblia de Alba*. Also see Jeremy Schonfield, "Biblia para la Concordia: La Biblia de Alba." *FMR* Edición española 4 / 1992, 83–108.

38. See the description of the Alba Bible on the Facsimile Editions website, http://www.facsimile-editions.com/en/ab/, with reproductions of a number of the illustrated pages.

39. The text of Rabbi Cohen's address is available at http://www.zenit.org/article-23837?l=english. Also see Pontifical Biblical Commission, "The Jewish People and their Sacred Scriptures in the Christian Bible" (2001), http://www.vatican.va/roman_curia/congregations/cfaith/pcb_documents/rc_con_cfaith_doc_20020212_popolo-ebraico_en.html.

40. See, for example, Melody D. Knowles and others, eds., *Contesting Texts: Jews and Christians in Conversation about the Bible* (Minneapolis: Fortress Press, 2007). This volume emerged from a 2005 conference in Chicago under the same name.

41. See http://divinity.vanderbilt.edu/people/bio/amy-jill-levine. Also see Amy-Jill Levine, "A Particular Problem: Jewish Perspectives on Christian Bible Study," in *Theology and Sacred Scripture*, ed. Carol J. Dempsey and William P. Loewe (College Theology Society Annual 47; Marryknoll, NY: Orbis Books, 2002), 12–23; as well as Levine's book *The Misunderstood Jew: The Church and the Scandal of the Jewish Jesus* (New York: HarperCollins, 2006).

42. Michael J. Cook, *Modern Jews Engage the New Testament: Enhancing Jewish Well-Being in a Christian Environment* (Woodstock, VT: Jewish Lights, 2008), xiii.

43. Klenicki, "The Biblia de Alba," 74.

44. *Biblia de Alba*, 19. Translation by Klenicki, "The Biblia de Alba," 66–68.

45. The quotation is from Rabbi Moses Arragel's speech on the occasion of the presentation of the *Biblia de Alba*, as translated by Klenicki, "The Biblia de Alba," 32.

III

IDENTITY

8

Jewish Identity

Shira Lander

León Klenicki, whose memory continues to be for a blessing, was a rare combination of *joie-de-vivre* and healthy cynicism. The most extended discussion I had with him was after we had both served on a delegation of international Jewish leaders to meet the newly elected Pope Benedict XVI at the Vatican on June 9, 2005. The day after our papal audience was Friday, and León invited me to join him and Myra for Shabbat dinner in Rome. I didn't know quite what to expect. I had read León's work and heard paeans about him from my father, a rabbinical colleague of León who was himself deeply devoted to interfaith work. Rabbi Klenicki loomed very large in the pantheon of interfaith relations pioneers. What I found in both him and Myra was a warmth, charm, and curiosity that embraced me, inspired me, and made me feel right at home. We recited the Sabbath blessings, and related our personal stories. Coming from very different backgrounds, we shared a profound conviction that repairing the Catholic-Jewish relationship was imperative to the health of both of our religious communities. We also shared a skepticism about whether meetings, such as the one we had just participated in, would accomplish anything beyond a public gesture. The real work of extensive conversation and probing study would need to be undertaken by teachers, religious leaders, and congregants, whose mundane personal interactions would be influenced by what they thought or believed about the other. This article is offered as a tribute to that ongoing work to which León contributed more than his fair share.

The question "Who is a Jew?" is as contentious now as it was during the centuries surrounding Christianity's emergence, and it is unlikely to be resolved in the near future. Despite attempts to fix a static definition, the definition is continually changing. Over the past

few millennia, Jews have constructed identity ethnically, anthropo-
logically, sociologically, and legally, but rarely theologically. That is
not to say, contrary to commonly held claims, that Judaism does not
use theology to develop its understanding of God or of God's relationship to the Jewish people; rather, Jewish self-understanding has
not typically relied on such discourse as its defining feature. Yet the
proliferation of Jewish theologians in the last century suggests that
this, too, is in flux.

Jews have understood themselves as the bearers of the ethnic
and spiritual heritage of the Biblical people known as *b'nei Yisrael*
(children of Israel). Particularly in the modern era, the Jewish people
is synonymous with the term used to denote the residents of the local-
ity known in ancient times as Judah, Yehud, Judea, and Palestine,
namely *Yisrael* (Israel). This perception has presented somewhat of a
theological stumbling block for Jewish-Catholic relations, since this
Jewish understanding of "Israel" conflicts with the dominant Catholic
one. Catholics understand "Israel" more broadly than do Jews.
According to the Dogmatic Constitution on the Church of the Second
Vatican Council, the theological category "Israel" includes the
Church, the "new Israel," along with the Jewish people, "Israel
according to the flesh."[1] This enlarged, more inclusive Israel—the
constitution declares—constitutes the "people of God."[2]

The Jewish apostle of Christ, Paul, was the first writer known to
us who articulated the notion of an expanded or eschatological Israel
(Rom 11:11), yet his understanding of the relationship between gentiles and Jews as part of that "Israel" is not altogether clear. Church
leaders over the past two millennia have variously interpreted the
relationship between Israel "according to the flesh" and Israel
"according to the spirit" as replacement, or supersession, and inclusion. The Second Vatican Council affirmed the inclusive, non-supersessionist view of Israel when it asserted: "Although the Church is
the new people of God, the Jews should not be presented as rejected
or accursed by God, as if this followed from the Holy Scriptures."[3]

For Jews, however, "Israel" generally excludes Catholics as
well as any other non-Jews on both ethnic and spiritual grounds.
Jewish rejection of Christian claims to be Israel was a source of controversy and sociological division for nearly two millennia. Until the
creation of the modern State of Israel, how Jews construed the category "Israel" recapitulated the difference and separation that

Christian officials repeatedly sought to produce and enforce.[4] Since 1948, however, some Catholics have challenged the legal boundary between Jew and Catholic. There have been some difficult test cases, such as Brother Daniel Rufeisen's claim to Jewish identity for the purposes of the modern State of Israel's Law of Return. In 1962, the Carmelite friar, born to Jewish parents, was denied immediate citizenship by the civil court, but proclaimed Jewish by the rabbinical court, which cited the strict *halakhic* (Jewish legal) interpretation of a Jew as one born of a Jewish mother. Later, in 1989, the Supreme Court of Israel ruled that people who had converted to another religion, including Messianic Judaism, were thereby not eligible for citizenship under the law. Although the State of Israel exercises no jurisdiction over Jews living elsewhere, Jews worldwide generally subscribe to the understanding of Jewish identity expressed by the Israeli Supreme Court's 1989 ruling. They therefore define a Jew as someone of Jewish ancestry who has not converted to another religion. Although the legal, or halakhic definition, limits the first part of this definition to those of maternal Jewish ancestry, most Reform Jews consider this gendered limitation to be obsolete. This definition of Jewishness is hybrid, combining the ethnic with the sociological. Curiously, what is missing from this understanding is any explicit theological component, a fact that alarms many rabbis whose own identities and understandings of Judaism are predominately theological. While the conversion clause of the Israeli court decision suggests certain theological boundaries, or *limes ad quo*, these boundaries constitute negative constraints rather than positive affirmations or creedal formulations. Furthermore, these negative theological constraints are determined by the (theological) formulations of other religions to which a Jew might convert, rather than by a set of Jewish theological principles.

Not all non-Jews have the same theological status in traditional Jewish understanding. Despite the tendency of some medieval (especially Sephardic) thinkers to consider Christian veneration before statues to constitute idolatry, Ashkenazic authorities, for the most part, consider Christians (and Muslims) to be monotheistic and not pagan (or polytheistic). The oft-quoted Talmudic dictum that "gentiles outside the Land of Israel are not idolaters" (*b. Hul.* 13b) is expanded in the Middle Ages to apply to all gentiles (*Tosafot* to *b. 'Avod. Zar.* 2a). This standard of what constitutes paganism is rather ironic given that Judaism did not traditionally use a belief litmus test as a barometer of Jewishness for itself. In Jewish law, a nonbelieving Jew may be a *min* (heretic), a *koferba-ikkar* (one who denies the fundamentals of faith; see *b. Pesah*. 168b), or an *apikoros*, a good rabbinic term imported from the Greek *Epicurean* (see *m. Sanh.* 10:1), but at the end of the day, he or she is still a Jew. This is why Jews who convert to Christianity need not undergo conversion upon renouncing their Christianity and reclaiming their Jewish identity (*Shulchan Arukh*, Yoreh Deah 268:12). This is the reason that the Israeli chief rabbinate considered Brother Daniel to be Jewish. While the consequences of nonbelief are traditionally construed as dire—no place in the world to come, that is, no posthumous salvation—the children of such a nonbeliever could be considered as Jewish as a rabbi's children. Nonetheless, this halakhic understanding is contravened by prevailing norms, as evidenced by the 1989 Israeli Supreme Court ruling on the Law of Return.

The Jewish custom of sitting *shiva* (traditional mourning ritual) for relatives who converted to Christianity also belies the understanding of Jewish identity as solely ethnic. Because this practice was based on an erroneous reading of an aggadah of Rabbi Isaac ben Moses of Vienna in *Or Zarua* regarding Rabbi Gershom ben Judah, who was wrongly thought to have observed *shiva* when his son had converted to Christianity rather than when his son had died, it has been largely abandoned.[5] The custom was made famous by its depiction in *Fiddler on the Roof* where Tevye exclaims, "Chava is dead to us!" once he has learned of her marriage to a Christian man. The story is adapted from Sholem Aleichem's *Tevye the Dairyman*, which uses more explicit language: "Get up, my wife, take off your shoes and let us sit down on the floor and mourn our child for seven days, as God has commanded."[6] In the contemporary period, such radical measures are uncommon, yet the understanding that a Jew who converts to another religious faith is no longer Jewish is pervasive. This understanding suggests that belief makes a difference when determining Jewishness, if only as an inadvertent result of the distinction between Jew and non-Jew as made in a Christian context. The boundary between Jew and non-Jew depends, in some measure, on the non-Jew's own self-definition, which, in the case of Christianity, entails faith. Boundaries are challenging in that way: they have a tendency to blur precisely what is attempting to be kept separate, and may even have the unintended result of each group influencing the other's self-definition. As Hebrew University professor Israel Yuval has observed, in the Middle Ages, "negation of the 'other' was an indispensable stage in the process of defining one's own identity."[7] In the modern world, Jews continue to define themselves in relation to Christianity, if sometimes unconsciously, but not by the principle of negation so much as exclusion. To a great extent, Jews understand themselves as "not Christian."[8]

Despite this faith aspect of Jewish identity, some contemporary Jews claim their Jewishness without any concomitant Jewish practice or belief. Some of these secular Jews may even identify themselves as "atheists," such as the pop singer Billy Joel, author Gina Welch, or Facebook creator Mark Zuckerberg.[9] This non-theological nature of modern Jewish identity is often perplexing to Catholics. Many rabbis and other Jewish participants in interfaith dialogue often acquiesce to Catholic theological expectations by asserting that the minimum requirement for Jewish belief is the oneness of God, as articulated in the *Sh'ma* (Deut 6:4) and are quick to dismiss "secular Judaism" as an oxymoron.

Along these lines, various Jewish thinkers have attempted to formulate essential principles of Jewish belief. Jewish philosophers—from the first-century Alexandrian Philo to the twelfth-century Spanish-Egyptian Moses Maimonides—have included belief in one God in their formulations of these principles.[10] Despite these attempts, no authoritative doctrine has ever been universally accepted. That being said, at various times and places, Jewish thinkers who have challenged aspects of Jewish belief have been excommunicated by their communities. In the seventeenth century, for example, the Jewish council of Amsterdam placed philosopher Baruch Spinoza under a ban (*herem*) for his monism and his critical approach to the Bible. No doubt political pressures contributed to this action, yet the community singled out his heretical opinions as the cause for sanction.[11] Two centuries later, the *Wissenschaft des Judentums* school would embrace Spinoza's hermeneutic, giving rise to both the Reform and Conservative movements of modern Judaism.[12]

Even though the complexity and dynamism of Jewish belief has not always been acknowledged in Jewish-Catholic dialogue, the following conclusions have emerged from the conversation (many of which are included in *Dabru Emet*, the culmination of work that I began while serving as the Jewish scholar at the Institute for Christian and Jewish Studies):

- The God that Jews and Catholics believe in is one;
- Jews and Catholics share Scriptures known to the former as *Tanakh* and to the latter as the Old Testament, as well as a deep commitment to its exegesis, albeit with different interpretive traditions;
- Jews and Catholics share a vision of peace and justice that is incumbent upon us to work toward;
- Jews and Catholics appreciate and respect the ethnic diversity that exists within each other's respective traditions;
- American Jews and Catholics share common immigrant experiences;
- Jews and Catholics share a commitment to education, inquiry, and scholarship;
- Jews and Catholics share a sense of the centrality of the family to religious life and spiritual development;
- Jews and Catholics share a sense of how the liturgical calendar governs the annual passing of time;
- Prayer and worship are central to Jewish and Catholic religious life.

That Jews and Catholics have reached this depth of mutual understanding and affirmation is a remarkable achievement. Members of these two communities continue to learn from each other and work together, despite the structural asymmetry of the communities, which sometimes produces unfortunate outcomes and creates unproductive tension. To give a recent example of the latter, on August 12, 2002, the Consultation of the Bishop's Committee for Ecumenical and Interreligious Affairs and the National Council of Synagogues, to which I have been a Reform representative since 1998, published a document titled "Reflections on Covenant and Mission" (henceforth RCM).[13] RCM resulted from the March 13, 2002, meeting of the joint consultation and was published with the intent that it "be read and discussed as part of an ongoing process of increasing mutual understanding."[14] The Catholic contribution to RCM addressed the validity of the Mosaic covenant, quoting John Paul II:

John Paul II has explicitly taught that Jews are "the people
of God of the Old Covenant, never revoked by God,"[15]
"the present-day people of the covenant concluded with
Moses,"[16] and "partners in a covenant of eternal love which
was never revoked."[17] The post–*Nostra Aetate* Catholic
recognition of the permanence of the Jewish people's
covenant relationship to God has led to a new positive
regard for the post-biblical or rabbinic Jewish tradition
that is unprecedented in Christian history.[18]

This recognition of the ongoing validity of the Jewish Mosaic
covenant garnered praise from those Jewish delegates present at the
meeting, as well as others in the Jewish and interreligious dialogue
communities.[19]

A second passage in RCM offered a nuanced understanding of
evangelization within the context of Catholic-Jewish dialogue:

Evangelization includes the Church's activities of presence and witness; commitment to social development and
human liberation; Christian worship, prayer, and contemplation; interreligious dialogue; and proclamation and catechesis.[20]

This latter activity of proclamation and catechesis—the "invitation to
a commitment of faith in Jesus Christ and to entry through baptism
into the community of believers which is the church"[21]—is sometimes
thought to be synonymous with "evangelization." However, this is a
very narrow construal and is indeed only one among many aspects of
the Church's "evangelizing mission" in the service of Gods' kingdom. Thus, Catholics participating in interreligious dialogue, a mutually enriching sharing of gifts devoid of any intention whatsoever to
invite the dialogue partner to baptism, are nonetheless witnessing to
their own faith in the kingdom of God embodied in Christ. This is a
form of evangelization, a way of engaging in the Church's mission.[22]

The document identifies dialogue as a form of evangelization. The description of dialogue as "mutually enriching" and non-
conversionary presumably reflected the writers' own experiences,
and was not an attempt to prescribe what dialogue *should* be for all
Catholics at all times.

Both RCM's approach to the Mosaic covenant and its understanding of non-conversionary evangelism in the context of Catholic-
Jewish dialogue elicited critique from some bishops who did not
participate in the consultation. Over the subsequent six years, dissent
roiled. In an attempt to consider these opposing views along with the
perspective of RCM, the Committee on Doctrine and the Committee
on Ecumenical and Interreligious Affairs of the United States
Council of Catholic Bishops issued a document on June 18, 2009,
titled "A Note on Ambiguities Contained in Covenant and Mission"
(henceforth "Note"). "Note" sought to address concerns that "some
theologians, including Catholics, have treated the document as
authoritative." [23]

After clarifying the document's unofficial status within the
Church, "Note" discusses RCM's portrayal of the Sinaitic covenant
as continuous with Jewish faithfulness to Torah and its understanding
of "evangelization" in the particular context of Catholic-Jewish dialogue. "Note" finds certain phrases in RCM worthy of disambigua-
tion, of which I will only discuss three. Item 5 of "Note" corrects
RCM's impression of "the enduring quality of the [that is, Israel's]
covenant" by asserting: "The long story of God's intervention in the
history of Israel comes to its unsurpassable culmination in Jesus
Christ, who is God become man." [24] This point of view may be aptly
characterized as supersessionist, since by stating that Jesus Christ is
the end of the Israelite narrative, it suggests that "history of Israel"
has no other trajectories except the Church. According to the stated
ecclesiology, the Synagogue—the complement of the medieval typology—is not a legitimate heir to "God's promises to Israel," which,
"Note" asserts, "is found only in Jesus Christ." [25] This may be what
Catholics affirm, but both Jews and Catholics need to openly
acknowledge that such a view negates a central Jewish claim. Can
Jews and Catholics form a meaningful relationship if each thinks the
other's claim to Israelite patrimony is unwarranted and illegitimate?
This issue constitutes an impasse to future Catholic-Jewish dialogue;
much more work needs to be done within the two respective communities before dialogue will be able to move forward. [26]

On the topic of evangelism, item 7 of "Note" quotes RCM's
description of interreligious dialogue as "devoid of any intention
whatsoever to invite the dialogue partner to baptism." [27] "Note" then
explains that

Though Christian participation in interreligious dialogue would not normally include an explicit invitation to baptism and entrance into the Church, the Christian dialogue partner is always giving witness to the following of Christ, to which all are implicitly invited.[28]

The word *implicitly* begs further clarification. The document goes on to invoke the famous passage in Romans 11:25–26 to account for the Catholic expectation of Jewish communal, rather than individual, conversion. I hesitate to inject my own biblical reading into Catholic theological debates, but this use of Paul's enigmatic passage puzzles me. It is likely that Paul believed that Jews who did not have faith that Jesus the messiah would return to accomplish his expected mission would, in fact, not be saved from condemnation in the final judgment. But this is a view that is rooted in imminent eschatology. If Paul had lived to see the destruction of the Temple, the selling of Jewish slaves into bondage, the wandering and sporadic persecution of Jews throughout the Middle Ages, and most importantly, the indefinite postponement of Jesus' expected return, would he still have believed that particularistic messianic faith was the key to salvation? The belief that Jews need to be baptized in order to be saved strikes me as an inversion of the argument between Peter and Paul about whether gentiles had to be circumcised to be included in Israel and, thereby, saved. The Church ultimately sided with Paul in the negative. It strikes me as ironic that the impulse toward inclusion, which prompted this decision, would result almost two thousand years later in the exclusion of non-baptized Israel from eschatological salvation. If Catholics believe that Jews have to be baptized to be saved, and Jews do not believe this, the dialogue faces yet another impasse. What fruit can a dialogue that fundamentally negates Jewish existence bear?

Jewish reactions were exacerbated by a vote taken at the June 2008 meeting of the USCCB, later recognized by the Vatican as in keeping with Catholic teaching, to replace the sentence in the American adult catechism, "Thus the covenant that God made with the Jewish people through Moses remains eternally valid for them," with:

To the Jewish people, whom God first chose to hear his word, "belong the sonship, the glory, the covenants, the giving of the law, the worship and the promises; to them belong the patriarchs, and of their race, according to the flesh, is the Christ." (Rom 9:4–5)[29]

The replacement of an unequivocal statement about the Mosaic covenant that recognizes its validity among current Jews with an almost two-thousand-year-old enigmatic Pauline passage about the ancient heritage of biblical Jews struck many in the Jewish community as a retreat.

On August 19, 2009, a coalition of American Jewish groups (American Jewish Committee, Anti-Defamation League, National Council of Synagogues, Orthodox Union, and Rabbinical Council of America) expressed concern about the "Note." The letter stated:

> A major source of concern is the document's assertion that the remark in the earlier "Reflections on Covenant and Mission" that interreligious dialogue is "devoid of any intention whatsoever to invite the dialogue partner to baptism" needs to be qualified....Since "Reflections" focused specifically on Jews, the latest statement informs us that Catholics engaging in dialogue with Jews must have the intention of extending an implicit invitation to embrace Christianity and that one can even imagine a situation in such a dialogue where this invitation would be made explicit....Section 10 of the new USCCB "Note"... appears to posit that the Mosaic covenant is obsolete and Judaism no longer has a reason to exist.[30]

In response to these concerns, the USCCB issued a revised version of its "Note" on October 13, 2009. The following passage from the original item 7 was deleted:

> For example, *Reflections on Covenant and Mission* [sic] proposes interreligious dialogue as a form of evangelization that is "a mutually enriching sharing of gifts devoid of any intention whatsoever to invite the dialogue partner to baptism." Though Christian participation in interreligious dialogue would not normally include an explicit invitation to baptism and entrance into the Church, the Christian dia-

logue partner is always giving witness to the following of
Christ, to which all are implicitly invited.[31]

This eliminates the problematic phrase "implicitly invited." The document leaves intact, however, the claim that it is mistaken for
Catholics to believe "the Church has a corresponding obligation not
to baptize Jews."[32] Concerns about the validity of the Jewish Mosaic
covenant are left unaddressed.

John Borelli, with whom I had the pleasure of working when he
served as associate director of the Secretariat for Ecumenical and
Interreligious Affairs of the U.S. Conference of Catholic Bishops, has
astutely observed about this whole affair: "Exchanging public statements is a poor way to conduct dialogue."[33] Offering a critique of the
process, both from the perspective of interreligious trust and episcopal protocol, Borelli has advocated further dialogical study instead of
"more unilateral actions that ignore the fruits of the Catholic-Jewish
dialogue of the past 45 years." Joint study can certainly help further
understanding about deeply complex and controversial issues, but
will it repair the breach of trust that has occurred in the relationships
between the Catholic and Jewish participants in this dialogue? Why
does the Jewish-Catholic relationship suffer when Catholics have
internal theological conflicts? Why are the two so intimately connected, to the extent that one cannot be discussed without implicating
the other? It seems to me that unraveling the mystery of Jewish-
Catholic symbiosis, gaining a better understanding of the relationship
itself, might go a long way to healing the relationship. The topics of
both covenant and mission touched this nerve, this core issue lying at
the root of all theological discussion. It would seem better to salve the
irritation at its root rather than casting at windmills.

Despite such tensions, as the second half of this century of
Jewish-Catholic relations dawns, we need to bear in mind the historical *novum* that this dialogue represents in addition to recognizing its
fragility. Jewish history bears witness to the errors of placing too
much hope in Catholic religious leadership without regard for the
laity. The dialogue of the past half-century has taught us that the laity
has a prominent and constructive role to play in the future of the relationship between these two communities.

Furthermore, the interpersonal dimension of this relationship
should not be taken for granted while cultivating institutional rela-

tions. The two paths are equally important, and may sometimes even overlap; one is neglected at the peril of the other. Jews and Catholics will, of course, stumble when walking this new path together, but the journey requires patience and understanding if any accomplishments are to contribute to the repair of this broken world, to *tikkunolam*.

NOTES

1. *Lumen Gentium* 2 (9), http://www.vatican.va/archive/hist_coun cils/ii_vatican_council/documents/vat-ii_const_19641121_lumen-gen tium_en.html (accessed January 4, 2011).

2. Ibid.

3. *Declaration on the Relation of the Church to Non-Christian Religions: Nostra Aetate, 4,* proclaimed by His Holiness Pope Paul VI, October 28, 1965, http://www.vatican.va/archive/hist_councils/ii_vatican_ council/documents/vat-ii_decl_19651028_nostra-aetate_en.html (accessed January 4, 2011).

4. See, for example, the Fourth Lateran Council, Canon 68; *Decrees of the Ecumenical Councils*, ed. Norman P. Tanner (Washington, DC: Georgetown University Press, 1990).

5. Alfred J. Kolatch, *The Second Jewish Book of Why* (Middle Village, NY: Jonathan David Publishers, Inc., 1985), 137–38.

6. *Sholem-Aleykhem's Tevye the Dairyman*, trans. Miriam Katz (Malibu, CA: Pangloss Press, 1994), 93.

7. Israel J. Yuval, "Jews and Christians: Shared Myths, Common Language," in *Demonizing the Other: Antisemitism, Racism and Xenophobia*, ed. Robert S. Wistrich (Abingdon, Oxford: Routledge, 1999: 2006), 104.

8. This may explain why most Jews reject the authenticity of messianic Jews or Jews for Jesus and feel deeply threatened by their presence.

9. Note the Facebook group titled "Atheist Jew" which, as of 1/13/11, counts 100 members.

10. Philo, *Decalogue* 65, and Maimonides, *Mishneh Torah, Sanhedrin*, chap. 10.

11. Rebecca Goldstein, *Betraying Spinoza: The Renegade Jew Who Gave Us Modernity* (New York: Schocken, 2006), 17.

12. Edward Breuer, "Post-medieval Jewish Interpretation," in *The Jewish Study Bible*, ed. Adele Berlin and Marc Zvi Brettler (New York: Oxford University Press, 2004), 1904.

13. "Reflections on Covenant and Mission," *Origins* 32 (2002): 218–24.

14. Although the document was originally available at http://www.

usccb.org/comm/archives/2002/02-154.htm#reflections, it is now only found on websites that have no affiliation with the USCCB. Quotations are from The Center for Christian-Jewish Learning at Boston College, http://www.bc.edu/dam/files/research_sites/cjl/texts/cjrelations/resources/documents/interreligious/ncs_usc cb120802.htm.

15. John Paul II, "Address to the Jewish Community in Mainz, West Germany," November 17, 1980, http://www.ccjr.us/dialogika-resources/documents-and-statements/roman-catholic/pope-john-paul-ii/297-jp2-80nov17.

16. Ibid.

17. John Paul II, "Address to Jewish Leaders in Miami," September 11, 1987, http://www.ccjr.us/dialogika-resources/documents-and-statements/roman-catholic/pope-john-paul-ii/308-87sep11.

18. The Consultation of the Bishop's Committee for Ecumenical and Interreligious Affairs and the National Council of Synagogues, "Reflections on Convenant and Mission" (document published August 12, 2002). Referred to as RCM.

19. Michael Kogan called the document "a revolutionary Catholic pluralism" in his article "Into Another Intensity: Christian-Jewish Dialogue Moves Forward," *Journal of Ecumenical Studies* 41 (2004): 14.

20. Pontifical Council for Interreligious Dialogue and the Congregation for the Evangelization of Peoples, *Dialogue and Proclamation*, 2, http://www.ccjr.us/dialogika-resources/documents-and-statements/roman-catholic/pope-john-paul-ii/308-87sep11. Note these similar comments from Pope John Paul II: "Mission is a single but complex reality, and it develops in a variety of ways. Among these ways, some have particular importance in the present situation of the church and the world," *Redemptoris Missio*, 41, http://www.vatican.va/holy_father/john_paul_ii/encyclicals/documents/hf_jp-ii_enc_07121990_redemptoris-missio_en.html. The pope went on to cite these various ways: "witness" (42–43), "proclamation" (44–47), "forming local churches" (48–49), "ecumenical activity" (50), "inculturation" (52–54), "interreligious dialogue" (55–57), "promoting development and liberation from oppression" (58–59).

21. Ibid., 10.

22. RCM.

23. Item 2, "A Note on Ambiguities Contained in Covenant and Mission." This quotation is taken from the unrevised version originally published on the USCCB website at www.nccbuscc.org/doctrine/covenant 09.pdf. The unrevised version has been replaced by the revised version at that same address.

24. "Note," unrevised version.

25. "Note," item 10.

26. Recent work, such as that in this volume's essays, by Catholic theologians like Philip Cunningham, John Pawlikowsky, and Mary Boys, and by Jewish theologians like León Klenicki, Michael S. Kogan, and Eugene Korn, need to be discussed more broadly within each community.

27. RCM.

28. Ibid.

29. "Backgrounder for Recognitio of Change in Adult Catechism," http://www.nccbuscc.org/mr/mediatalk/backgrounder_recognitio.shtml (accessed January 14, 2011).

30. "Letter to U.S. Conference of Catholic Bishops: Jewish Organizations Express Concern about Future of Interfaith Dialogue," http://www.adl.org/Interfaith/usccb_letter.asp. Representatives of the (Orthodox) Rabbinical Council of America and Union of Orthodox Jewish Congregations of America expressed similar concerns over "Note" in a meeting with representatives of the U.S. bishops on June 25 in New York.

31. "Note," original version.

32. "Note," item 9; revised version.

33. John Borelli, "Troubled Waters," *America,* February 22, 2010, 20.

9

Toward the Future as People of God and Partners in Covenant

Elizabeth Groppe

Images of rubble and chaos filled the news in the aftermath of the earthquake that devastated Haiti on January 12, 2010. In this most impoverished country in the Western Hemisphere, people who had already suffered tremendous hardship faced yet another catastrophe. Rising in response to the challenge were both the Haitians themselves and people from all over the world, who gave aid in whatever manner they were able. In Cincinnati, one powerful sign of love and hope amid televised images of the ruins of Port-au-Prince was that of the adoption of two children from a Haitian orphanage by Chris and Lauri Pramuk. Chris is my colleague in the theology department at Xavier University and Lauri is a pediatrician.

Their adoption has brought new life to infant Henry David and six-year-old Sophia—and to the Pramuk's biological children, Isaiah and Grace. Before Henry and Sophia arrived at their new home, six-year-old Grace told her parents she would share everything with Sophia, and sometimes Sophia and Grace indeed delight in their new sisterhood. The relationship, however, is not without its tensions. When a visitor asks Sophia to name her favorite color, Grace interjects, "She can't pick pink."

"Yel-low," Sophia answers in the English she is rapidly learning.

In the interactions of Grace and Sophia, developmental psychologists can recognize patterns similar to those observed in biological siblings, as each enacts the process of developing a unique identity as a person-in-relation to others. The process of identity formation involves both the articulation of a person's uniqueness vis-à-vis others and the expression of commonalities that unite us to the group to which we belong. A *Xavier* magazine article about the Pramuk family includes not only Grace's interjection that Sophia "can't pick pink," but also a photo of Grace with blonde braids adorned with colored beads—just like the beaded braids of Sophia.

Christians have interpreted the biblical account of the sibling rivalry between Jacob and Esau as the story of the relationship between the church and the synagogue, and in the historical development of this relationship, we can indeed see dynamics similar to those that mark the process of two brothers or sisters developing their identities vis-à-vis the other. This essay highlights two very different approaches to this sibling relationship from within the historical complexity of the two-thousand-year history of Christian-Jewish relations: the second-century theology of Justin Martyr, and the theology of the Second Vatican Council. I will conclude with a reflection on postconciliar developments in Catholic-Jewish relations that invite us to envision a future of Christians and Jews as brothers and sisters who are partners in covenant.

JUSTIN MARTYR AND TRYPHO THE JEW: "YOUR PEOPLE SHOULD NOT BE A PEOPLE"

Justin Martyr's *Dialogue with Trypho* (155–160 CE) is a key document in scholarly efforts to reconstruct the emergence of Christianity as a religious body clearly distinct from the Jewish community.[1] Christian historian Timothy Horner identifies *Dialogue* as one of the first attestations of a self-consciously independent Christianity, while Jewish scholar Daniel Boyarin finds Justin engaged in a process of forging a Christian self-identity by construing Judaism as Christianity's binary opposite.[2] *Dialogue*, he suggests, is one of the earliest extant documents in which the border lines of Christianity and Judaism are drawn with the thick ink of a cartographer's pen.

Unlike the original followers of Jesus Christ, Justin was not of a Jewish background. He was born in a Roman colony in Palestine to Greek-speaking parents, and as a youth, his quest for truth ended in Platonism. One day, however, he encountered an old man who engaged him in a dialogue about God and the soul that persuaded him that Platonism does not have a coherent philosophy. Those who do know the truth, the elder told Justin, are those who spoke through the inspiration of the Holy Spirit. These prophets are worthy of belief because of the miracles they worked and because the events that they foretold have now transpired. "They exalted God, the Father and Creator of all things, and made known Christ, his Son, who was sent by him."[3]

In *Dialogue*, Trypho notices that Justin wears the cloak of a philosopher and initiates a discussion, introducing himself as "a Hebrew of the circumcision, a refugee from the recent war."[4] This allusion establishes as a backdrop for the dialogue, the Bar Kochba revolt against the Roman emperor Hadrian in 133 to 135 CE, which resulted in the death or enslavement of thousands of Jews and the expulsion of Jews from Jerusalem.

The primary focus of Justin's dialogue are texts from Scripture—not the New Testament, which has not yet been canonized, but the Septuagint, a Greek translation of the scrolls of the Law, the Prophets, and the Writings. In rambling style, Justin tells Trypho of the coming to pass of the events the prophets foretold: the birth of a child from a virgin (Isa 7:10–17); the transfer of Elijah's spirit (Matt 17:10–13); the affliction of a man of sorrows wounded for our iniquities (Isa 53:5); the Just One delivered for our transgressions (Isa 53:12); the extension of God's promise of salvation from Israel to all the nations (Isa 52:10; 51:4–5; Zech 2:11); and the desolation of Jerusalem (Isa 64:10–12).[5]

But Justin's reliance on the Septuagint to establish the truth of his Christian philosophy presents him with a problem: the Scriptures are teeming with divine commandments and teachings that he does not follow. He cannot dismiss the requirement for circumcision or the texts of the Mosaic Law as teachings of a God other than the God of Jesus Christ, the position taken by Marcion, for he believes that he and Trypho worship the same God.[6]

Justin resolves the problem by emphasizing that the Scriptures themselves speak of a new covenant: "Behold the days shall come, said the LORD, and I will make a new covenant with the house of Israel, and with the house of Judah: it will not be like the covenant which I made with their fathers, in the day that I took them by the hand to lead them out of the land of Egypt" (Jer 31:31–32). Justin prefaces his citation of these words of the prophet Jeremiah with Isaiah's promise of light and salvation for the nations (Isa 51:4–5), transposing a promise Jeremiah spoke to the house of Israel into a promise for the gentiles.[7] Indeed, Justin describes those who have been led to God through the crucified Christ as the "true spiritual Israel."[8]

This new covenant of the spiritual Israel is qualitatively superior to the Mosaic Law. Trypho has only a circumcision of the flesh, whereas members of the spiritual Israel have circumcised hearts (Jer 4:4; Deut 10:16–17) from which idolatry and every other sin have been excised.[9] The old covenant was a religion of carnal deeds, whereas the new covenant washes away anger, avarice, jealousy, and hatred from the soul.[10] "The law promulgated at Horeb," Justin concludes, "is already obsolete and was intended for you Jews only, whereas the law of which I speak is simply for all men. Now a later law in opposition to an older law abrogates the older; so, too, does a later covenant void an earlier one."[11]

Why did God, who is immutable, ordain precepts that were intended to be superseded? The commandments concerning Temple sacrifices, Justin explains, were not a reflection of the ultimate will of God who asks only a sacrifice of praise (Ps 49:1–23), but rather a law for a weak people prone to the worship of idols.[12] And circumcision of the flesh was given as a mark to distinguish the Jews for the desolations that they now suffer,[13] afflictions that are justified because Trypho and his people "have murdered the Just One, and his prophets before him; now you spurn those who hope in him, and in him who sent him."[14] Circumcision is a sign that "your people should not be a people, and your nation not a nation" (Hos 1:9).[15]

THE SECOND VATICAN COUNCIL (1962–1965): SPIRITUAL TIES OF THE PEOPLE OF THE OLD AND NEW COVENANTS

Over the course of the centuries following Justin's dialogue with Trypho, Christian approaches to Judaism took a variety of forms, including both the harsh polemic of John Chrysostom's homilies and Augustine's theology of the Jews as a witness people who should be protected because of their providential role in carrying prophetic texts into diaspora. But I leap forward to 1958, when Pope John XXIII's announcement of the convocation of the Second

Vatican Council inspired Jules Isaac to travel to Rome. Isaac, a French Jewish scholar who lost his wife and children to the Nazi genocide, delivered to the pope a dossier that documented the elements of the Christian tradition that contributed to a contemptuous attitude toward Judaism.[16] Isaac appealed for a purification of this tradition that was in his judgment so counter to the Gospel of love. The pope instructed Cardinal Augustin Bea's Secretariat for Promoting Christian Unity to prepare materials on the Jewish people for conciliar consideration, and over the course of the Council, this initiative ultimately bore fruit in the promulgation of *Nostra Aetate*, the Declaration on the Relation of the Church to Non-Christian Religions, approved by the Council in October of 1965.[17]

For the first time in the history of Church councils, *Nostra Aetate* affirms the "spiritual ties which link the people of the new covenant to the stock of Abraham," the good olive tree onto whom the wild olive branches of the Gentiles have been grafted (Rom 11:17–24). The Israelites are the sons and daughters of God to whom "belong the glory, the covenants, the giving of the law, the worship, and the promises" (Rom 9:4–5) and this covenant is enduring, for "God does not take back the gifts he bestowed or the choice he made" (4). *Nostra Aetate* emphasizes that "neither all Jews indiscriminately at that time [of Jesus Christ], nor Jews today, can be charged with the crimes committed during his passion" (4). It is true "that the church is the new people of God, yet the Jews should not be spoken of as rejected or accursed as if this followed from holy scripture" (4).

This ecclesiology of the Church as the new people of God is central to another conciliar document, *Lumen Gentium*, the Dogmatic Constitution on the Church. Decades of scholarly labor had prepared the way for *Lumen Gentium*; in a concerted effort of *ressourcement*, or biblical and theological renewal through return to the sources, European theologians recovered dimensions of the theology of the Church that had been neglected in the post-Reformation period. One of these dimensions was the theology of the Church as the people of God, an ecclesiological tradition imbued with longstanding assumptions about the relationship of Judaism and Christianity. Drawing from this tradition, *Lumen Gentium* approaches the narratives of the Old Testament as a typological preparation and foreshadow of the Christ event; the history of the Jewish people is "a preparation and figure of that new and perfect covenant which was to be ratified in

Christ, and of the fuller revelation which was to be given through the Word of God made flesh" (9).

Recounting the history of salvation, *Lumen Gentium* explains that God desires "to make men and women holy and to save them, not as individuals without any bond between them, but rather to make them into a people who might acknowledge him and serve him in holiness" (9). God, therefore, made a covenant with the Jewish people and "made them holy for himself" (9). In Christ has come a fuller revelation, a new covenant sealed in his blood (1 Cor 11:25) in which God calls together a people "made up of Jews and Gentiles which would be one, not according to the flesh, but in the Spirit, and it would be the new people of God" (9). Christ is the head of this new messianic people whose law is love (John 13:34) and whose destiny is the Kingdom of God, begun on earth and brought to perfection at the end of time when creation is free from corruption. God desires that all who are now scattered among the nations be gathered as one (John 11:52) in a new universal people of God (13). Although this messianic people does not yet include everyone, the Church is a visible seed of unity, hope, and salvation that prefigures and promotes universal peace (9 and 13), and those "who have not yet accepted the Gospel are related to the people of God in various ways" (16). First among these are "that people to whom the covenants and promises were made, and from whom Christ was born in the flesh (see Rom 9:4–5), a people in virtue of their election beloved for the sake of the fathers, for God never regrets his gifts or his call (see Rom 11:28–29)" (16).

POSTCONCILIAR DEVELOPMENTS:
A VISION OF PARTNERSHIP

In the decades following the Council, there have been a number of important developments in Catholic-Jewish relations. *Nostra Aetate* encouraged biblical and theological discussions between Christians and Jews in order to foster mutual understanding and appreciation, and in 1974 the Commission of the Holy See for Religious Relations with the Jews was established.[18] A number of episcopal bodies have expressed remorse for the legacy of Christian anti-Judaism.[19] Pope John Paul II reached out to the Jewish community on multiple occasions, including a pilgrimage to Israel in March of 2000 in which he prayed at the Western Wall in sorrow for the suffering of the Jewish people and committed the Catholic Church to "genuine brotherhood with the people of the Covenant."[20] Catholic universities have established institutes for Christian-Jewish learning, and theologians have built relationships with members of the Jewish community and engaged in theological exchange of a character and quality unprecedented before Vatican II.[21] Biblical scholars have emphasized that Jesus of Nazareth was a faithful Jew, and Jewish scholars, such as Paula Fredriksen, Amy-Jill Levine, Alan Segal, and others have made important contributions to New Testament scholarship.[22] Jews have also shared their stories and traditions and opened themselves to dialogue with Christians. In September of 2000, an interdenominational group of leading rabbis and Jewish scholars published *Dabru Emet* ("To Speak the Truth"), a statement on Christians and Christianity that acknowledged the dramatic changes that have taken place in Christian approaches to Judaism and offered a reflection on the possibility of a new relationship.[23]

The developments of these past forty-five years are Catholicism's first sustained theological engagement with post-biblical Judaism as a living religion. There is debate among scholars as to whether the character of Trypho in Justin's dialogue was a real person or a literary construction, but in succeeding centuries, most Christian perceptions of Judaism were based on theological stereotypes rather than Judaism as it is actually lived and practiced.[24] Today the Catholic Church engages in authentic dialogue with Judaism and definitively rejects Justin Martyr's position that God abrogated the covenant with Israel. At the same time, it is the Catholic faith that covenantal history culminates in the incarnation of the Word of God in Jesus Christ and the paschal mystery of death and resurrection. Catholic theology today faces the very difficult challenge of eliminating all vestiges of supersessionism while at the same time affirming a trinitarian soteriology of the redemption of all creation through Christ and the Spirit.

Although work in this area is ongoing, it is clear that a Catholic ecclesiology of the people of God that is consistent with postconciliar developments will affirm the irrevocable character of Israel's existence as God's people and the reality that Judaism is in the words of Pope John Paul II not an ancient relic but a "living heritage" of faith.[25] *Lumen Gentium*'s typological theology of the biblical people Israel as a preparation and figure of the new covenant reflects the relationship of the Old and New Testaments, but it is not adequate to the relationships of mutual learning and enrichment that have developed between Catholics and Jews in the decades after the Council. In a 1985 statement, the Commission of the Holy See for Religious Relations with the Jews affirmed the value of typological exegesis when properly practiced but also noted that "typology...makes many people uneasy and is perhaps the sign of a problem unresolved."[26] This unease results in part from the Church's newfound appreciation for rabbinic Judaism as a religious development that has been an ongoing source of spiritual vitality beyond the biblical period.

These postconciliar developments invite us to find our Christian identity as the people of God in a true partnership with the Jewish people. *Lumen Gentium* envisions the unification of all humanity as God's one people, and this is not a *fait accomplit*. In our broken world, the Jews are the original people of God, chosen according to one rabbinic account not because God's love is exclusive but because other peoples refused to accept God's *Torah*.[27] "The concept of chosen people," Wayne Dosick explains, "means *not* that Jews were chosen for special privilege, but for sacred responsibility: to be *or la'goyim* [*sic*], a 'light unto the nations' (after Isaiah 42:6, 49:6), a faith community reflecting God's light of love and law."[28] Through the incarnation of the Word in human flesh and the paschal mystery of death and resurrection, God has taken all humanity into the divine embrace. "The mission of Jesus," wrote then-Cardinal Joseph Ratzinger, "consists in bringing together the histories of the nations in the community of the history of Abraham, the history of Israel. His mission is unification, reconciliation....[A]ll nations, without the abolishment of the special mission of Israel, become brothers and receivers of the promises of the Chosen People; they become People of God with Israel through adherence to the will of God."[29] Jews do not believe that Jesus Christ is the messianic source of this reconciliation, but the Jewish and Christian traditions nonetheless share a vision of all people of the earth united in right worship of God. Jews and Christians serve this eschatological destiny together through the power of the *Torah*/Word[30] and the *Shechinah*/Spirit of God, active in distinct ways in both the Jewish and Christian communities. In the end, stated Cardinal Walter Kasper in his former capacity as president of the Commission of the Holy See for Religious Relations with the Jews, "Israel and the Church will be reunited," but in "the current eschatological interim, two concurrent parts of God's one people...[are] co-existing as rivals in the positive as well as in the conflict-ridden sense of the word."[31]

On this side of eternity, there are irreducible and irreconcilable differences between Jews and Christians and deep fissures throughout the human community. Yet even as we stand in a world far different from that of our eschatological hope, the proleptic communion of the people of God must take visible and social form. In the present, the Church is a sign and sacrament of the eschatological unity of the people of God when it fosters communion among its members who come from a great multiplicity of nations, prefiguring and promoting universal peace.[32] The Church must act boldly to give visible and social expression to this communion, transcending the fault lines of nation, ethnicity, and class that all too often shape the boundaries of our world. The Jewish people, in turn, serve the eschatological communion of God's people when they are *or goyim*, a beacon of light reflecting God's love and law unto all nations. Christians and Jews have begun to find creative new ways to give visible expression to the peoplehood that we are called to share, such as the establishment of formal partnerships between churches and synagogues and joint efforts to work for *tikkun olam*, the healing and repair of our broken world. "As partners in dialogue," Pope John Paul II stated in an address to Jewish leaders in Miami, "as fellow believers in the God who revealed himself....[W]e are called to collaborate in service and to unite in a common cause wherever a brother or sister is unattended, forgotten, neglected, or suffering in any way, wherever human rights are endangered or human dignity offended; wherever the rights of God are violated or ignored."[33]

CONCLUSION

Western psychologists once construed the process of human development primarily as a process of growth in autonomy and individuation. This approach is giving way to a much more relational vision of human maturity, a vision that is more consistent with Christian theologies of humans as persons-in-communion and the relational philosophies of Jewish scholars, such as Martin Buber and Emmanual Levinas.[34] For Ruthellen Josselson, a professor of clinical psychology, human development is not a process of growing autonomy from others but increasing complexity of relationships.[35] This is a helpful lens through which to consider the relation of the church and synagogue. The mature Catholic Church need not articulate its own identity in binary opposition to Judaism as if our status as people of God can only be gained by denying that of the Jews. Nor is it sufficient to describe the people Israel only as a foreshadow of the Christian Church. Rather, the identity of both the Church and the Jewish people is found in multiple layers of complex historical relationship between the biblical people Israel, the Christian Church, and the rabbinic Judaism of the post-biblical era. From this complicated and painful history, we have the opportunity to emerge as partners in covenantal commitment to the healing of a fractured world.

Rabbi Abie Ingber, founding director of Xavier's Office of Interfaith Engagement, recalls a gathering at the home of Chris and Lauri Pramuk in December of 2009 that was not only a Christmas party for the theology department but also an inclusive holiday celebration. He was struck both by the warm welcome he received and by the photos of two Haitian children he noticed on the Pramuk's refrigerator. At this point, Chris and Lauri had initiated an adoption procedure that they were told could take as long as two years. When news of the earthquake came in January, Rabbi Ingber extended to the Pramuks an offer to do whatever he could to assist with their efforts to get the children out of Haiti. In the coming days, he worked around the clock for Sophia and Henry, contacting legislators in Washington, DC, and organizing support from within the Xavier community. He was at the gate of the airport to greet the plane that carried the newly united Pramuk family home. Reflecting on the experience, which he describes as a special privilege, he cites the words of Stefan Zweig, a Jewish author who was murdered during the Holocaust: "All hardships become lighter if borne in common and all goodness becomes better if practiced in unison."

This story of goodness practiced in unison is not yet complete. In January of 2011, Rabbi Ingber and Lauri Pramuk intended to lead a group of thirteen Xavier premed students in an interfaith medical mission to Haiti. Heart to Heart International (HHI), host of the travel program, had to cancel the trip because they could not provide the required security, and Ingber's Office of Interfaith Engagement instead took physicians and premed students to Guatemala in March. They were living witness to the fact that although there are differences between Jews and Christians that are irreconcilable on this side of eternity, we are nonetheless both part of the one people of God, called to witness to God's desire for the perfection of the redemption of the world.

NOTES

1. Justin Martyr, *Dialogue with Trypho*, trans. Thomas B. Falls (Washington, DC: Catholic University of America Press, 2003).

2. Timothy Horner, *Listening to Trypho: Justin Martyr's Dialogue Reconsidered* (Leuven: Peeters, 2001), 7; Daniel Boyarin, *Border Lines: The Partition of Judaeo-Christianity* (Philadelphia: University of Pennsylvania Press, 2004), 1–73.

3. Justin Martyr, *Dialogue*, 7.3.

4. Ibid., 1.3.

5. See, for example, Justin Martyr, *Dialogue*, 43.4–8; 13; 12.1; 119.3. The biblical citations include these: "Look, the young woman (*'almah*) is with child and shall bear a son, and shall name him Immanuel" (Isa 7:14). "And the disciples asked him, 'Why, then, do the scribes say that Elijah must come first?' He replied, 'Elijah is indeed coming and will restore all things; but I tell you that Elijah has already come, and they did not recognize him, but they did to him whatever they pleased. So also the Son of Man is about to suffer at their hands.' Then the disciples understood that he was speaking to them about John the Baptist" (Matt 17:10–13). "But he was wounded for our transgressions, crushed for our iniquities; upon him was the punishment that made us whole; and by his bruises we are healed" (Isa 53:5). "He poured out himself to death, and was numbered with the transgressors; yet he bore the sin of many, and made intercession for the transgressors" (Isa 53:12). "The LORD has bared his holy arm before the eyes of all the nations; and all the ends of the earth shall see the salvation of our God" (Isa 52:10). "Listen to me, my people, and give heed to me, my nation; for a teaching will go out from me, and my justice for a light to the peoples. I will bring near my deliverance swiftly, my salvation has gone out and my arms will rule the peoples; the coastlands wait for me, and for my arm they hope" (Isa 51:4–5). "Many nations shall join themselves to the LORD on that day, and shall be my people; and I will dwell in your midst. And you shall know that the LORD of hosts has sent me to you" (Zech 2:5). "Your holy cities have become a wilderness, Zion has become a wilderness, Jerusalem a desolation. Our holy and beautiful house, where our ancestors praised you, has been burned by fire, and all our pleasant places have become ruins. After all this, will you restrain yourself, O LORD? Will you keep silent, and punish us so severely?" (Isa 64:10–12).

6. See, for example, Justin Martyr, *Dialogue*, 11.1.

7. Justin Martyr, *Dialogue*, 11.3.

8. Ibid., 11.5. This, notes Judith Lieu, is the first extant Christian claim to the name "Israel." Lieu, *Image and Reality: The Jews in the World of the Christians in the Second Century* (Edinburgh: T & T Clark, 1996), 136.

9. Ibid., 15.7, 28.2–3, 19.3.

10. Ibid., 14.2.

11. Ibid., 11.2.

12. Ibid., 22.1–11.

13. Ibid., 16.2.

14. Ibid., 16.4.

15. Ibid., 19.5.

16. Jules Isaac, *The Teaching of Contempt: Christian Roots of Anti-Semitism*, trans. Helen Weaver (New York: McGraw Hill, 1965, c. 1964).

17. *Vatican Council II: Constitutions, Decrees, Declarations*, ed. Austin Flannery (Northpoint, NY: Costello, 1996). On the development of *Nostra Aetate*, see Thomas Stransky, "The Genesis of *Nostra Aetate*: Surprises, Setback and Blessings," *America*, October 24, 2005, 8–12.

18. See http://www.vatican.va/roman_curia/pontifical_councils/chrs tuni/sub_index/index_relations_jews.htm.

19. See http://www.bc.edu/research/cjl/cjrelations/backgroundresour ces/documents/catholic.html

20. See http://www.bc.edu/dam/files/research_sites/cjl/texts/cjrela tions/resources/documents/catholic/johnpaulii/westernwall.htm.

21. For testimony of some of these scholars, see John C. Merkle, ed., *Faith Transformed: Christian Encounters with Jews and Judaism* (Collegeville, MN: Liturgical Press, 2002).

22. See, for example, John P. Meier, *A Marginal Jew: Rethinking the Historical Jesus* (New York: Doubleday, 1991). Jewish scholarship on the New Testament and Christian origins includes Paula Fredriksen, *Jesus of Nazareth, King of the Jews: A Jewish Life and The Emergence of Christianity* (New York: Knopf, 2000); Amy-Jill Levine, *The Misunderstood Jew: The Church and the Scandal of the Jewish Jesus* (HarperSanFrancisco, 2006); Alan Segal, "Jesus in the Eyes of One Jewish Scholar," in *The Historical Jesus Through Catholic and Jewish Eyes*, ed. Leonard J. Greenspoon, Dennis Hamm, and Bryan F. LeBeau (Harrisburg, PA: Trinity Press International, 2000), 147–54.

23. The statement that originally appeared in the *New York Times* is reprinted together with scholarly essays in *Christianity in Jewish Terms*, ed. Tikva Frymer-Kensky et al. (Westview, CO: Westview Press, 2000).

24. On this point, see David M. Neuhaus, "Engaging the Jewish People: Forty Years since *Nostra Aetate*," in *Catholic Engagement with*

World Religions, ed. Karl J. Becker and Ilaria Morali (Maryknoll, NY: Orbis, 2010), 399.

25. Pope John Paul II, *Spiritual Pilgrimage: Texts on Jews and Judaism 1979–1995*, ed. Eugene J. Fisher and León Klenicki (New York: Crossroad, 1995), 14.

26. Commission of the Holy See for Religious Relations with the Jews, *Notes on the Correct Way to Present Jews and Judaism in Preaching and Catechesis in the Catholic Church* (1985), II.3.

27. See, for example, *Sifre: A Tannaitic Commentary on the Book of Deuteronomy*, trans. Reuven Hammer (New Haven, CT: Yale University, 1986), 343, 352–53.

28. Wayne Dosick, *Living Judaism* (San Francisco: Harper, 1995), 19.

29. Joseph Ratzinger, *Many Religions—One Covenant*, trans. Graham Harrison (San Francisco: Ignatius, 1999), 27–28.

30. "Torah," explains Rabbi Abraham Joshua Heschel, has two senses: the supernal Torah and the Torah revealed at Sinai. The supernal Torah existed before the creation of the world and is equated with Wisdom (Prov 8:22). The Greek-speaking Jew Philo referred to this Torah as *Logos*. According to the Rabbis, Moses received Torah at Sinai—but not all of the Torah. See Heschel, *God in Search of Man: A Philosophy of Judaism* (New York: Farrar, Straus, and Giroux, 1955), 262, 276 n. 7; also his *Heavenly Torah: As Refracted Through the Generations* (New York: Continuum, 2005), 327.

31. Kasper, "The Relationship of the Old and New Covenant as One of the Central Issues in Jewish-Christian Dialogue," lecture given at the Centre for the Study of Jewish-Christian Relations, Cambridge, UK, December 6, 2004, http://www.bc.edu/dam/files/research_sites/cjl/texts/cjrelations/resour ces/articles/Kasper_Cambridge_6Dec04.htm.

32. *Lumen Gentium*, 13.

33. Pope John Paul II, "Address to Jewish Leaders in Miami," in *Spiritual Pilgrimage*, 109.

34. See, for example, Catherine Mowry LaCugna, *God for Us: The Trinity and Christian Life* (San Francisco: HarperCollins, 1991); Martin Buber, *I and Thou: A New Translation with a Prologue and Notes*, trans. Walter Kaufmann (New York: Scribner, 1970); Emmanuel Levinas, *Entre Nous: Thinking-of-the-Other*, trans. Michael B. Smith and Barbara Harshav (New York: Columbia University Press, 1998).

35. Ruthellen Josselson, *The Space Between Us: Exploring the Dimensions of Human Relationships* (San Francisco: Jossey-Bass, 1992); *The Meaning of Others: Narrative Studies of Relationships*, eds. Ruthellen Josselson, Amia Lieblich, and Dan McAdams (Washington, DC: American Psychological Association, 2007).

IV
THEOLOGY

10

The Dreadful Past...
The Jewish Future

Post-Shoah Reflections on David Hartman's
Theologies of Suffering[1]

Adam Gregerman

In the wake of the Shoah, I struggle to look confidently toward the future without being devastated about the past. Unprecedented and unimaginable suffering raises terrible questions about God's goodness and omnipotence, and casts doubt upon fundamental religious claims. Many, with great sensitivity as well as anguish, have delved into these questions, which have been so prominent in theological reflection over the last half-century. The subject is inescapable. Steven T. Katz writes, the Shoah "raises the most difficult intellectual, phenomenological, and existential issues with which reflective men [*sic*] have to deal."[2] David Halivni puts the Shoah in the broadest of terms: "Every aspect of spiritual life is affected by [it]."[3] For Jews, the Shoah has, therefore, led to profound, sometimes radical, reconsiderations of traditional religious beliefs, most of all about God's nature and covenant with the Jewish people. It has also ushered in remarkable changes in the ways Jews and Christians, after centuries of estrangement and the occurrence of mass slaughter of Jews in "Christian" Europe, relate to and view the religious claims of each other. Because of the enormity of the event, it can dominate—and sometimes overwhelm—both Jewish theology and Jewish-Christian relations.[4]

It is a painful challenge to my own Jewish faith, as I struggle with a tradition that, while accommodating terrible earlier losses (for example, military defeat and exile), is unprepared for loss on this scale. Even though I was not personally affected by the event (no one in my family was a victim or survivor), and I have not experienced religious persecution, the challenge is unavoidable. As an observant Jew, I regularly join in prayer that praises God's might and God's love for the Jewish people. I feel the tension between traditional claims and actual events when I pray to God as "shield of our salvation in every generation" and thank God for "miracles which daily attend us."[5] It is tempting to do this unthinkingly, but when I reflect on what I say, I find it difficult because of the sad facts of history.

Admittedly, I often choose not to dwell on this tension, but get caught up with (or distracted by) the cycle of Sabbath and holidays or family rituals. Recently, my wife Rahel and I had the great joy of creating a ceremony to welcome our new baby girl into the covenant with the Jewish people. We also built a *sukkah* for the first time in our new home. These celebrations and rituals are the "stuff" of Jewish living, and the content that infuses a religious life seemingly separate from theological speculation. Still, this tension cannot be entirely bracketed, for Jewish religious life rests on a relationship with a God in covenant with the people of Israel. This relationship is shaped by convictions about God's nature (for example, divine love of Israel), experiences of God's actions (for example, deliverance from Egypt), and expectations (for example, eschatological redemption, intervention on behalf of the afflicted). While Jewish religious faith and specifically views of God should not be evaluated solely by the adequacy of explanations for innocent suffering, these challenges are enormously serious.

As a Jew, must I ignore or minimize the theological challenge of the Shoah to these traditional claims about God in order to sustain a viable religious life? Should I seek a persuasive theodicy that defends these views? What is the cost—psychologically, theologically, or even exegetically—of these choices?

DIVERSITY WITHIN JEWISH TRADITION: DAVID HARTMAN'S APPROACHES TO SUFFERING

To explore some of these questions, I want to engage critically with the thought of modern Jewish theologian David Hartman (1931–2013). His award-winning book *A Living Covenant: The Innovative Spirit in Traditional Judaism* responds creatively to the

challenge of unmerited suffering.[6] Hartman, who is not usually cate-
gorized as a post-Shoah theologian, is nonetheless grappling with the
event, though in a complex and largely indirect way. Nearly the entire
second half of his book is devoted to the general topic of suffering,
though, significantly, he rarely mentions the Shoah itself.[7] He writes
for contemporary Jews, but his examples of suffering are typically
ancient, from the rabbinic and biblical periods. This approach is paradoxical—intensively discussing suffering and loss while almost
entirely avoiding the unprecedented recent event—and highly reveal-
ing. Because of his decision to focus on suffering, I believe the Shoah
is never far from his view, nor is he able to ignore completely the
theological challenge it offers to traditional claims about God. In a
post-Shoah world, his defense of "A Living Covenant" with a living
God suggests his recognition of the prominence of radical claims
about the "death of God."[8] I believe that the fact that Hartman so seldom refers explicitly to the Shoah, despite devoting approximately
one hundred pages to the theme of suffering, is not an oversight but
a careful effort to limit the danger it poses to his defense of a traditional yet modern Jewish faith.

Hartman's analysis of suffering helps us to understand this
seeming paradox. It must be seen in terms of his overall purpose for
writing, which is to help Jews to cultivate "a viable way of life."[9]
Such a life is based on traditional religious observance and reinterpretation of sacred texts. The virtues of such a religious system are
demonstrated not by arguments for its "metaphysical truth" but by its
contribution to the Jews' "psychological and existential vitality."[10]
Although he is a philosophically trained theologian, Hartman recognizes the limits of abstruse theological speculation, especially for
answering perhaps insoluble questions or for providing guidance for
religious living. He, therefore, emphasizes observance of the *mitzvot*
as a practical way of life that promotes joy and a sense of meaning-
fulness. He wants to help Jews to continue to live "Jewishly," and to
draw closer to God through daily rituals and prayer, rather than by
engaging in inconclusive theologizing or awaiting God's intervention
in history.

I find much that is appealing and constructive about Hartman's
views, above all a practical focus on what is conducive to Jewish
faith. To return to the topic of suffering, he faces it by shifting the
terms of the discussion in ways noted above. That is, he attends to the

question of the suffering of the innocent not in order to "solve" it but in order to limit its potential to undermine Jews' ability to maintain their commitment to God and *mitzvot*. He, therefore, sidesteps the morass of unsatisfying theodicies. In a key move intended to bracket the most painful or difficult theological questions, he rejects "philosophical theology" in favor of "religious anthropology."[11] The former phrase, like the metaphysical speculation that he also criticizes, includes efforts to "reconcil[e] what seems to be an incompatibility of facts and beliefs. How is it logically possible to claim that God is the just Lord of History in the light of the senseless evil manifest in the world?" This philosophical approach opens up doubts about God's power or benevolence and, without much hope of convincing resolution, threatens Jewish faith. By contrast, the latter phrase, "religious anthropology," eschews theological speculation and emphasizes that which is useful for maintaining one's faith. Taking the covenant between God and the Jewish people as the starting point, Hartman offers a religious anthropology that enables the suffering Jew to practically "respond to events" in order to preserve "continuity, stability, and predictability" in that relationship. Doubts about God brought on by suffering and which are shocking or challenging are necessarily minimized because the goal is to "*sustain* commitment to a way of life predicated on God's covenantal love and justice."[12]

Reviewing classical Jewish texts, he surveys various options without endorsing any one in particular.[13] Perhaps Jews can be satisfied if they "eliminate every expectation of reward in this world" and yearn for the rewards of the next world. On the other hand, Jews can discover that, despite suffering, "everyday reality can also contain joy" if they follow the *mitzvot*. Alternatively—and provocatively—he suggests that even unmerited or inexplicable suffering nonetheless provides opportunities to repent and to "examine one's conduct" in order to avoid a sense of despair. Hartman also lowers expectations about what God might do to end suffering. In contrast to the biblical "Exodus model" of divine intervention in history on behalf of suffering Israelites, he endorses a "Sinai model" in which God, having given the Torah as a guide to the Jews, no longer intervenes in history.[14] All of these responses are intended to buttress Jews' faith despite suffering. Hartman does not claim that one perspective is true, only that they are all potentially useful.

HARTMAN AND THE CHALLENGE OF THE SHOAH

I appreciate Hartman's shift away from theodicies and his emphasis on a viable, living Judaism. He prizes continuity in the face of historical events and losses—a key aspect of any religious system—and aims to minimize the shock of disappointment of finding one's beliefs potentially undermined. However, in the wake of the Shoah, I also find his approach inadequate. By taking traditional faith as a given and avoiding serious consideration of the unique challenge of the Shoah, his analysis is severely circumscribed. Hartman's almost complete refusal to allow this experience of incomparable Jewish suffering to intrude on his thinking suggests that, for faith to abide in a broken world, perhaps one must avert one's eyes from the abyss. His ultimately practical goal—that Jews find "some approach that will enable them to maintain their commitment to the *mitzvot*"— in effect precludes a direct confrontation with the shock of the Shoah.[15] While Hartman does not say he will not address the event, in one of his only direct comments on the Shoah, he appears to dismiss its significance out of hand: "If Jewish theism was not destroyed by two thousand years of exile, it should not be imagined that even the Holocaust could destroy it."[16] I agree that a traditional faith such as Judaism depends on steadfastness and continuity. However, I yearn for serious attention to the reasons why so many Jews, myself included, find the static portrait of a covenanting God troubling in the wake of the Shoah. Even when Hartman recognizes that (generic) occasions of "acute persecution and catastrophe" might undermine commitment to Jewish life, he puzzlingly does not apply this observation to the greatest challenge to Jewish faith in history.[17]

Because his claims are grounded in biblical and rabbinic texts, I want to consider his interpretations of some of these texts, and specifically his efforts to grapple with the challenge of innocent suffering to Jewish faith. This provides me an opportunity to survey the tensions in his approach in light of my own (but not only my own) powerful sense that the Shoah is a *novum* in Jewish history and must be faced squarely. A few themes recur that I find relevant in the post-Shoah era. Prominent among these is Hartman's interest in minimizing the shock of suffering by demonstrating how earlier Jews, in coping with disappointment and loss, offer a model to modern Jews. For example, he draws on a vivid scene from the Book of Nehemiah.

In the fifth century BCE, an assembly of Jews, returned from exile, gathers to make a public statement. Though subjugated by foreigners and "in great distress," they affirm their commitment to God and to the Torah (9:36—10:1). Hartman interprets this as evidence of abiding faith despite their oppression and the perceived failure of God's promises to protect them.[18] Contemporary Jews, Hartman says, ought to emulate them.

There are two difficulties with this interpretation. First, Hartman omits to mention that these Jews offer the type of explanation for suffering that Hartman otherwise rejects. They are afflicted by God, they say, "because of [their] sins" (Neh 9:37). Their suffering is not a challenge to their faith in God's justice and goodness. Rather, it confirms it, a type of claim that is widely rejected in the post-Shoah period as "blaming the victims."[19] Second, Hartman appeals to their steadfast faith as a model for Jews today. Their losses, he says, did not threaten their affirmation of "the ongoing covenantal drama of Jewish history." In a post-Shoah period, however, Hartman's claim that ancient, colonized Jews' holding onto their faith offers a "great spiritual bequest" to contemporary Jews is, I believe, unacceptably irenic. For some contemporary Jews, the incomparably worse afflictions during the Shoah undermine the relevance to them of ancient Jews' responses to drastically different experiences. There is an enormous difference in the losses each group faced: ancient Jews' hopes for security and independence were dashed by foreign oppression; modern Jews' hopes for acceptance in non-Jewish society were dashed by the genocidal slaughter of millions.

The claim that modern Jews should emulate ancient Jews and accept a less-than-satisfying reality appears elsewhere. For another model of admirable piety, Hartman quotes Talmudic praise of Jews who thanked God for small portions of food even though they did not receive a full meal (as promised in Deuteronomy 8:10). The rabbinic text puts these words in God's mouth: Jews "are particular to say grace if the quantity [of bread they eat] is [equivalent to only] an olive or an egg."[20] While the original purpose of the text was to explain God's wisdom in electing the Jews, Hartman makes a different point. He praises the Jews' faithfulness to God even when afflicted or hungry. They accept "the partial and incomplete conditions of unredeemed history" in spite of the imperfections of life and the lack of divine intervention to change them. The Jews focus on what they have received, not on what they lack.

Again, Hartman's praise for their gratitude to God is unsuitable to the contemporary theological challenge. Millions of Jews, only a few generations ago, received not a "meager meal" or "an incomplete meal"[21] but, to continue the metaphor, no meal at all. The analogy of insufficient material support grievously understates the seriousness of the loss that I believe we must face in the wake of the Shoah. The suffering that threatens faith in God's covenant with Israel is not just that God, Hartman says, was "not visibly triumphant" in intervening to end the Jews' suffering and to satisfy all their desires. The gap between expectations and reality in the Shoah is nearly unbridgeable. In his use of this text and elsewhere,[22] Hartman consistently minimizes that distance and fails to face the full shock of these events. This undermines the relevance of his model in relation to the most painful and pressing Jewish doubts. I appreciate his desire to refrain from offering a theodicy and to shift the discussion to maintaining Jewish faith in a God who does not directly intervene in history. I also do not want to deny that some Jews even in Auschwitz praised God, as do some survivors. However, his examples of faith that can withstand suffering rest on a limited view of the depth of the rupture that I, and others, feel has occurred.

I want to shift to another theme in Hartman's work illustrated by his interpretation of another Talmudic text. While his Sinai model presumes divine non-intervention in history, even to end suffering, Hartman is unable fully to let go of the idea of an interventionist God. On the contrary, he upholds a minimal level of divine intervention at least to limit the oppression of Israel. Hartman's inconsistency between non-intervention and limited intervention is significant, for it illustrates his unease with a completely absent God. This raises serious and unanswered questions about why and when God might choose (or not choose) to aid the afflicted people. It also threatens Hartman's optimistic assumptions about human freedom. Such freedom can have truly dreadful consequences, both practically and theologically, which raise doubts about God's failure to limit it.

This tension appears in his interpretation of a rabbinic text discussing the different glorious attributes applied to God.[23] Rabbis ask why Jeremiah and Daniel omitted terms such as *awesome* and *mighty* that were earlier used for God by Moses. Strikingly, one rabbi says that they were unwilling to "ascribe false things" to God because they lived at times when the people were oppressed. After Jeremiah and Daniel, the "men of the Great Assembly" properly reapplied to God all of the attributes mentioned by Moses. How could they call God "awesome" and "mighty" when they too were humiliated and power-less and lived under foreign oppression? The rabbinic text says that one should not suppose that God's non-intervention, evident in the people's suffering, reveals God's inability to intervene. Rather, God partly manifests these attributes through *voluntary non-intervention* and partly through *covert intervention*: "Therein lie [God's] mighty deeds, that he suppresses his wrath, that he extends long-suffering to the wicked [that is, the nations that oppress Israel]. Therein lies his awesome power, for but for [the nations'] fear of him, how could [Israel] persist among the nations [who would otherwise seek to destroy them]?" God, though seemingly not active, allows the nations freedom of action to oppress Israel but ensures that they limit them-selves so that God might not intervene and take vengeance on them. In the language of the text, God is involved in history through "mighty deeds" of self-restraint along with "awesome power" that encourages the nations, out of fear of God, to restrain their violence. Israel's suffering is painful, but not beyond the purview of God, who ultimately ensures the people's survival.

In his use of this text, Hartman, contrary to what he says else-where, is engaged in philosophical theology, and a very traditional version of it. Despite his best efforts, Hartman veers into attempts to explain why suffering occurs and implicitly to exculpate God from responsibility for it. He says God's partial withdrawal from history, though allowing for suffering, gives Jews a chance to maintain their faith in God. The evil they face is subsumed into a fundamentally good, purposive theological system that encourages their develop-ment of a "mature faith."[24] This system is somehow under God's providence and reflects God's will and intentions for the development of this faith. This is because God, even passively or distantly, ulti-mately is responsible for the world and would only have allowed such a system if it was conducive to some greater religious good.

This is actually a free-will theodicy. According to Hartman's interpretation of this text, human freedom, granted by God when God voluntarily ceased intervening in history, explains why suffering occurs (in this case, caused by the nations that oppress Israel). This, however, raises the same questions asked of all free-will theodicies: why is God's grant of human freedom preferable to limiting (even some) freedom in order to prevent the unimaginably evil deeds that can result?[25] Would it not be better for God to intervene, especially when God can do so? That is why Hartman's praise for "God's patience," in his comment on this text, makes sense only when the suffering is minimized. When the suffering gets too great—in the words of the text, when it threatens Israel's "persistence"—it no longer seems worth it, and indeed contradicts the limits in the text. Hartman, however, attends only to the religious benefits of the freedom of God's withdrawal and not the costs. This model is, therefore, defensible only in the case of limited suffering. Unbridled, devastating violence cannot be accommodated by it. In the case of the Shoah, I find it impossible to see God's might and power in *allowing* this to happen. The massive destruction of nearly an entire continent's Jewry seems incompatible with a divinely ordained limitation on violence.[26]

FACING SUFFERING AFTER THE SHOAH

While I have been critical of some of Hartman's arguments, I do not want to minimize the significance of his contribution. His project is valuable, prompting reflection on this important topic and responding to a real need for a modern defense of traditional Jewish faith. It is also frustrating. This is precisely why I have chosen to focus on it. It illustrates the remarkable challenge of writing theology after the Shoah and the struggle to look hopefully toward the future while relying on traditional sources and claims. Hartman looks toward the future but seems not to grapple with the past. This is often seen in his interpretations of classical Jewish sources, which he uses without much attention to the shock of twentieth-century events and the ways they undermine the uses to which he puts these sources.

He has his reasons for doing so. As an advocate of a practical religiosity, Hartman aims to help Jews to "take the disappointments [in God] in stride."[27] But I am disappointed in God, and I cannot avert my eyes from the suffering that prompts this, as I believe Hartman averts his. Though the tradition seems inadequate to answer terrible questions about divine absence and innocent suffering, I yearn for some frank admission by Hartman of the depth of suffering and the anguish it causes many post-Shoah Jews. Of course, this yearning reveals something about me as well as about him. For me, contemplating the abyss of the Shoah is simultaneously unavoidable and agonizing: unavoidable, for loss on such a scale cannot but be faced theologically (politically, pastorally, and so on); agonizing, for it challenges my faith in the covenant between God and Israel and the traditional image of God. Hartman, because of his circumscribed focus, in effect, sides with the view that it is too agonizing.

How else to account for our differences? By treating commitment to Judaism and God as a given, Hartman's argument is most suitable for those already convinced of central Jewish affirmations about God's love, the covenantal relationship, and the joy of *mitzvot*. I begin in a more ambivalent place. I share joy in Jewish living and relate to God in these distinctly Jewish categories and terms of *mitzvot* and covenant. However, I do not have as much optimism about the possibilities of a life of faith as Hartman or confidence in traditional religious affirmations. These differences in perspective explain some of my resistance to resolving these problems as he does, by bracketing the shock of disconfirmation or forcing traditional texts into a modern theology. He wants to find resources in the tradition that will buttress his faith in a living covenant and quiet the deafening screams lamenting the triumph of evil. I am far less willing than he is to deflect my "attention from absorption with the irrational forces" in order to concentrate on a life of *mitzvot*.[28] The irrational forces haunt me, hinting at something terrible about both human depravity and God's powerlessness and unfaithfulness to the covenant.[29]

However, this does not mean that doubt defeats faith or nullifies my Jewishness. Rather, I embrace a paradox of living with both. As an observant Jew, I follow the *mitzvot* and live a religious life. It is organized around celebration of Shabbat and the holidays, attendance at synagogue, and study of Torah. I celebrate God's deliverance of Israel from Egypt and the remarkable persistence of Jewish faith despite terrible losses. My doubts about God, along with a commitment to a religious life, do not prove that theology does not matter. Rather, it is important but not determinative. Or, to be specific, theodicy does not exhaust the full range of Jewish theology. It is one facet of a multifaceted religious identity that is only partly theological. The identity includes a wider range of beliefs and activities, some easily separated from theological reflection, either inherently or by sometimes averting my own eyes from the theological issues. The tension remains unresolved, one of the most serious of my life.

I approach such an inquiry then with humility, recognizing my inability to systematically defend or reconcile all my claims or commitments. This can be difficult but is perhaps inevitable, and should be embraced as reflecting different ways of living "Jewishly." This is not unprecedented or untraditional, for Jews have long held that consistency is not the highest value. While not endorsing total relativism, rabbis welcomed diverse and sometimes contradictory views. The tradition is comfortable with genuine attempts to wrestle with the irresolvable in a spirit of truth-seeking.[30] In particular, this approach is supported by the non-creedal nature of Judaism, which, in comparison with Christianity, downplays the importance of theological speculation in favor of ritual and praxis.

Furthermore, in grappling with paradox, I am influenced by recent essays by Catholic scholars Gregor Maria Hoff and Terrence Tilley on Jewish-Christian relations. They both struggle with competing claims about, on the one hand, salvation of all humanity in Christ alone and, on the other, a refusal to say Jews who do not believe in Christ are rejected by God.[31] Rather than force a reconciliation between these claims, they grant that, as finite humans, we are precluded from making definitive, universally true statements about God and God's will. There are unavoidable limits to our speech about God. That is why our efforts to reflect on "experiences or thoughts about the Ultimate Mystery" and topics such as soteriology and theodicy must involve "paradox, contradiction, and not fully compatible concepts."[32] This is inherent to the nature of the subjects being discussed. Much as they, in their own ways, hold fast to seemingly paradoxical ideas, I too refuse to sacrifice Jewish life in its entirety in the name of a superficial consistency. Doubts about God in the wake of terrible suffering do not undermine Judaism entirely, nor do all contradictions need to be resolved for one to live a rich religious life.

The differences between Hartman and me are in the end not large; our levels of observance are probably quite similar, and we share an interest in cultivating viable religious lives.[33] However, I believe my own approach to suffering more frankly preserves these tensions between faith and doubt than does Hartman's. He cautiously considers suffering but then tries to redirect the focus elsewhere. Yet in the wake of the Shoah, I doubt whether one can face suffering, and the terrible suffering of the Shoah in particular, and then redirect one's focus away from it. Still, I continue to engage in a religious life of worship, study, and practice, partially but not completely unaffected by these theological questions. The absence of persuasive answers to immensely difficult and important questions is genuinely troubling but not disastrous. There can be no solution to the theological challenge of the Shoah, but I refuse to let it dominate everything as much as I refuse to avert from eyes from the challenge.

NOTES

1. I am grateful to have been asked to contribute to a volume in memory of Rabbi León Klenicki. With a painful awareness of the traumas of the past, he successfully strived for decades to improve relations between two long-estranged religious communities. May his successes encourage both Jews and Christians to continue his work, and may his memory be for a blessing.

2. Steven T. Katz, *Post-Holocaust Dialogues: Critical Studies in Modern Jewish Thought* (New York and London: New York University Press, 1983), 169, also 42–43.

3. David Weiss Halivni, *Breaking the Tablets: Jewish Theology after the Shoah*, ed. Peter Ochs (Lanham, MD: Rowman & Littlefield, 2007), 117.

4. See Edward Kessler, *An Introduction to Jewish-Christian Relations* (Cambridge: Cambridge University Press, 2010), 124–44; Steven L. Jacobs, ed., "Studies in the Shoah," in *Contemporary Christian Religious Responses to the Shoah* (Lanham, MD: University Press of America, 1993).

5. This is a quotation from the daily *Modim* prayer of thanksgiving.

6. David Hartman, *A Living Covenant: The Innovative Spirit in Traditional Judaism* (Woodstock, VT: Jewish Lights, 1997). The book was first published in 1985 and won the National Jewish Book Award in Jewish Thought. It has been the subject of numerous reviews and full-length essays.

7. There are only a few references; some are incidental, and a few are substantive; see ibid., 202–3, 77.

8. Ibid., 203. The most prominent Jewish exponent of "death of God" theology is Richard Rubenstein.

9. Ibid., 193, 200.

10. His phrase "metaphysical truth" refers to the Talmud, though it reflects Hartman's goal.

11. Hartman, *Living Covenant*, 187–88. Italics added. See further Zachary Braiterman, *(God) After Auschwitz: Tradition and Change in Post-*

Holocaust Jewish Thought (Princeton, NJ: Princeton University Press, 1998), 54.

12. Emphasis added.

13. Hartman, *Living Covenant*, 193–96. On his presentation of a range of options, see David Blumenthal, "Review of David Hartman's 'A Living Covenant,'" *AJS Review* 12 (1987): 305.

14. Hartman, *Living Covenant*, 230–31.

15. Ibid., 194.

16. Ibid., 203.

17. Ibid., 224.

18. Ibid., 214.

19. Ibid., 213. See also Steven T. Katz, Shlomo Biderman, and Gershon Greenberg, eds., *Wrestling with God: Jewish Theological Responses during and after the Holocaust* (Oxford and New York: Oxford University Press, 2006), 359; Braiterman, *(God)*, 30–31.

20. Hartman, *Living Covenant*, 220–21. He quotes *b. Ber.* 20b.

21. Ibid., 220.

22. See ibid., 47, 186.

23. Ibid., 216–17. He quotes *b. Yoma* 69b.

24. Ibid., 221.

25. See Katz, *Post-Holocaust Dialogues*, 270–83.

26. On the unprecedented and "irredeemable destruction" that occurred in the Shoah, see Halivni, *Breaking the Tablets*, 18.

27. Hartman, *Living Covenant*, 194.

28. Ibid., 196.

29. David Blumenthal writes, "Hartman's view takes the dark side of human nature and human history too lightly," in Blumenthal, "Review of David Hartman 'A Living Covenant,'" 303.

30. A well-known example is the preservation of mutually exclusive legal opinions in rabbinic texts, as well as the stunning affirmation that divergent opinions are nonetheless "the words of the living God" (*b. Erub.* 13b).

31. Gregor Maria Hoff, "A Realm of Differences: The Meaning of Jewish Monotheism for Christology and Trinitarian Theology," in *Christ Jesus and the Jewish People Today: New Explorations of Theological Interrelationships*, ed. Philip A. Cunningham and others (Grand Rapids, MI: William B. Eerdmans, 2011); Terence Tilley, "Doing Theology in the Context of the Gift and the Promise of *Nostra Aetate*," *Studies in Christian-Jewish Relations* 6 (2011).

32. Hoff, "A Realm of Differences," 213.

33. Hartman is a modern Orthodox Jew. I am a Conservative Jew toward the "right" end of the observance spectrum.

11

God's Presence in
Israel and Incarnation

Christological Reflections in Dialogue[1]

Hans Hermann Henrix

During the last two decades of his life, Rabbi León Klenicki participated intensely in the Christian-Jewish exchange in Europe. Several times, he held a guest lectureship at the Catholic theological faculty in Leuven, Belgium, he taught at Cambridge, and finally was happy to come to Germany. Once, as we were taking a walk, he admitted to me: "When I was a young man and rabbi, I was convinced that only the German people was capable of such a monstrosity as the Shoah. But during the years of the military junta in Argentina, it dawned on me that this could be possible in every people." Thus, he came to a second openness toward theologians from Germany and could greet them with disarming friendliness.

León Klenicki was often a guest at the *Bischöfliche Akademie* of the Aachen diocese. At academy conferences, he drew the participants' attention to anti-Jewish ways of thinking in some aspects of Latin American theology; he spoke on the question of God after Auschwitz; and he explained Jewish uneasiness regarding the passion plays of Oberammergau. During his last visit to Aachen, he commented on the project *"Dabru Emet*: A Jewish Statement on Christians and Christianity." He had signed the document, but he did not conceal his difficulties with certain statements in it. Thus, he questioned the thesis that "Jews and Christians worship the same God"; he preferred to say, "Jews and Christians worship God." León summed up his understanding of Christians and Christianity as follows:

Jewish thinking, the Jewish people, must overcome what Christians have done to Jews through the centuries, and seek to understand Christianity and its call to serve God. It also entails a reflection on Jesus, his vocation and call, still a difficult endeavor for Jews. The Christian-Jewish relationship has undergone a particular transformation. It has gone in general from argument to dialogue, from conflict to a situation of meeting, from ignorance and alienation to encounter, a conversation between equals. The road has not been smooth, and problems and misunderstandings still abound. But mainly, there is a desire to listen and to respond, to see the other as a person of faith and not an object of contempt.[2]

I would like to honor León, the friend, as a person of faith with a reflection on Christian Christological theology. Over many centuries, Christian theology's reflection on Jesus Christ as a motive for separation from Judaism was often used polemically. In dialogue after the Shoah, there is an abiding challenge to Christian theology to reflect on Jesus Christ in the sense of an ecumenically understood motive for closeness to Judaism. What can this mean? The following considerations are an attempt to seek an answer to this question.

PROFOUND DIFFERENCE AND STRONG CONNECTING LINK: ON THE CHRISTIAN-JEWISH DIFFERENCE AND PROXIMITY IN FAITH IN THE INCARNATION OF THE SON OF GOD

The most profound difference of belief manifests itself in the face of the strong connecting links between Christians and Jews. The Christian belief in Jesus Christ who as a consequence of his crucifixion and resurrection is affirmed and proclaimed, not only as the promised Messiah, but also as the consubstantial Son of God, appears to many Jews as something radically "unjewish": they see him as an absolute contradiction, if not a blasphemy, to the strict monotheism as it is referred to every day, particularly by devout Jews, in the "Shema Israel." The Christian must understand this, even if he himself sees no contradiction to monotheism in the teaching of Jesus, Son of God.[3]

This is how, in their 1980 declaration on the relationship of the Church to Judaism, the German bishops described—in the words that Franz Rosenzweig once used—the "bond of community and non-community"[4] between Judaism and Christianity where Christian faith in Jesus Christ is concerned. In so doing, they gave two titles to Jesus Christ: Messiah and Son of God.

The difference between Christianity and Judaism centers on these two Christological titles, which are of unequal weight. The difference in the understanding of Incarnation is more fundamental. Because of the varying significance given to the messianic theme in the Jewish and Christian traditions, this title does not hold such a fundamental place. Messianic expectation is not as essential to Judaism as the Christological question is to Christianity. Because of the different importance given to the messianic issue in the two traditions, it is not surprising that the central issue in the Jewish-Christian dialogue of our time does not lie in the title of Messiah, but rather in Jesus Christ's other title, that of Son of God, and with that the question regarding God in the narrower sense. Christian-Jewish divergence is centered around the understanding of God and more specifically on the theme of God's presence in history, that is, the Incarnation of the Son of God in Jesus Christ. Thus, the Orthodox Jewish philosopher Michael Wyschogrod said:

> The most difficult outstanding issues between Judaism and Christianity are the divinity of Jesus, the Incarnation, the Trinity, three terms which are not quite synonymous but all of which assert that Jesus was not only a human being but also God. Compared to this claim, all other Christian claims, such as Jesus as the Messiah, become secondary at most.[5]

JEWISH REACTION TO THE "IDEA" OF INCARNATION

Christian-Jewish dialogue today, which has progressed to considering the issues around God and the Incarnation, has given rise to various Jewish responses without mitigating the seriousness of the difference. Christian theologians should be aware of the fact that there are several ways of thinking that can be distinguished in the

Jewish objection as regards the Incarnation of the Son of God. One important reaction is at the philosophical level. Emmanuel Levinas, coming from the specific premises of his philosophy as well as from his understanding of revelation, examined the value of the "idea" of the Incarnation (of the Son) of God and thought: God's presence in the world's time would be "too much" for God's poverty and "too little" for God's glory, without which God's poverty is no abasement. The Jewish philosopher denied that God in his duration can become a "presence" in time and in the world. He held on to God remaining an "Otherness that cannot be assimilated, absolute difference to everything that manifests itself." Consequently, he spoke of "God's original priority or original ultimate validity as regards the world, which cannot receive and shelter him"; thus God "cannot...become incarnate," cannot "enclose himself in an end, a goal."[6]

Jean-François Lyotard makes another point. Although not a Jew, he is nevertheless an important thinker in relation to the Shoah, Judaism, and Jews. He sees the teaching of the Incarnation as turning God's transcendence into an object and as a destruction of the prohibition to make images. When the Word has become clear and distinguishable "in God become man," God's being God is made harmless; one no longer has to listen for the "voice" in a constant search, and instead one has given space to the seeing of an image.[7] Wyschogrod describes another, *a posteriori* position: Judaism cannot accept the Incarnation of the Son of God because it does not hear this story, because the Word of God as it is heard in Judaism does not tell this story, and because Jewish faith does not testify to it.[8] So from the point of view of tradition and history, the Incarnation is not a Jewish topic of discussion. That is why, already in the 1930s, Martin Buber spoke of the absence of God's Incarnation as being something specifically Jewish: "The absence of an Incarnation [*Inkarnationslosigkeit*] of the God who reveals himself to the 'flesh' and who is present to it in a reciprocal relationship...[is]...what ultimately separates Judaism and Christianity. We 'unify' God by professing his unity in our living and our dying; we do not unite ourselves to him. The God whom we believe, to whom we are given in praise, does not unite with human substance on earth."[9] Moreover, some Jews believe that the fruits of Christian belief in the Incarnation were historically bad.[10]

Catholic theology certainly listens attentively to Jewish reactions to the doctrine of the Incarnation of the Son of God.[11] When theologians reflect on the possibilities and limits of a Christian reception of these Jewish responses, they do so not least of all with reference to the Council of Chalcedon's (451) understanding of Christ and to so-called Chalcedonian hermeneutics.

The famous decree of the Council of Chalcedon states:

> Following the saintly Fathers, we all with one voice teach the confession of one and the same Son, our Lord Jesus Christ: the same perfect in divinity and perfect in humanity, the same truly God and truly man, of a rational soul and a body; consubstantial with the Father as regards his divinity and the same consubstantial with us as regards his humanity; like us in all respects except for sin; begotten before the ages from the Father as regards his divinity, and in the last days the same for us and for our salvation from Mary, the virgin God-bearer as regards his humanity; one and the same Christ, Son, Lord, only-begotten, acknowledged in two natures which undergo no confusion, no change, no division, no separation; at no point was the difference between the natures taken away by their union, but rather the property of both natures is preserved and comes together into a single person and a single subsistent being.[12]

This conciliar guideline remains important when Christian theology tries to respond to Jewish discussion of the doctrine of the Incarnation of the Son of God.

In Jewish thinking today, we encounter a tradition, which, among others, was brought to mind by the inner-Jewish argument around the already-quoted *Dabru Emet*. The document *Dabru Emet—Speak Truth* begins its series of theses with the theocentric statement that "Christians also worship the God of Abraham, Isaac, and Jacob, creator of heaven and earth" and that "through Christianity, hundreds of millions of people have entered into relationship with the God of Israel."[13] This thesis was welcomed by many Christians, whereas it met in part with sharp Jewish criticism.[14] Thus, for example, the recognized Orthodox scholar David Berger expressed the opinion in a commentary that it might be customary to emphasize that Christians adore the God of Abraham, of Isaac, and of Jacob, the creator of heaven and earth, but "it is essential to add that worship of Jesus of Nazareth as a manifestation or component of that God constitutes what Jewish law and theology call *avodah zarah*, or foreign worship—at least if done by a Jew."[15] In adding this last part, Berger is alluding to the Talmudic position, according to which "non-Jews outside of the Land of Israel are not considered to be idol worshippers. They are only staying with the customs of the fathers" (*b. Hul.* 13b). However, with that he is indirectly characterizing Christian worship of God as idol worship or foreign worship. In so doing, Berger falls behind a medieval position within Judaism that further developed the Talmudic understanding of Christianity and which normally forms the unspoken background for present-day Jewish contributions to the discussion around God.

During the early Middle Ages, Jewish authors used the Hebrew concept *shittuf* to designate their impression that the Christian worship of Jesus Christ as equal Son of God introduced a non-divine element into God himself. Halakhically, or according to religious law, the concept *shittuf* can be understood as a term that is friendly toward Christians. With that term, the authors expressed that, from a Jewish point of view, Christianity was not idol worship or idolatry (*avodah zarah*), which would have meant that contact with its members was prohibited; rather, it was *shittuf* (a connection, a communion, an association). As such, it was seen as introducing into God an element of mingling, by which something was joined to God, associated with God, united to God, thus obscuring the clear revelation of the one and only God.[16] The concept of *shittuf* reflected Jewish unease with the Incarnation (of the Son) of God, which was so impressively expressed in our day by Emmanuel Levinas. His reaction should be heard in relation to the concept of *shittuf* and should be taken into consideration as regards a Christology based on "Chalcedonian hermeneutics."

THE PROFILE OF CHRISTIAN BELIEF IN THE INCARNATION

When Christians say in faith, "We believe in the Incarnation, that the Son of God became flesh or became man in Jesus Christ," they consider an intimacy between God and his creation, which as an event in the history of the world did not fall to earth like a meteorite, but that came toward us within a specific history of intimacy between God and the world, that is, within the encounter between the God of Israel and the people of Israel. This specific presence of God forms that history of encounter and intimacy. In the Hebrew Bible, this is described as God's dwelling in or among the people of Israel. "Then have them make a sanctuary for me, and I will dwell among them" (Exod 25:8). His dwelling designates here a special form of God's presence. As Benno Jacob states in a commentary on the Book of Exodus, it is "the completion of human beings with His spirit and essence as a representative residing among them."[17] Exactly this idea is developed further in Exodus 29:42–46 and made concrete in the concept of covenant: "There [the tent of meeting] I will meet with the people of Israel, and it shall be sanctified by my glory....And I will dwell among the people of Israel, and will be their God" (Exod 29:43, 45). Dwelling among the people of Israel is a consequence of the exodus from Egypt: so God can be "their God."[18] When Solomon began building the house of God, the Temple in Jerusalem, God said, "Concerning this house you are building, if you will walk in my statutes and obey my ordinances and keep all my commandments and walk in them, then I will establish my word with you. And I will dwell among the children of Israel" (1 Kgs 6:12–13). God thus has two dwelling places for his intimate presence: the Temple and the people of Israel.[19]

Christian faith dares to state that the event of the Incarnation of the Son of God—Jesus Christ, the one son of the Jewish people as concrete and personal space and place of God's indwelling—brought about change, not only within history, but to history itself. This is expressed in the Gospel according to John in the climactic sentence for New Testament theology: "And the Word became flesh and dwelt among us." This double statement in John 1:14 must be taken entirely seriously: the Word's becoming flesh is just as important as its dwelling among us. The testimony about the Word becoming flesh says what "was already said in the testimony about God 'pitching his tent' and his name 'in the midst' of Israel. It doesn't mean anything else, both mean the same thing."[20] The first half of the verse says in a "Christian" way what the second half says in a "Jewish" way. During the course of the Church's history, biblical language was transformed into other categories of speech, so that "Jewish" categories are in the end expressed "philosophically." The belief that God, the creator of everything in heaven and on earth, descended through the Son and that his Son and Word became flesh and human, is foreign to the Jewish understanding of God. Israel, in whose midst the event of becoming flesh and human occurred, and from whose midst it went out toward the nations, did not, on the whole, speak *in this way* about God's proximity, even though it had and has deep and intimate insights into this proximity. The majority of the Jewish people did not hear *this*, because the Word of God as they understood it did not tell them this.

Regarding the Jewish-Christian relationship in professing the proximity of God, Wyschogrod did not shy away from choosing a phrase to characterize Judaism, which at first glance sounds like an antithesis to what Buber said about the "lack of Incarnation": The God of Israel is

> a God who enters into the human world and who, by so doing, does not shy away from the parameters of human existence, including spatiality. It is true that Judaism never forgets the dialectics, the transcendent God....But this transcendence remains in dialectic tension with the God who lives with Israel in its impurity (Lev 16:16), who is the Jew's intimate companion, whether in the Temple of Solomon or in the thousands of small prayer rooms.... Thus, Judaism is incarnational—if we understand this concept as meaning that God enters into the human world, that he appears in certain places and lives there, so that they thereby become holy.

According to Wyschogrod, there are no reasons "within the essence of the Jewish idea of God," which exclude *a priori* God's "appearance in human form."[21] According to this position, the idea of the Incarnation in general is not antithetical to Judaism.[22]

A CHRISTIAN ATTEMPT TO RESPOND TO JEWISH CONSIDERATIONS

What can a Christian say in response to Jewish reaction to the Christian belief in the Incarnation of the Son of God in Jesus Christ and to the Jewish understanding of God's dwelling among the people of Israel or even to the incarnational self-understanding of a Jewish thinker like Michael Wyschogrod? The answer will not be philosophical but theological. We can begin with Wyschogrod. It was not the victory of a philosophical idea, but rather the free decision of the sovereign

God of Israel to take up his dwelling in the one Son of the Jewish people, Jesus of Nazareth, in such a way that we can no longer speak of God without including God's relationship to this Son, and in naming God's taking up of his abode, we cannot come up with a better concept than that the Word or the Son of God became flesh. Here we should again remember the double statement in John 1:14: "And the Word became flesh and dwelt [lived] among us." According to Johannine understanding, the testimony concerning the Word that was made flesh says the same thing as the testimony regarding God's dwelling or living in Israel. This was the testimony given from the midst of Israel to the Christians from among the Nations, as the free deed of the God of Israel to the son of the Jewish people, Jesus of Nazareth.

In view of Levinas' proposition that the Incarnation is too much for God's poverty and too little for God's glory, the Christian answer consists in the simple and philosophically defenseless counter-question: but what if the God of Israel was pleased to enter into a presence or proximity, which in fact does seem to be too much for divine poverty, and to dare a presence, which seems to be too little for God's glory, without which God's poverty is no abasement? This is Christian belief. Responsible reflection on this topic prohibits triumphalism as, for example, the claim that our belief is better, greater, or deeper than that of our friend León or that of other Jews and of Judaism. Such a judgment will only become apparent at the end of our lives or—for all of us—at the end of history, when our faith will be weighed by the Lord of history. May our faith not be timid but humble, without claiming to be better, without being polemical as regards the faith of our friend León.

Levinas' objection to the idea of "a God man" is part of the uneasiness that found expression in the Middle Ages in the concept of *shittuf*. This concept arose out of the impression that Christian worship of Jesus Christ as the equal Son of God introduced an element of mingling into God's self.[23] Christian theology will not be able to respond to this Jewish concern in a satisfactory way, but it should be sensitive to the dangers of mingling and fusing the relationship between the human and the divine natures in Jesus Christ.

It seems to me that use of the concept of *shittuf* touches on the Council of Chalcedon in its emphasis on the one and same Christ "in two natures; and we do this without confusing the two natures, without transmuting one nature into the other," which the Council then

reinforced by adding: "The distinctiveness of each nature is not nul-
lified by the union" (DH 302).[24] In his Christology, Walter Cardinal
Kasper emphasized that Chalcedon unambiguously held on to the
statement that "God and man do not form a natural symbiosis. In the
Incarnation, God does not become a principle within the world; he is
neither made into a spatial reality nor into one of time. God's transcendence is upheld as much as is the human person's independence
and freedom."[25] The Council of Chalcedon expressed a sensitivity
that does not do away with the Jewish concern, but that does indicate
something that is objectively related: it does not mean some being in
between that is formed by mingling the divine and the human, but
rather, the one and same Christ "in two natures that are not mingled."

THE INCARNATION OF THE SON OF
GOD AS BECOMING A JEW

Along with his differences with the Christian understanding of
the Incarnation, Wyschogrod affirmed that Jesus must never be separated from his people, the Jewish people. In fact, that did happen
often enough and it still happens when the Incarnation is spoken of in
a way that makes the Son of God in Jesus Christ into a "human being
in abstracto, in general and in a neutral way."[26] The Son of God,
God's Word, became a human being in Jesus of Nazareth; he did not
become a human being *in abstracto*, in general or in a neutral way.
Rather, he became Jewish flesh, a Jew, the son of a Jewish mother,
and as *such* he became a concrete human being.

The fact that the Son of God became a Jew is a foundational fact
in Christian theology. Theology is only gradually coming to the
recognition that the concreteness of the Incarnation of the Son of God
in Jesus Christ has to be taken seriously. Over the last decades, several documents of the Church's magisterium have touched on this
topic. Thus, the Vatican's *Notes on the Correct Way to Present the
Jews and Judaism in Preaching and Catechesis in the Roman
Catholic Church* of June 24, 1985, began thinking about the Jewish
roots of Christianity with a christological reflection:

> Jesus was and always remained a Jew, his ministry was
> deliberately limited 'to the lost sheep of the house of Israel'

(Mt 15:24). Jesus is fully a man of his time, and of his environment—the Jewish Palestinian one of the first century, the anxieties and hopes of which he shared. This cannot but underline both the reality of the Incarnation and the very meaning of the history of salvation, as it has been revealed in the Bible (cf. Rom 1:3–4; Gal 4:4–5)....Thus the Son of God is incarnate in a people and a human family (cf. Gal 4:4; Rom 9:5). This takes away nothing, quite the contrary, from the fact that he was born for all (Jewish shepherds and pagan wise men are found at his crib: Lk 2:8–20; Mt 2:1–12) and died for all (at the foot of the cross there are Jews, among them Mary and John: Jn 19:25–27, and pagans like the centurion: Mk 15:39 and parallels).[27]

The Vatican document teaches us to consider the reality of the Incarnation in a very concrete way. If this is done, one automatically comes to the Jewish milieu of the land of Israel in the first century and becomes aware of the family and people of Jesus of Nazareth.

Pope John Paul II reflected deeply on the concrete reality of the Incarnation of the Son of God in his many statements concerning the relationship of the Church to Judaism. On April 11, 1997, he received the Pontifical Biblical Commission in audience, and in his address he spoke of the New Testament's inseparable link with the Old Testament. By emphasizing that Jesus became a Jew, he described the Incarnation of the Son of God as follows:

Jesus' human identity is determined on the basis of his bond with the people of Israel, with the dynasty of David and his descent from Abraham. And this does not mean only a physical belonging. By taking part in the synagogue celebrations where the Old Testament texts were read and commented on, Jesus also came humanly to know these texts; he nourished his mind and heart with them....Thus he became an authentic son of Israel, deeply rooted in his own people's long history....To deprive Christ of his relationship (with the Old Testament) is therefore to detach him from his roots and to empty his mystery of all meaning.[28]

John Paul II underlined that Jesus' human identity has its specific place in the history of Israel. This specific place is part of the "mystery" of the Incarnation. The pope took up the fundamental theological category of "mystery" in order to give weight to his emphasis. In Jesus Christ, the Incarnation does not go immediately and directly to the human in general. Rather, Jesus Christ is "an authentic son of Israel," the Son of God become a human being.

Pope Benedict XVI also engages in more detailed theological exploration of Jesus' human identity and the concreteness of the Incarnation in his book *Jesus of Nazareth*. This is evident in his dialogue with Rabbi Jacob Neusner on the subject of the Sermon on the Mount.[29] For the pope, the preponderance of the Sermon on the Mount is found in Matthew 5:17—7:27; after "a programmatic introduction in the form of the Beatitudes," the Sermon reveals the "Torah of the Messiah" (100). In his conversation with Neusner on the matter of disputes regarding the observance of the Sabbath, the pope explains what the expression "Torah of the Messiah" means. First, he corrects a "conventional interpretation" of the saying attributed to Jesus by Mark (2:27): "The Sabbath was made for humankind, and not humankind for the Sabbath." The pope says that many interpret this as meaning that Jesus "broke open a narrow-minded legalistic practice, and replaced it with a more generous, more liberal view" (106); they then use the text as a basis for the "image of the liberal Jesus." In the conflict around the Sabbath, however, Benedict claims that "we are dealing not with some kind of moralism, but with a highly theological text, or to put it more precisely, a Christological one" (110).

Neusner's sharp objection to seeing Jesus taking the "place of the Torah" seems to have led Benedict to claim: "The issue that is really at the heart of the debate is thus finally laid bare. Jesus understands himself as the Torah—as the word of God in person" (110). The pope seems to be in the process of developing an unusual key category or even a new title for Christ: "Jesus who is himself God's living Torah" (169). When Benedict says that "Jesus understands himself as Torah," and adds "as the word of God in person," he links this understanding to the "tremendous prologue of John's Gospel" (110). Thereby, a new light is shed on the person of Jesus. This new light leads to a deepening of the meaning of the Christological Logos title. Jesus Christ's title as Torah in person—read with a non-supersessionist approach— announces an abiding reference to Israel, to whom God entrusted the

Torah. By calling Jesus Christ "God's living Torah," we might also speak of the Torah incarnate. Benedict has traced a path that should be continued critically in theological discussion. It stimulates reflection on the concreteness of Incarnation and leads to one aspect of the Son of God becoming a human being as a Jew.

If one turns to the most difficult issue in the present-day Christian-Jewish relationship and dialogue, one has to face the Jewish reflections on the Christian "idea" of the Incarnation of the Son of God in Jesus Christ. Reflection on these considerations allows Christian belief in the Incarnation to be shown more clearly. At the same time, the question arises whether the most profound difference in the understanding of God does not also include an element of proximity and of unity, even of something Jews and Christians have in common. This really does come about both regarding the kinship of faith in God's descent as self-abasement and in the directive to Christians to remain receptive to the possibility of reinforcing the connectedness when interpreting their profession of faith in the Incarnation of the Son of God. That is a comforting experience in the theology and dialogue of our time.

NOTES

1. Translated by Katherine Wolff, Kiryat Yearim, Israel.

2. León Klenicki, "Redet Wahrheit—Gedankennach Unterzeichnung des Dokuments. Aufdem Wege zu einem jüdischen Verständnis des Christentums" (*Dabru Emet:* A Reflection After Signing It—Towards a Jewish Understanding of Christianity), in *Fensterzur Welt. Fünfzig Jahre Akademie arbeitin Aachen*, ed. Hans Hermann Henrix (Aachen: Einhard, 2003), 309–21. Also, León Klenicki, "*Dabru Emet*. Une appréciation personelle," *Théologiques* 11 (2003): 171–86.

3. German Bishops' Conference, *The Church and the Jews*, April 28, 1980, IV.2, www.bc.edu/research/cjl/meta-elements/texts/cjrelations/resources/documents/catholic/german_church_jews.html.

4. Thus, Franz Rosenzweig, in his famous letter of October 31, 1913, to his cousin Rudolf Ehrenberg; Franz Rosenzweig, *Briefe und Tagebücher*, vol. 1, 1900–18: *Der Mensch und sein Werk: Gesammelte Schriften*, ed. Rachel Rosenzweig and Edith Rosenzweig-Sheinmann with Bernhard Casper (The Hague: Martinus Nijhoff, 1979), 132–37, 127.

5. Michael Wyschogrod, *Abraham's Promise: Judaism and Jewish-Christian Relations*, ed. with intro. by R. Kendall Soulen (Grand Rapids,

MI, and Cambridge, UK: Eerdmans, 2004), 166; Michael Wyschogrod, "Inkarnation aus jüdischer Sicht," *Evangelische Theologie* 55 (1995): 13–28; similarly, Eugene B. Borowitz, *Contemporary Christologies: A Jewish Response* (New York and Ramsey, NJ: Paulist Press, 1980), 31–32; Alon Goshen-Gottstein, "Judaisms and Incarnational Theologies: Mapping out the Parameters of Dialogue," *Journal of Ecumenical Studies* 39 (2002): 219–47; Amy-Jill Levine, *The Misunderstood Jew: The Church and the Scandal of the Jewish Jesus* (New York: Harper, 2007), 7, 16, 20. See the analogous view of Christian theologians: Friedrich-Wilhelm Marquardt, *Das christliche Bekenntnis zu Jesus, dem Juden: Eine Christologie*. Band 1 (Munich: Kaiser, 1990), passim; Julie Kirchberg, *Theologie in der Anredeals Weg zur Verständigung zwischen Juden und Christen* (Innsbruck and Vienna: Tyrolia, 1991); Clemens Thoma, "Juden und Christen beten denselben Gottan: Monotheismus und Trinität," in *Juden und Christen im Gespräch über "Dabru emet—Redet Wahrheit,"* ed. Erwin Dirscherl and Werner Trutwin (Paderborn and Frankfurt a.M.: Bonifatius/Lembeck, 2005), 89–102; Hans Hermann Henrix, *Judentum und Christentum: Gemeinschaft wider Willen* (Regensburg: Pustet, 2008), 157–58.

6. Quotations from Emmanuel Levinas, "Menschwerdung Gottes?," in Emmanuel Levinas, *Zwischen uns: Versuche über das Denken an den Anderen* (Vienna: Carl Hanser, 1995), 73–82.

7. Jean-François Lyotard and Eberhard Gruber, *Ein Bindestrich: Zwischen "Jüdischem" und "Christlichem"* (Düsseldorf: Parerga, 1995).

8. Michael Wyschogrod, "Warum war und ist Karl Barths Theologie für einen jüdischen Theologen von Interesse?" *Evangelische Theologie* 34 (1974): 222–36, 226; Michael Wyschogrod, *The Body of Faith: Judaism as Corporeal Election* (New York: Seabury, 1983), 113; similarly, *Jeshajahu Leibowitz, Gespräche über Gott und die Welt* (Frankfurt: Insel, 1990), 74, or Peter Ochs, "The God of Jews and Christians," in *Christianity in Jewish Terms*, ed. Tikva Frymer-Kensky et al. (Boulder, CO, and Oxford: Westview Press, 2000), 49–69.

9. Martin Buber, "Die Brennpunkte der jüdischen Seele" (1930), in Martin Buber, *Der Jude und sein Judentum: Gesammelte Aufsätze und Reden* (Gerlingen, Germany: Lambert Schneider, 1993), 196–206.

10. See Clemens Thoma, *Die theologischen Beziehungen zwischen Christentum und Judentum* (Darmstadt, Germany: Wissenschaftliche Buchgesellschaft, 1989²), 111 or Zwi Werblowsky, *Juden und Christen am Ende des 20: Jahrhunderts* (unpublished manuscript, November 5, 1999), 2–5.

11. See *Emmanuel Levinas—eine Heraus forderung für die christliche Theologie*, ed. Josef Wohlmuth (Paderborn: Schöningh, 1998); Josef Wohlmuth, *Die Tora spricht die Sprache der Menschen: Theologische Aufsätze und Meditationen zur Beziehung von Judentum und Christentum*

(Paderborn: Schöningh, 2002); Jean-Bertrand Madragule Badi, *Inkarnation in der Perspektive des jüdisch-christlichen Dialogs* (Paderborn: Schöningh 2006); Hans Hermann Henrix, "Jesus Christ in Jewish-Christian Dialogue," *Theology Digest* 53 (2006): 103–12; Hans Hermann Henrix, "The Son of God became Human as a Jew: Implications of the Jewishness of Jesus for Christology," in *Christ Jesus and the Jewish People Today*, ed. Philip A. Cunningham et al. (Grand Rapids, MI, and Cambridge, UK: Eerdmans, 2011), 114–43.

12. Quoted according to *Decrees of the Ecumenical Councils*, ed. Norman P. Tanner at http://www.piar.hu/councils/ecum04.htm#Definition %20of%20the%20faith.

13. Tikva Frymer-Kensky et al., eds., "*Dabru Emet*: A Jewish Statement on Christians and Christianity," in *Christianity in Jewish Terms* (Boulder, CO, and Oxford: Westview Press, 2000), xv–xvii.

14. See the volumes of commentaries: Frymer-Kensky, *Christianity in Jewish Terms*; *Dabru emet—redet Wahrheit: Eine jüdische Herausforderung zum Dialog mit den Christen*, ed. Rainer Kampling and Michael Weinrich (Gütersloh, Munich: Kaiser/Gütersloh, 2003); as well as Edward Kessler, "*Dabru Emet*," in *A Dictionary of Jewish-Christian Relations*, ed. Edward Kessler and Neil Wenborn (Cambridge: Cambridge University, 2005), 119.

15. David Berger, "*Dabru Emet*: Some Reservations about a Jewish Statement on Christians and Christianity," www.bc.edu/research/cjl/metaelements/sites/partners/ccjr/berger02.htm.

16. For an understanding of the concept of *shittuf*, Clemens Thoma, "Schittuf," *Lexikon der jüdisch-christlichen Begegnung*, ed. Jakob J. Petuchowski and Clemens Thoma (Freiburg: Herder, 1989), 359–62; Michael Signer, "Trinity, Unity, Idolatry? Medieval and Modern Perspectives on *Shittuf*," in *Lesarten des jüdisch-christlichen Dialoges: Festschrift zum 70. Geburtstag von Clemens Thoma*, ed. Silvia Käppeli (Bern, Switzerland: Peter Lang, 2003), 275–84; Edward Kessler, "Shittuf," 404.

17. Benno Jacob, *Das Buch Exodus* (Stuttgart: Calwer, 1997), 859.

18. Christoph Dohmen, *Exodus 19–40* (Freiburg: Herder, 2004), 247.

19. For the exegetical discussion of the statements of the Hebrew Bible on God's "dwelling" and on its derivates, such as *shekinah*, see, for example, Johan Brinkman, *The Perception of Space in the Old Testament: An Exploration of the Methodological Problems of Its Investigation, Exemplified by a Study of Exodus 25 to 31* (Kampen, Netherlands: Kok Pharos, 1992); Bernd Janowski, *Gottes Gegenwart in Israel* (Neukirchen-Vluyn: Neukirchener Verlag, 1993), esp. 11–147, 214–46, 247–80; Susanne Owczarek, *Die Vorstellung vom, Wohnen Gottes in mitten seines Volkes,* in

der Priesterschrift (Frankfurt: Peter Lang, 1998); Rolf Rendtorff, *Theologie des Alten Testaments. Ein kanonischer Entwurf.* Band 2 (Neukirchen: Neukirchener Verlag 2001), 89–104; and Clemens Thoma, "Gott wohnt mitten unter uns: Die Schekhina als zentraler jüdischer Glaubensinhalt," *Freiburger Rundbrief*, NF 14 (2007): 82–85.

20. Thus in Friedrich-Wilhelm Marquardt, *Das christliche Bekenntnis zu Jesus 1*, 115–16.

21. Michael Wyschogrod, "Inkarnation aus jüdischer Sicht," 22; see also Michael Wyschogrod, *The Body of Faith*, 10, 11–14, 211–15.

22. Elliot R. Wolfson picks up Wyschogrod's thought; see Elliot R. Wolfson, "Judaism and Incarnation: The Imaginal Body of God," in *Christianity in Jewish Term*, 239–54. See also Meir Y. Soloveichik, "God's First Love: The Theology of Michael Wyschogrod," in *First Things: A Journal of Religion, Culture and Public Life* 197 (2009), 43–48; www.first things.com/article/2009/10/gods-first-love-the-theology-of-michael-wyschogrod.

23. Michael Wyschogrod expressed the Jewish concern when he said, "There is a good reason for the severity of the Jewish rejection of the incarnation. No matter how close God comes to humankind in the Hebrew Bible, no matter how much God is included in human hopes and fears, he still remains the eternal judge of the human being, whose nature is to be in the image of God (cf. Gen 1:26f.), but who may not be mingled with God....In the light of this, the statement that a human being was God can only give rise to most profound concern in the Jewish soul"; Michael Wyschogrod, "Ein neues Stadium im jüdisch-christlichen Dialog," *Freiburger Rundbrief* 34 (1982): 22–26; similarly Michael Wyschogrod, "Christologie ohne Antijudaismus?" *Kirche und Israel* 7 (1992): 6–9; and *Abraham's Promise*, 165–78.

24. For more on this, see Hans Hermann Henrix, "The Son of God became Human as a Jew," in *Christ Jesus*.

25. Thus, by Walter Kasper, *Jesus der Christus*, vol. 3, *Gesammelte Schriften* (Freiburg: Herder, 2007), 350.

26. Hans Hermann Henrix, *Gottes Ja zu Israel: Ökumenische Perspektiven christlicher Theologie* (Berlin and Aachen, Germany: Einhard, 2005), 11.

27. Commission for Religious Relations with the Jews, *Notes on the correct way to present the Jews and Judaism in preaching and catechesis in the Roman Catholic Church*, June 24, 1985, www.vatican.va/roman_curia/ pontifical_councils/chrstuni/relations-jews-docs/rc_pc_chrstuni_doc_ 19820306_jews-judaism_en.html; the phrase "the Jewish Palestinian one of the first century" means the first-century land of Israel.

28. Pope John Paul II, "Address to Members of the Pontifical Biblical

Commission," April 11, 1997, www.vatican.va/holy_father/john_paul_ii/speeches/1997/april/documents/hf_jp-ii_spe_19970411_pont-com-biblica_en.html.

29. Joseph Ratzinger and Pope Benedict XVI, *Jesus of Nazareth: From the Baptism in the Jordan to the Transfiguration*, trans. Adrian J. Walker (New York: Doubleday, 2007). In a number of places, the book includes the pope's discussion with Jacob Neusner and his book *A Rabbi Talks with Jesus* (Montreal: McGill-Queen's University Press, 2000).

V

SPIRITUALITY: LITURGY

12

Constructing Memory in Jewish Liturgy

Ruth Langer

Every spring, on the Fourteenth of Adar,[1] the Jewish community celebrates the minor festival of Purim, recalling the salvation of the Persian Jews from the plots of King Ahasuerus's (Xerxes) evil minister, Haman, as recorded in the biblical Book of Esther.[2] The primary element of this celebration is the communal reading of this book, symbolically blotting out the name of Haman with raucous noise each time it occurs. This holiday is great fun: children and some adults dress in costumes; its mandates include giving gifts of food to each other (sort of a reverse trick-or-treating), giving gifts to the poor, and drinking more than during most of the rest of the year. Indeed, there is a custom of drinking until one cannot distinguish between blessing Esther and cursing Haman. This is a holiday that lives in a tension liturgically between memory and blotting out memory.

This blotting out of memory lies, not just in the drinking and noise making, but in the focus on rejoicing itself. It derives from another aspect of the holiday. The Sabbath preceding Purim is named *Shabbat Zakhor*, "Remember Sabbath," based on its special additional Scripture reading from Deuteronomy 25:17–19:

> Remember what Amalek did to you on your journey out of
> Egypt, how he attacked you on the way, when you were
> faint and weary, and struck down all who lagged behind
> you; he did not fear God. Therefore when the Lord your
> God has given you rest from all your enemies on every
> hand, in the land that the Lord your God is giving you as

an inheritance to possess, you shall blot out the remembrance of Amalek from under heaven; do not forget.

This is reinforced in the *haftarah*, the reading from the Prophets
paired with this passage, from 1 Samuel 15, where Saul is commanded to attack the Amalekite nation and utterly destroy them in
retribution for the assault in the wilderness. The king of the
Amalekites, at this point, is named Agag. Esther 3:1 identifies Haman
as an Agagite, that is, as one of his descendents. Drawing on this,
Jewish tradition understands anyone like Haman who seeks the utter
destruction of the Jews also to be an Amalekite, to be like the ancient
king who cruelly attacked the refugee Israelites on their flight from
Egypt. Deuteronomy, though, confusingly commands that when one
reaches a point of safety from this persecution, one retains memory
of it, but also blots out this memory, that is, forgets it. This is indeed
a conundrum, one that has given rise to many good sermons. In this
context, it provides an opportunity for trying to tease out the historical role and contemporary ethical mandate of this memory and forgetting in Jewish liturgy.

WHAT DOES JEWISH LITURGY "REMEMBER"?

Jews, in general, are more aware of the outline of Jewish history, especially its tragedies, than they are of Jewish theology or even
how Jewish liturgy is constructed. Historical consciousness and its
attendant memory are thus quite central to Jewish identity—which is
best described as a national, ethnic identity in which religion, itself
variously defined by a spectrum of groups in today's society, plays a
role. The degree to which religion plays a role in defining Jewish
identity correlates significantly with the definition of religion
involved. This itself is a significant and complex topic, but not one
that can be properly explored here. We can note, though, that a two-
day symposium at Concordia University in the spring of 2011 on the
topic of "History, Memory, and Jewish Identity" included not a single paper title addressing issues of liturgy and ritual. Instead, they
focus on various periods of Jewish experience and the ways that their
events shaped Jewish memory and identity.[3]
Today's Jewish liturgy, that which one encounters in a syna-

gogue service, emerged into its current structure in the aftermath of the Roman destruction of the Jerusalem Temple in the year 70 CE. The actual language of the fixed prayers probably emerged in the following centuries, taking perhaps the better part of a millennium to reach its familiar form in all its details. However, these prayers were orally transmitted, leaving few shreds of evidence by which to reconstruct their emergence. Only in the nineteenth century, as Jews were emancipated and sought to join Western society, did these now accepted forms begin to receive any substantial revision, and then only by those who came to identify themselves as Reform (or Liberal or Progressive) Jews. Today, a wider spectrum exists, ranging from the various Orthodox or traditional groups who consider the received texts to be mandatory, to Conservative Jews who allow some changes, to the Reconstructionist and Reform movements who allow much more substantial creativity.[4] However, even radical creativity among more liberal movements is to some degree derivative of the traditional received liturgy. My discussion here, then, for the sake of simplicity, will focus on traditional modes of liturgical expression, with occasional references to the liberal.[5]

For all traditional forms of Judaism, the destruction of the Jerusalem Temple, the subsequent exile, and the consequent loss of any ability to fulfill God's biblical commandments for sacrificial worship formed and forms the central existential crisis. A key message of the resultant liturgy is that we are living in a world in desperate need of divine messianic intervention. This is not just because Jews are scattered and often persecuted; without a Temple in Jerusalem, even Jews who do live in peace and without persecution cannot fulfill all of God's biblical commandments. While this does not create a situation of sin,[6] it does create a situation where life before God is not in its ideal form. Regular elements of the liturgy— the petitionary and supplicatory elements of the weekday prayers and the central blessing of the additional service on Sabbaths and holidays—voice a memory of crisis in the past that shapes an understanding of the present and articulates as well a "memory" of the future. This last is an assurance that the God who redeemed Israel in the past will do so again. Exactly what form this messianic worship will take can be only a matter of speculation, although there are certainly some who expect and even actively seek a full restoration of the Herodian Temple and its rites.[7]

The rabbis layered this response to their personal situation onto a daily memorialization of key elements of the pentateuchal narrative as well. God created the world, redeemed Israel from Egypt, and revealed the Torah at Mount Sinai—in the past—but continues to act as creator, revealer, and redeemer in the present and in the future. Many understand these to be the three pillars of Jewish theology. They find expression in key daily prayers as well as in the lectionary cycle, and in the shaping of the liturgical year.

In addition, the rabbis had a few received models for historical celebrations. Best known of these are Hanukkah, the celebration of the defeat of the Seleucids who tried to destroy Jewish religious practice in the 160s BCE, celebrated with special lights in the dark of winter for eight nights; and the celebration of Purim with which we began. The rabbis also instituted fast days, most importantly in mourning for the destructions of the first and second Temples on the Ninth of Av in the heat of summer, but with more minor fasts for events related to this.[8]

This, then, is the memory that the rabbis of the first several centuries CE wanted to articulate liturgically and inculcate among Jews. As far as we can determine, they were largely successful, at least by the end of the first millennium. The texts of these prayers became fixed and mandatory. No additions to them had their status, and deletions rendered them invalid.

NON-JEWS IN JEWISH LITURGY AND RITUAL LIFE

The rabbis decreed that all prayers must be recited in the first person plural. Even an individual praying alone recites them as part of the entire community of Israel.[9] Therefore, liturgically, for Judaism, the "other" cannot be another Jew, but must be those outside the Jewish community. Except in Scripture readings, though, these "others" mostly remain unnamed. The primary exception is the biblical Egyptians who were certainly "other," but they are also mostly ancient historical figures. Jews living in Egypt in late antiquity and later generally did not equate their neighbors with Pharaoh and his henchmen, although there remained a sense of diffidence about moving from the Land of Israel to Egypt. Today, some liberal prayer books delete the specific references to the Egyptians.[10] In contrast, the rabbis considered their Roman oppressors, first pagan Rome and then Christian Rome, to be the descendents of the biblical Esau, but neither Esau nor Rome play an explicit role in the memories evinced by the central statutory prayers.[11] Even on the Ninth of Av, the primary texts come from the Book of Lamentations, reflecting on the destruction of the first Temple. There, too, the Babylonians remain unnamed.

It is precisely here that we must confront the major tension in Jewish liturgical memory. On the one hand, what we might term the "sacred memory" of the biblical and particularly pentateuchal narrative is present, yet, as framed, it largely "blots out" or ignores the other. On the other hand, we live in history, a history of which the Jewish community is, in general, very conscious. How do these two elements merge?

A particularly powerful example takes us back to the celebration of Purim. Eighteenth-century Hasidic rabbis taught that those who hear the reading of the scroll of Esther on Purim should not understand it as stories about historical miracles, but rather that they consider themselves to be participants in the events.[12] This might be considered simply a Jewish example of what in Christian liturgy is called *anamnesis*, a memory of the past that is made present in ritual action today.[13] However, this Hasidic teaching goes further and suggests that one must be conscious that, through the merit of participating in the reading with this intention, God will perform miracles continually, in every generation. Two significant presuppositions underlie this statement. One is the understanding of the performance of God's commandments with proper intention that Hasidism shares with other forms of kabbalistically informed Judaism: that human actions performed with correct intentions (*kavvanot*) influence the interaction of the heavenly *sefirot* (emanations of God), with direct consequences for life on earth. Thus, the intention here is not *anamnesis* but rather activating these powers of blessing.

The second presupposition is more important to our topic here: that Jews are constantly in need of God's miraculous intervention to save them from the next Haman. This trope appears even more explicitly directly in the text of the Passover Haggadah. Referring to God's promise to save Israel, it says, "For not only once somebody rose against us to annihilate us, but in every generation they rise against us to annihilate us; but the Holy One, praise to Him, rescues us from their hands."[14] There is a power and a danger in this. Its power lies in its personalizing and keeping fresh the message of God's continuous providential and loving care for Israel, particularly in forms relevant to the holiday itself. This should not be minimized. Its danger lies in its potential to eliminate the element of "blotting out the memory" of the "other." The "other" gains a name and a face, and when that is a persecuting dangerous "other," this memory presents its own dangers. A contemporary figure becomes Haman or Amalek, and particularly in our world where Jews are no longer powerless, "blotting out the memory" can go beyond the figurative and become simply an indiscriminate "blotting out."

It is, then, worth delving more deeply into this tension between remembering and blotting out. This move to naming the other and embedding specific memories of history in the liturgy did not begin in the eighteenth century. It seems to have its roots from around the time that fixed prayers emerged that omitted precisely such information. While the rabbis in Babylonia felt that these statutory modes of prayer that largely avoided specific historical memories needed to take central stage, synagogues in the Land of Israel from the middle of the first millennium developed ways of enriching and even replacing some of these prayers with liturgical poetry (*piyyut*). This poetry became a vehicle, not just for creative study of Scripture (its primary role), but also for response to current realities.

Yannai was a sixth-century poet who lived approximately when the Byzantine Emperor Justinian (reigned 527–565) was decreeing further limitations on the practice of Judaism.[15] Yannai wrote poetry for every Sabbath that focused on that week's lectionary. When the readings discussed Jacob's brother Esau, his poetry described Esau's, that is, Byzantine Rome's, wickedness and prayed for its demise.[16] Yannai's poetry was eventually lost, and then rediscovered a century ago.[17] Of his successors, Elazar b'Rabbi Kalir's poetry had the most impact because it entered the liturgical rites of central Europe. Kalir continued to present Esau as Rome and Christian Rome as a subtle motif, especially in his laments written for the Ninth of Av, the anniversary of the destruction of the Temple.

However, as of the early seventh century, the centers of world Jewry came under a generally benign Muslim rule. Jews' immediate living "other" changed and, for the most part, became one that either did not demand a liturgical response or that response was embedded in poetry that European Jews did not adopt.

This method of recording and then rehearsing memory reemerges in Europe in the High Middle Ages, again largely in response to negatives. As Christianity gained confidence and political power in the High Middle Ages, it started placing more and more pressure on the Jews living in Christian lands to convert, seeking to construct a Christian society that excluded blasphemers, infidels, and Christ-killers. While today's scholars are suggesting that, for the most part, life did indeed go on fairly normally most of the time, what Jewish memory records from this period is a series of disasters.[18]

The Crusades, for Jews, were not a glorious time; instead, in 1096, peasant crusaders decided that they needed to kill off the infidel in their own midst. They massacred the Jewish communities of the Rhineland, even denying the prerogatives of local bishops, as in Mainz, to shelter them in his castle. The communities affected were the intellectual center of Jewish Europe, where leading rabbis taught and trained students. As a result, even today on the Ninth of Av, while mourning the destruction of the Temples, Jews also recite laments for these Rhineland communities. The rabbis themselves were massacred in 1096; in 1242 in Paris, on orders of the pope and king, the texts they taught were burned. The liturgy of the Ninth of Av also contains a wrenching lament recalling this massacre of the Talmud, the destruction of cartloads of books that the Church deemed blasphemous but which represent the core of the Jewish curriculum.[19]

Individual communities recalled their own local disasters in this way, as well as their salvations from near disasters. The anniversary of the disaster became a local fast day, the anniversary of a miraculous salvation they celebrated as a Purim. For the most part, though, these memories lasted only as long as the local community continued to exist. Almost all Jews in Europe from the thirteenth to the sixteenth centuries were expelled from their homes—either from entire countries or more locally. This generally left no intact community to preserve local memories. Only the most important memories of disasters or salvations became universalized, sometimes with their liturgical poetry transposed to other dates on the calendar.[20]

The Church and European governing powers, not only destroyed communities, but they deliberately destroyed Jewish memory. As one might imagine, Jewish liturgical texts constructed to memorialize communal disasters or narrow escapes would not portray the perpetrators positively. We know that Christian concern about the nature of

Jewish life deepened from the mid-thirteenth century on, usually when baptized Jews brought details to the attention of Church and civil authorities, using their insider knowledge in the process. Beginning in the fourteenth century, these accusations led to occasional local censorship of Jewish liturgical texts; from 1553 on, censorship of all Hebrew books was universal in the Catholic world, followed soon by the Protestants, in response both to the changed nature and proliferation of the now-printed word and sensitivities to heresy arising from their own theological debates. The result of this process was the censorship from Jewish prayer books of any prayers or segments thereof that were deemed anti-Christian. This erased another set of memories.[21]

In some cases, scholars today can reconstruct these erased memories from manuscripts, but they remain something just for the history books. As a consequence, as with the older statutory prayers, the surviving poetry does not really name the "other," even when it narrates historical events. We may know well who perpetrated the atrocities memorialized in the laments for the Crusades martyrs, but the poetry does not name them. The historical laments focus instead on descriptions of what the Jews themselves endured. Designed to bring the worshipper to join in the poet's grief, these texts communicate immense pain. They generally conclude by petitioning God to exact justice; perhaps because it was useless in their world, they do not seek to elicit a human anger that would lead to activism.[22]

CONTEMPORARY IMPLICATIONS

Events of the past century have drastically reshaped the Jewish world, destroying the historic Jewish communities of both Europe and Arab lands. However, the Holocaust and the realities of life in the contemporary Jewish State of Israel provide opportunities and mandates for Jews today to construct memories related to this changed reality thoughtfully and responsibly, and this especially includes memory that gives new presence to the "other." In Jewish understanding, both the Holocaust and the birth of the State of Israel (and its continuing search for peaceful existence) intersect with God's commandment to "remember what Amalek did to you" but, once given secure life in the land, "to blot out the memory of Amalek" and not to forget. Jews have a long tradition of understanding Amalek "to symbolize any enemy of the Jews."[23] Thus, Hitler fit this category. Many understood Arafat this way as well, certainly while the PLO operated as a terrorist organization, and continue to extend this to terrorist elements among Palestinian society. What do we now remember?

To begin with the easier category: how do Jews deal with the memory of the Holocaust? It is an unhealed sore in the community that requires, to my mind, some kind of more adequate liturgical response than has yet emerged. But Holocaust perpetrators are mostly deceased, and Nazism is at least illegal if not dead in most places. Germany itself, as a country, has done yeoman's work in confronting and repenting for its past, as has much of the Christian world, led especially by the Catholic and Evangelical Lutheran Churches. Jewish memory here requires careful nuance.

In the aftermath of the Crusades, the crusaders did not repent, nor did the Christian perpetrators of other atrocities suffered by Jews throughout the centuries, and Jews retain the pain. Thus, today's repentance of the perpetrators is a radically new element; it challenges these reflexes of Jewish memory. Mourning for the lost individuals, communities, and civilization is still necessary. The command is "Remember what Amalek *did to you.*" The suffering does not disappear, and the memory of the lost needs to be honored. At the same time, though, we might blot "Amalek" himself from the picture and move beyond personalizing the persecutor, because today we have reached, or are in the process of reaching, a better and secure place. Because of the repentance of the perpetrators, we can now remember while also leaving room for rebuilding relationships. This is not precisely the Deuteronomist's intent, but it works liturgically. It requires skillful and thoughtful construction of memorial observances that hold these various ethical imperatives in proper tension.

As to Israel and the Palestinians, the situation is volatile and complex. Certainly, many Palestinians want to live in peace, but the Hamas charter still calls for Israel's destruction,[24] and acts of violence are still perpetrated or attempted constantly, whether bombings, stabbings, or in rocket attacks from Gaza. Are the perpetrators today's Amalekites? Their actions, in targeting civilians and children do have Amalekite characteristics.[25] In medieval times, when Jews were powerless, liturgy would have inscribed the memory of the victims and called on God for justice; that would be the end. However, today,

Israelis have the power to enforce justice on the human level. Much of the country struggles deeply with the moral quandaries this creates.

On the one hand, self-defense is morally correct. Sitting back and waiting for divine intervention when one has the means to save oneself is suicidal, hence, itself a grave sin and not an appropriate response. Memory and prayer are thus insufficient. On the other hand, full activism is also problematic. God commanded the biblical king Saul to spare not a single Amalekite in war and punished Saul when he spared the life of the Amalekite king (1 Sam 15). Today, though people—including Jews—may commit atrocities that have Amalekite characteristics, there are no literal Amalekites. Therefore, understanding the commandment to wipe out the memory of Amalek cannot be correctly applied as a command to destroy a living human community, even in a situation of war. It cannot be a mandate for genocide or even for a defensive response to genocide. The application of this commandment, then, to the Israel-Palestine situation, awaits a time, hopefully in the not-too-distant future, when this can be applied, as between Jews and Christians and Jews and Germans, to the process of reconciliation, to remembering by also blotting out the memory of that which constructed the conflict. After all, the Deuteronomic command applies precisely to the period when the danger has passed, not to the process of getting there.

The tension between memory and forgetting in Jewish life is thus not theoretical. It has real implications for Jewish relations with the "others" of our world today.

NOTES

1. This lunar month precedes the month in which Passover falls, so Purim usually is celebrated in March. In cities that were walled "from the days of Joshua," most notably Jerusalem, the holiday is celebrated a day later to recall the extension granted to the Jews of Shushan to save themselves. See Adele Berlin, *The JPS Bible Commentary, Esther* (Philadelphia: The Jewish Publication Society of America, 2001), 87–88.

2. Mordecai, Esther's cousin and guardian, is identified in 2:5–7 among the descendants of the exiles from Jerusalem in 597 BCE. Ahasuerus is usually identified as Xerxes I (reigned 486 to 465 BCE). However, scholars question whether to read this story as history. See Berlin, xxxiii–xxxiv, 25.

3. The program is available at http://religion.concordia.ca/jewishid/program/ (accessed May 22, 2011).

4. For a discussion of these changes, see my "Prayer and Worship," in *Modern Judaism: An Oxford Guide*, ed. Nicholas de Lange and Miri Freud-Kandel (Oxford: Oxford University Press, 2005), 231–42.

5. Where I capitalize the term, I am referring to an identified movement in the contemporary Jewish world. I employ here "traditional" and "liberal" more as descriptive adjectives.

6. Sin, in Jewish understanding, is best understood as a failure to fulfill a divine commandment. This commandment, though, has to be applicable to the person and possible to fulfill.

7. See, for example, the website of "The Temple Institute," http://www.templeinstitute.org/main.htm, and especially its "Statement of Principles," http://www.templeinstitute.org/statement.htm (accessed May 22, 2011).

8. Like the Seventeenth of Tammuz (when the walls of Jerusalem were breached), the Fast of Gedalia on the Third of Tishrei (when the Jewish governor of Judea was killed), or the Tenth of Tevet (the beginning of the siege of Jerusalem).

9. *M. Ber.* 7:3; *y. Ber.* 7:3, 11b–c; *b. Ber.* 29b–30a and 49b–50a.

10. Most notable in this category is the prayer book of the contemporary Israeli Conservative (Masorti) movement, which prints the words "The water covered their enemies, leaving not one of them" in gray, with a note in the margin acknowledging that some omit these words. See *Va'ani Tefilati, An Israeli Siddur* (The Masorti Movement and The Rabbinical Assembly of Israel; Tel Aviv: Miskal–Yedioth Ahronoth Books and Chemed Books, 2009), 41, 119. Compare the evening service (pp. 75 and 104), where much more is in gray.

11. The exception is the appending of Obadiah 1:21 to the morning recitation of Exodus 15. However, we do not know when or how this verse entered the liturgy. If it entered after the rise of Islam, as is possible, it becomes difficult to read it as anti-Roman.

12. In their discussions of the meaning of the Mishnah's prohibition on reading Esther liturgically *lamefra'* (in reverse order), attributed to second-generation Hasidic rebbes, or perhaps to the Besht himself, see R. Kalonymos Kalman ha-Levi Epstein, *Ma'or va-Shemesh, Rimzei Purim*, citing R. Ze'ev Wolf ha-Levi of Zhitomir's *'Ohr Hameir*, and R. Zvi Elimelech Shapira of Dinov, *B'nei Yissachar, Ma'amarei Hodesh Kislev-Purim 4, Hallel ve-Hoda'ah 9* (both from Bar Ilan Responsa Project CD-ROM, version 18). My thanks to Rabbi Benjamin Samuels for alerting me to this interpretation.

13. After the Greek of Jesus' instruction at the Last Supper, as recalled by Paul in 1 Cor 11:24, "and when he had given thanks, he broke

128 TOWARD THE FUTURE

[the bread] and said, 'This is my body that is for you. Do this *in remembrance* of me'" (emphasis added).

14. See, for example, *The Scholar's Haggadah: Ashkenazic, Sephardic, and Oriental Versions*, with a historic-literary commentary by Heinrich W. Guggenheimer (Northvale, NJ: Jason Aronson, Inc., 1998), 38–39.

15. Justinian largely continued existing Roman imperial legislation about Jews, but added several novellae of significance. For a summary see "Justinian I," *Jewish Virtual Library*, http://www.jewishvirtuallibrary.org /jsource/judaica/ejud_0002_0011_0_10500.html (accessed May 24, 2011).

16. On Yannai's treatment of Esau, see Laura S. Lieber, *Yannai on Genesis: An Invitation to Piyyut* (Cincinnati: Hebrew Union College Press, 2010), 270–85.

17. On this discovery, see Adina Hoffman and Peter Cole, *Sacred Trash: The Lost and Found World of the Cairo Geniza* (New York: Nextbook, Schocken, 2011), 103–25. On Yannai, see Lieber, *Yannai on Genesis*, esp. part I.

18. See, for example, Jonathan Elukin, *Living Together, Living Apart: Rethinking Jewish-Christian Relations in the Middle Ages* (Princeton, NJ: Princeton University Press, 2007).

19. In *The Authorised Kinot for the Ninth of Av*, ed. Abraham Rosenfeld, 2nd ed. (New York: Judaica Press, 1970), see #24, pp. 127–30; #27, pp. 132–34; #31, pp. 139–42; #35, pp. 148–49; #43 (on the burning of the Torah), pp. 161–62.

20. "Purims, Special," *Encyclopaedia Judaica*, ed. Michael Berenbaum and Fred Skolnik, 2nd ed. (Detroit: Macmillan Reference USA, 2007), 16:742–44.

21. See my *Cursing the Christians? A History of the Birkat Haminim* (New York: Oxford University Press, 2012), chs. 3–4.

22. One wonders, though, whether the manuscripts of pre-censored texts would contain different sorts of material. These have not yet been published.

23. Bernard M. Levinson, *Jewish Study Bible*, p. 423, to Deuteronomy 25:17–19.

24. See "MidEast Web Historical Documents: Hamas Charter, The Covenant of the Islamic Resistance Movement (Hamas), 18 August 1988," *MidEast Web*, http://www.mideastweb.org/hamas.htm (accessed May 24, 2011).

25. This careful nuance was developed by Rabbi Benjamin Samuels in his introduction to Parshat Zakhor on March 19, 2011, Congregation Shaarei Tefillah, Newton Centre, Massachusetts.

13

Reviving the Catholic Observance of the Feast of the Circumcision of Jesus

Philip A. Cunningham

INTRODUCTION

I am delighted to contribute to this volume in honor of Rabbi León Klenicki. When we first met in the late 1980s, León was particularly interested in Catholic liturgy, including attitudes toward the "Old Testament" conveyed explicitly and implicitly by the lectionary. León's concern eventually led to plans for the publication by the Stimulus Foundation and Paulist Press of a series titled The Word Set Free, to which I was honored to contribute the first volume, *Sharing the Scriptures*.[1] It seems appropriate, then, that the editors of this collection have invited me to write on a liturgical topic. Since my encounters with León typically stimulated new insights, it also seems fitting that I try to reflect imaginatively about something that was once a subject of our conversation: the removal of the Feast of the Circumcision of Jesus from the Catholic liturgical calendar after the Second Vatican Council.

Pope Paul VI, wishing to reemphasize the ancient tradition of venerating Mary as God-bearer during the Christmas season, removed the Feast of the Circumcision from the liturgical calendar and renamed the first day of the year as the "Solemnity of Mary, the Mother of God." He also allowed the day to be marked as a World Day of Peace.[2] This change was ironic because the same Council issued the landmark Declaration on the Church's Relationship to Non-Christian Religions, *Nostra Aetate*. One feature of that document is a strong emphasis on the Jewishness of Jesus. Thus, the post-conciliar Church has both promoted a vivid awareness that "Jesus

129

was and always remained a Jew"[3] but has also ceased liturgically observing his circumcision into the covenantal life of the children of Israel.

In 1975, the Catholic bishops of the United States noted that:

> Christians have not fully appreciated their Jewish roots. Early in Christian history a de-Judaizing process dulled our awareness of our Jewish beginnings. The Jewishness of Jesus, of his mother, his disciples, of the primitive church, was lost from view. That Jesus was called Rabbi; that he was born, lived and died under the Law; that He and Peter and Paul worshipped in the Temple—these facts were blurred by the controversy that alienated Christians from the Synagogue. How Jewish the church was toward the mid-point of the first century is dramatically reflected in the description of the "Council of Jerusalem" (Acts 15). The question at issue was whether Gentile converts to the church had to be circumcised and observe the Mosaic Law?[4]

This essay suggests that considering a restored observance of the Feast of the Circumcision in the Roman Catholic Church could do much to counter the lingering effects of this early Christian de-Judaization. The word *restored* is important here. Commemorating the circumcision of Jesus would be a retrieval of an ancient custom. In addition, although at times in history the event was presented as the supersessionist replacement of Judaism by a Torah-free and universal Christianity, other voices spoke about it in ways that could be quite instructive in a post–*Nostra Aetate* Church.

COMPLEX CONVERGENCES

Catholic-Jewish relations take place in contexts where the theological and liturgical questions raised by this dialogue intersect with issues of gender, ethnicity, and other sociopolitical realities.[5] That complicated web of intersections is beyond the scope of this essay. However, we must acknowledge that remembering Jesus' circumcision occurs today in a context in which recent legislative initiatives in several countries have proposed banning the practice of infant male circumcision as inhumane. Such proposals, not only focus on the medical benefits or hazards of the procedure, but often intersect with debates about the role of religions in secular societies, as well as accompanying issues of race, religion, and ethnicity. The debate has deployed such expressions as *mutilation, traumatized, control over one's own body, religious freedom, anti-Semitism,* and *Islamophobia.* In 2011, public controversy prompted the Swedish Council of Christians and Jews to invite comments from the International Council of Christians and Jews. In consultation with members of the ICCJ Executive Board, president Deborah Weissman composed a statement that was issued by the ICCJ in January of 2012.[6]

The subject of male circumcision also raises questions of gender, which have also been posed by Jewish scholars.[7] Circumcision can symbolize and enact male hegemony, privileging maleness in such a way that one Jewish writer states that circumcision "is fundamentally about gender and power."[8] Nonetheless, for all that the ritual is fraught with ambiguity in relation to gender and power, most Jews have their sons circumcised, all the while finding ways to create rituals that also honor their daughters.[9]

From the perspective of interfaith relations, the issues of gender surrounding circumcision as a religious rite of initiation are for Jews to debate in terms of their own self-understanding. Having said that, we must acknowledge that for Catholics to imagine the restoration of a Feast of the Circumcision of Jesus, in some way enters into that ambiguity, this time risking the privileging of maleness in a Roman Catholic context in relation to the male identity of Jesus. Nonetheless, even these complexities tell us something about the incarnation of the Word as a Jew and his initiation into the life of covenant between God and the people Israel.

A BRIEF SKETCH OF THE FEAST'S HISTORY

The commemoration of the circumcision of Jesus first appeared during the hegemony of the Roman Empire. In December, Romans celebrated Saturnalia in honor of the agricultural god Saturn, astrologically associated with the movement of the sun through the constellation Capricorn around the winter solstice. Several days of festivity marking the start of increasing daylight included lighting candles, exchanging gifts, and disregarding class distinctions so that slaves and masters came together to dine and engage in sports and games. After Julius Caesar decreed a new calendar and established January as the first month, the celebratory atmosphere extended to Kalends, the first day of the New Year on January 1. The general air of overturning social conventions and mocking authority figures continued on the popular level in the centuries after the collapse of the empire in the West.

Although there is debate over which played the primary role—the winter solstice or the counting of nine months from the Feast of the Annunciation around the vernal equinox—it is evident that, by the fourth century, Christians associated celebrating the nativity of Jesus with the Roman winter solstice on December 25. By this time, the Saturnalia involved the solstitial "Birthday of the Invincible Sun." Christians related the Invincible Sun to the one whose resurrection had conquered the darkness of death and whose coming was thought to be foretold at the end of the last book of their Old Testament: "There will arise the Sun of Righteousness with its healing rays" (Mal 4:2 [Heb 3:20]).[10] The Eastern fathers Athanasius, Basil the Great, Cyril of Alexandria, Didymus the Blind, Eusebius, Gregory of Nyssa, John Chrysostom, Origen, and others all made use of Malachi's phrase "Sun of Righteousness" in reference to Christ.[11]

The narrative found in Luke 2:21 connects the Nativity to the next event in Jesus' life: "After eight days had passed, it was time to circumcise the child; and he was called Jesus, the name given by the angel before he was conceived in the womb" (see Lev 12:3). Counting eight days from December 25 leads to January 1 as the day to mark Jesus' naming and incorporation into Israel. Thus, while pagans were carousing during the Kalends, Christians were continuing to celebrate and ponder the incarnation, specifically Jesus' circumcision in the flesh and his naming as *Yeshua*, "God saves." Christians had also been debating whether it was proper to call Mary the *Theotokos*, "she who bears the one who is God," and so there were Marian dimensions to early Christian reflection on the incarnation and circumcision. Many of these interconnections can be seen in a later Greek Orthodox prayer, a *theotokion*, which praises Mary as the God-bearer: "You are a cloud of light, all-holy Virgin, bearing the Sun of Righteousness. He dispels the dark ignorance of idolatry, shining upon us with the light of divine knowledge."[12] Thus, enlightened, Christians should clearly observe the New Year very differently from the dark antics of their pagan neighbors.

Early in the Church's history then, the Feast of the Circumcision was connected to the New Year, with the continuing celebration after eight days (an octave) of the physical incarnation of God's Word in Jesus, and with Mary as the God-bearer. Various medieval texts show how the feast was understood in later periods. Early in the twelfth century, Bernard of Clairvaux preached about the Word's self-emptying (*kenosis*) in becoming human by "abbreviating" his divine prerogatives:

> For He was "abbreviated" in taking flesh, and is still further "abbreviated" in receiving the circumcision of the flesh....[B]y undergoing the rite of circumcision, He gave further proof of His human nature, but the adorable name of Jesus which He then received is above every other name, and declares the glory of His majesty.[13]

Bernard's meditation shows that the circumcision and naming of Jesus were linked together, as indeed they are in Luke 2:21. But they are also connected to the nativity and incarnation, the unity of the divine and the human. Related ideas are found the next century in Jacobus de Voragine's very popular collection of the lives of the saints. Compiled around 1260, though added to subsequently, his book *The Golden Legend* presents four reasons why the Circumcision of the Lord is "an important and solemn" observance:

> Firstly, this day is [part of] the Octave of the Nativity....
> Secondly, the Circumcision recalls to us the conferring of a new name upon the Lord, for our salvation....
> Thirdly, the Circumcision celebrates the first shedding of Christ's blood for men.
> Fourthly, the Feast of the Circumcision honors our Lord's circumcision itself....He wished to show that He had really taken human form: for blood can come forth only from a real body. He also wished to show us that we too should accept spiritual circumcision, that is, that we should apply ourselves to the work of our purification. Again, the Lord allowed Himself to be circumcised in order to take away from the Jews any excuse of their actions toward Him: for if He had not been circumcised,

they could have said to Him, "We did not receive thee, because thou wert different from our fathers."

Lastly, Our Lord wished to show that the Law of Moses was holy: for he had come not to destroy the Law, but to complete and to fulfill it.[14]

De Voragine's fourth point unsurprisingly reflects the prevailing ideas of the time, some of which reveal inner tensions. Thus, though the blood shed in the circumcision is seen to declare Jesus' authentic humanity, Jesus "the Lord" is described as having "allowed" the ritual, as if as an eight-day old infant he had control over what was done to him. Also, while indicating that Christ did not come to destroy the Torah (though note the possible implications of the past tense, "*was* holy"), de Voragine wants to reinforce that "the Jews" had no defense for later allegedly rejecting Jesus on the grounds that he wasn't truly Jewish. Desiring to leave "the Jews" without excuse is clearly polemical and reflects the influence of supersessionism and possibly of the deicide charge.

Around 1270, Thomas Aquinas, in his *Summa Theologiae*, also considered the question of Christ's circumcision:

For several reasons Christ ought to have been circumcised. *First*, in order to prove the reality of His human nature, in contradiction to the Manicheans....*Secondly*, in order to show His approval of circumcision, which God had instituted of old. *Thirdly*, in order to prove that He was descended from Abraham, who had received the commandment of circumcision as a sign of his faith in Him. *Fourthly*, in order to take away from the Jews an excuse for not receiving Him, if He were uncircumcised. *Fifthly*,..."to exhort us to be obedient"...[so] He was circumcised on the eighth day according to the prescription of the Law (Lev 12:3). *Sixthly*, "that He who had come in the likeness of sinful flesh might not reject the remedy whereby sinful flesh was wont to be healed." *Seventhly*, that by taking on Himself the burden of the Law, He might set others free therefrom, according to Gal 4:4, 5: "God sent His Son...made under the Law, that He might redeem them who were under the Law."[15]

We see here Aquinas echoing some of de Voragine's points, including those that presuppose the replacement of Judaism by Christianity.

While reflecting supersessionist understandings, these medieval perspectives also convey a theological conviction of great relevance today: the circumcision of Jesus attests to the Jewish humanity of the Word-made-flesh. They also impart the pastoral or ethical admonition for church members to purify themselves spiritually so that their actions reflect their faith in Christ. It is not necessary here to give a detailed history of how the interlaced themes and feasts mentioned above were variously celebrated. In different centuries, Christians in various countries in Europe observed January 1 as either a feast honoring the motherhood of Mary, as the circumcision of Jesus, as the bestowing of the name "God saves" upon the child, and/or as the Octave Day of Christmas.

CONTEMPORARY CONSIDERATIONS

In the years since Paul VI's decree, there has been much interest in the Jewishness of Jesus and the early Church by Jews and Christians alike.[16] Although he was not addressing the question of restoring the Feast of the Circumcision, Pope John Paul II offered some pertinent comments on Jesus' Jewishness that provide compelling theological and pastoral reasons for doing so. Speaking to the Pontifical Biblical Commission as it was working on a major study that would be published a few years later as *The Jewish People and Their Sacred Scriptures in the Christian Bible*, he noted:

1. a temptation to a Marcionist separation of Jesus from the story of Israel and of the Old Testament "is making its appearance again in our time";
2. a related docetic danger of viewing Jesus "like a meteor that falls to earth" if his participation in the "history of the People of Israel" were to be disregarded;
3. an enduring "ignorance that Christians have nothing in common with Jews"; and
4. the fact that Jesus' human identity cannot be appreciated apart from his formation as "an authentic son of Israel."[17]

The Catholic liturgical calendar certainly takes up some of these themes, but no observance substantively explores the significance of Jesus' Jewishness for Catholic-Jewish relations today. The post– *Nostra Aetate* Church would obviously avoid earlier supersessionist motifs. It could not accept the logic of a homily given in the Vatican on the Feast of the Circumcision in 1493 that Jesus' dying words in the Gospel of John, "It is finished," referred to the termination of Judaism and its initiatory rite.[18] The modern revival of the feast would stress Jesus' Jewish identity as a Torah-observant son of Israel from a Torah-observant family, the vitality of ongoing Jewish covenantal life, and the relationship between Jews and Christians.

The restoration of the feast would also provide a formal liturgical grounding or preparation for the "Day of Judaism" that is currently being marked in several European countries around January 17.[19] The revived Feast of the Circumcision would usher in the Day of Judaism with a sacerdotal liturgy, not only for Europeans, but for Catholics around the globe.

POSSIBLE SCRIPTURE LECTIONARY READINGS FOR A RESTORED FEAST OF THE CIRCUMCISION

As described above, January 1 has been associated with the Octave of Christmas, the Circumcision, the Name of Jesus, Mary the Mother of God, the World Day of Peace, and New Year's Day. One could imagine a three-year lectionary cycle for January 1 (or the nearest Sunday) that rotates among three of these themes or optional sets of readings at the celebrant's discretion. In any case, the following readings assume that the liturgy is focused on the ritual event of Jesus' circumcision.

First Reading (Lev 12:1–4, 6–8)

The LORD spoke to Moses, saying: Speak to the people of Israel, saying:

If a woman conceives and bears a male child, she shall be ceremonially unclean seven days; as at the time of her menstruation, she shall be unclean. On the eighth day the flesh of his foreskin shall be circumcised. Her time of blood purification shall be thirty-three days; she shall not touch any holy thing, or come into the sanctuary, until the days of her purification are completed.

When the days of her purification are completed, whether for a son or for a daughter, she shall bring to the priest at the entrance of the tent of meeting a lamb in its first year for a burnt offering, and a pigeon or a turtledove for a sin offering. He shall offer it before the LORD, and make atonement on her behalf; then she shall be clean from the flow of her blood. This is the law for her who bears a child, male or female. If she cannot afford a sheep, she shall take two turtledoves or two pigeons, one for a burnt offering and the other for a sin offering; and the priest shall make atonement on her behalf, and she shall be clean.

Commentary

Since one aspect of a post–*Nostra Aetate* revival of the Feast of the Circumcision is to recall that Jesus "wished to submit himself to the law (Gal 4:4), that he was circumcised and presented in the Temple like any Jew of his time (Luke 2:21, 22–24), that he was trained in the law's observance,"[20] this passage from Leviticus demonstrates that the purpose of the restored feast is to celebrate the participation of Jesus in the Sinai covenantal life of Israel with God. In order to think of Jesus as embodying the Torah, as Pope Benedict XVI has recently written,[21] his own commitment to living according to the Torah must be made explicit. The suggested reading includes the commands concerning the mother's postpartum purification, in order to provide additional connections with the proposed Gospel reading.

Responsorial Psalm (Ps 119:1–5, 12–16, 129–33)

Refrain: Happy are those whose way is blameless; who walk in the law of the LORD.

Happy are those whose way is blameless; who walk in the law of the LORD
Happy are those who keep his decrees, who seek him with their whole heart,
Who also do no wrong, but walk in his ways.
You have commanded your precepts to be kept diligently.

O that my ways may be steadfast in keeping your statutes!
[*Refrain*]

Blessed are you, O LORD; teach me your statutes.
With my lips I declare all the ordinances of your mouth.
I delight in the way of your decrees as much as in all riches;
I will meditate on your precepts, and fix my eyes on your ways.
I will delight in your statutes; I will not forget your word.
[*Refrain*]

Your decrees are wonderful; therefore my soul keeps them.
The unfolding of your words gives light; it imparts understanding to the simple.
With open mouth I pant, because I long for your
commandments.
Turn to me and be gracious to me, as is your custom toward
those who love your name.
Keep my steps steady according to your promise, and never
let iniquity have dominion over me. [*Refrain*]

Commentary

This psalm in praise of the Torah and fidelity to it seems like a
perfect response to the First Reading in a revived Feast of the
Circumcision. It presumably reflects Jesus' own sentiments as he
"nourished his mind and heart"[22] with the traditions of his people. It can
remind Christians that Jesus himself loved the Torah and conversed
with Jewish contemporaries about how best to observe its commands.
The liturgical use of this psalm counteracts the hoary Christian carica-
ture of Judaism as a joyless legalism to which Jesus was opposed.
Clearly, such thoughts are far from the heart of the psalmist.

Second Reading (Rom 15:5–13)

May the God of steadfastness and encouragement grant
you to live in harmony with one another, in accordance
with Christ Jesus, so that together you may with one voice
glorify the God and Father of our Lord Jesus Christ.
Welcome one another, therefore, just as Christ has welcomed you, for the glory of God. For I tell you that Christ
has become a servant of the circumcised on behalf of the

truth of God in order that he might confirm the promises given to the patriarchs, and in order that the Gentiles might glorify God for his mercy. As it is written:

"Therefore I will confess you among the Gentiles, and sing praises to your name"; and again he says,

"Rejoice, O Gentiles, with his people"; and again, "Praise the Lord, all you Gentiles, and let all peoples praise him," and again Isaiah says, "The root of Jesse shall come, the one who rises to rule the Gentiles; in him the Gentiles shall hope."

May the God of hope fill you with all joy and peace in believing, so that you may abound in hope by the power of the Holy Spirit.

Commentary

Although the second reading from one of the New Testament epistles typically runs continuously over a season independently of the Old Testament and Gospel readings, on major feasts the epistle can directly relate to them. Here the Apostle Paul reiterates that Jesus served his own Jewish people, thereby confirming divine promises to the patriarchs and giving the Gentile nations reason to thank and praise God's mercy. The birth of the Church, including those Gentile communities founded by Paul, has become possible precisely because Jesus "became an authentic son of Israel."[23]

Sequence (Luke 1:67–75, 79)

Celebrant:

Zechariah was filled with the Holy Spirit and spoke this prophecy:

All:

Blessed be the Lord God of Israel,
for he has looked favorably on his people and redeemed them.
He has raised up a mighty savior for us
in the house of his servant David,
as he spoke through the mouth of his holy prophets from of old,
that we would be saved from our enemies and from the hand of all who hate us.

Thus he has shown the mercy promised to our ancestors,
    and has remembered his holy covenant,
the oath that he swore to our ancestor Abraham,
    to grant us that we, being rescued from the hands of our
        enemies,
    might serve God without fear, in holiness and righteousness
        before him all our days.
By the tender mercy of our God,
    the dawn from on high will break up on us,
    to give light to those who sit in darkness and in the shadow
        of death,
    to guide our feet into the way of peace.

Commentary

In Catholic liturgical tradition, a "sequence" is a hymn or chant that introduces the Gospel reading. Although, in the past, many major holy days had sequences, today the most familiar one is probably that on Pentecost, *Veni Sancte Spiritus* ("Come, Holy Spirit"), which begins, "Come, Holy Spirit, and send forth from heaven the rays of your light."

Interestingly, the narrative of Jesus' circumcision, found only in the Gospel of Luke, does not at that point elaborate upon the event's significance. However, the Lucan infancy narrative is structured as a step parallelism with the annunciation, birth, circumcision, and naming of Jesus contrasted with the earlier annunciation, birth, circumcision, and naming of John the Baptist. On the occasion of John's circumcision, his father Zechariah proclaims a poetic prophecy that actually comments more upon the deeper meaning of the ensuing circumcision of Jesus. Zechariah sings that the imminent birth of Jesus would save the Jewish people from their traditional Gentile enemies, as covenantally promised to the patriarchs, so that they could worship God in peace.

This text carries additional resonances in the post–*Nostra Aetate* Church, which has vigorously rejected anti-Semitism. Moreover, echoing the Romans lection, the coming of Jesus will guide the Gentile nations who sit in darkness into the light of the pathways of peace. The image of Jesus as the dawn breaking from on high also echoes the feast's ancient associations with Malachi's "Sun of Righteousness."

Since the few words about the circumcision of Jesus in the

Gospel reading do not convey all these rich themes, the inclusion of this Sequence before the Gospel would frame the deeper significance for Christians of Jesus' initiation into Israel's covenantal life.

Gospel (Luke 2:6–7, 21–24)

The time came for her to deliver her child. And she gave birth to her firstborn son and wrapped him in bands of cloth, and laid him in a manger, because there was no place for them in the inn.

After eight days had passed, it was time to circumcise the child; and he was called Jesus, the name given by the angel before he was conceived in the womb. When the time came for their purification according to the law of Moses, they brought him up to Jerusalem to present him to the Lord (as it is written in the law of the Lord, "Every firstborn male shall be designated as holy to the Lord"), and they offered a sacrifice according to what is stated in the law of the Lord, "a pair of turtledoves or two young pigeons."

Commentary

The motif of Jesus and his family as pious, Torah-observant Jews is an important one for Luke. He deliberately notes that almost all the characters in his infancy narrative fit that description: Zechariah, Elizabeth, Mary, Joseph, Simeon, and Anna. The observance of the circumcision ritual develops this motif. Luke follows the order of Leviticus 12:2–6, and so the circumcision is followed immediately by the purification of Mary and presentation in the Temple. Although there is a separate feast on February 2 of the Presentation of Jesus in the Temple, the suggested Gospel reading for this revived Feast of the Circumcision includes that scene providing an additional connection with the first reading from Leviticus. Not only is Jesus circumcised according to the Torah of Moses, but his mother is also halakhically purified. This highlights the Jewishness of Mary as well. As the preeminent character in Luke's account who hears the word of God and keeps it, she models both the ideal Jewess in covenant with God and the ideal disciple of her son (see Luke 11:27–28). The mention of the offering of a pair of turtledoves or pigeons is a further link to Leviticus, expressing another favorite Lucan theme: the family of Jesus is poor; they cannot afford a sheep.

Homily Hints

The brief commentaries on the recommended lections suggest a number of possible homiletic approaches. The Feast of the Circumcision of Jesus, as noted for many centuries, emphasizes the reality of the incarnation. The Word-made-flesh is an actual human being. Contrary to various heresies envisioning Jesus as a purely celestial figure who could not possibly experience human limitations or pain or needs, the feast reiterates that Jesus is fully human. Even today, when it could be argued that many Christians are functional docetists, this core dogma of Christian teaching should be explicitly reiterated.

Moreover, the Word was enfleshed in *Jewish* flesh. His participation in Israel's covenantal life with God was marked with the traditional sign in the flesh of his circumcision. As all the evangelists variously describe, Jesus' story is within Israel's story. As he grew in wisdom and in grace, he learned to love the God of Israel and to pray to God as "Abba." His life and death were in the service of the inbreaking reign of the God of Israel.

The same is true for his mother, Mary. As the evangelist clearly expressed in the words exclaimed by Mary in the *Magnificat*, her motherhood was due to the favor of God her savior, "in remembrance of his mercy, according to the promise he made to our ancestors, to Abraham and to his descendants forever" (Luke 1:54–55). Mary's story is also embedded within the story of her people. Recalling this Marian theme is most appropriate given the long association of January 1 with praise of Mary as *Theotokos*. Furthermore, Jesus was born a Jew because he was born of a mother who was a Jewess. Mary not only gives birth to the one who is God, but observes Torah and imparts her own Jewish heritage to him.

Equally significant is the traditional linkage of the circumcision with the naming of Jesus. As the Lucan infancy narrative shows, the name "God saves" or "God rescues" declares that the birth of Jesus into the world reflects God's own fidelity to the people Israel. God's covenantal relationship with the Jewish people, Luke believes, is what prompts the coming of the one who will bring peace and reconciliation to both Israel and all the nations. If there is a pastoral hesitancy at Masses for Children in focusing on the act of circumcision itself, the homilist could spotlight the naming of Jesus as the expression of his Jewishness and of God's concern for the divine covenant with the people Israel.

Indeed, a point made by *Nostra Aetate* is very pertinent here. Jews and Christians are religiously connected for several reasons, one of which is the Jewishness of Jesus, of Mary, and of the earliest disciples and apostles. This means that Christians should regard Jews today as their brothers and sisters[24] who have a long and praiseworthy history of seeking to do God's will as understood through the Torah.[25]

Another question in restoring the Feast of the Circumcision is whether it could raise the issue of why Christians do not practice the same religious ritual that Jesus did. A homilist in the post–*Nostra Aetate* Church would obviously not want to suggest that defining Jewish rites had ended or lacked any spiritual significance. One would also not want to get into a long discourse over how the debate over circumcision unfolded in the Pauline churches[26] or in subsequent centuries. It should suffice to say that the early apostles realized after the resurrection of Jesus that the time had come to open their fellowship to non-Jewish Gentiles without demanding circumcision or Torah-observance of them. Christ's death and resurrection made it possible for Gentiles to enter into relationship with the God of Israel as Gentiles. The Church has maintained this tradition ever since.

However, this does not mean that the example of Jesus' circumcision has no direct implications for the life of Christian faith. Just as circumcision ritually incorporates a Jewish boy into the life of God's people Israel, baptism incorporates Christians, children, and adults alike, into the life of God's people, the Church. Both Jews and Christians see the respective initiating rites as pledges to live as God wants covenanted people to live. Recalling the long-lived practice of contrasting Christian behavior with the raucousness of New Year's celebrations, a revived Feast of the Circumcision could be the occasion for encouraging church congregations to live according to the ethical principles that, in reality, Christians have mostly inherited from the traditions of Judaism.

NOTES

1. Philip A. Cunningham, *Sharing the Scriptures*, The Word Set Free, vol. 1 (New York and Mahwah, NJ: Paulist Press/Stimulus, 2003).

2. See Paul VI, *Marialis Cultus*, 5, February 2, 1974.

3. Pontifical Commission for Religious Relations with the Jews, "Notes on the Correct Way to Present Jews and Judaism in Preaching and Catechesis in the Roman Catholic Church" (1985), III, 12.

4. National Conference of Catholic Bishops, "Statement on Jewish-Christian Relations," November 20, 1975. Available at http://www.ccjr.us/dialogika-resources/documents-and-statements/roman-catholic/us-confer ence-of-catholic-bishops/479-nccb1975.

5. See Ange-Marie Hancock, "When Multiplication Doesn't Equal Quick Addition: Examining Intersectionality as a Research Paradigm," *Perspectives on Politics* 5 (2007): 63–79; at http://www.jstor.org.ezproxy.cul.columbia.edu/stable/pdfplus/20446350.pdf?acceptTC =true.

6. See http://www.iccj.org/redaktion/upload_pdf/2012032118015 20.booklet2_circumcision.PDF.

7. See, for example, Howard Eilberg-Schwartz, *The Savage in Judaism: An Anthropology of Israelite Religion and Ancient Judaism* (Bloomington and Indianapolis: Indiana University Press, 1990), 141–76. On the complicated history of debate about circumcision, see Shaye J. D. Cohen, *Why Aren't Jewish Women Circumcised? Gender and Covenant in Judaism* (Berkeley, Los Angeles, London: University of California Press, 2005), 207–23.

8. Miriam Pollack, "Circumcision: Identity, Gender, and Power," *Tikkun*, June 27, 2011. Available at http://arclaw.org/newsletter/vol-9/no-1 /jewish-perspectives/circumcision-identity-gender-and-power.

9. See Judith Plaskow, "Bringing a Daughter into the Covenant," in *Womanspirit Rising*, ed. Carol Christ and Judith Plaskow (New York: Harper and Row, 1979), 179–84; Lawrence A. Hoffman, *Covenant of Blood: Circumcision and Gender in Rabbinic Judaism* (Chicago and London: University of Chicago Press, 1996); Riv-Ellen Prell, "Reading the Covenant: A Review of *Covenant of Blood: Circumcision and Gender in Rabbinic Judaism*," *The Reconstructionist* 63 (1998): 88–91.

10. Thus Eusebius of Caesarea, "Oration in Praise of the Emperor Constantine" VI 20: "Hence it is that the mystic and sacred oracles reveal him to be the Sun of righteousness, and the Light which far transcends all light."

11. There are literally dozens of allusions to Malachi 4:2 in the Eastern fathers. To give only one example for each of the fathers named here: Athanasius, *Expositiones in Psalmos* (2035:061), Migne, *Patrologia Graeca* (hereafter MPG), 27, p. 400, ln. 13; Basil, *Homilia in martyrem Julittam* (2040:023), MPG 31, p. 253, ln. 35; Cyril, *Commentarius in Isaiam prophetam* (4090:103), MPG 70, p. 573, ln. 41; Didymus, *Commentarii in Job (incatenis)* (2102:014), MPG 39, p. 1120, ln. 35; Eusebius, *Commentarius in Isaiam* (2018:019), in *Eusebius Werke*. Band 9: *Der Jesajakommentar*, ed. J. Ziegler (Berlin: Akademie-Verlag, 1975); Gregory of Nyssa, *Deperfectione*

Christiana ad Olympium monachum (2017:026), in *Gregorii Nysseniopera*, ed. W. Jaeger (Leiden: Brill, 1963), vol. 8, 1, p. 185, ln.1; John Chrysostom, *Expositiones in Psalmos* (2062:143), MPG 55, p. 451, ln. 58; and Origen, *Expositio in Proverbia (fragment aecatenis)* (2042:075), MPG 17, p. 188, ln. 53. My thanks to Demetrios Tonias for these references.

12. See http://www.fordham.edu/Halsall/basis/triodion/lent2sun.txt.

13. *Sermons of St. Bernard on Advent and Christmas: including the famous treatise on the incarnation called "missus est"* (London: R. & T. Washbourne and New York: Benzinger, 1909): http://www.archive.org/stream/sermonsofstberna00bernuoft/sermonsofstberna00bernuoft_djvu.txt.

14. Jacobus de Voraigne, *The Golden Legend*, pt. 1, trans. Granger Ryan and Helmut Ripperger (London, New York, Toronto: Longmans, Green, and Co., 1941), 82–83.

15. See III, q. 37, art. 1, *responsio*, http://www.gutenberg.org/files/19950/19950.txt.

16. The number of publications on Jesus and his times by both Jewish and Christian scholars is enormous. I would note, in particular, the research by James H. Charlesworth, Daniel Boyarin, Paula Fredriksen, Richard Horsley, Amy-Jill Levine, John Meier, Ben F. Meyer, Mark Nanos, E. P. Sanders, and N. T. Wright, among many, many others.

17. John Paul II, "Address to the Pontifical Biblical Commission," April 11, 1977, §3–4. For a complete anthology of John Paul II's work on Jews and Judaism, see *The Saint for Shalom; How Pope John Paul II Transformed Catholic-Jewish Relations: The Complete Texts 1979–2005*, presented by the Anti-Defamation League, ed., and with commentary by Eugene J. Fisher and León Klenicki (New York: Crossroad, 2011).

18. Cardulus, *Oratio de circumcisione*, cited by Leo Steinberg, *The Sexuality of Christ in Renaissance Art and in Modern Oblivion* (New York: Pantheon, 1983), 58, n. 65.

19. See http://www.jcrelations.net/Day+of+Judaism+in+the+Churches+of+Europe.222.0.html?L=3.

20. PCRRJ, "Notes" (1985), III, 13.

21. See the discussion in Hans Hermann Henrix, "The Son of God Became Human as a Jew: Implications of the Jewishness of Jesus for Christology," in *Christ Jesus and the Jewish People Today: New Explorations of Theological Interrelationships*, ed. Philip A. Cunningham et al. (Grand Rapids, MI: Eerdmans, 2011), 120–22, 131–38.

22. John Paul II, "Address to the Pontifical Biblical Commission," April 11, 1977, §3.

23. Ibid.

24. John Paul II, "Address at the Great Synagogue of Rome," April 13, 1986, §4.

25. See PCRRJ, "Notes" (1985), VI, 25.

26. Though I might note the broad consensus in current Pauline scholarship that emphasizes Paul's abiding Jewishness. He argued that Gentiles being baptized into the churches need not undergo circumcision, but never wrote that Jews-in-Christ should cease circumcising their male children. The Acts of the Apostles makes this same distinction in narrating that Paul circumcised his companion Timothy because his mother was Jewish (Acts 16:1–3). For a fine overview of recent developments in Pauline studies, see Magnus Zetterholm, *Approaches to Paul: A Student's Guide to Recent Scholarship* (Minneapolis: Fortress Press, 2009). See also Pamela Eisenbaum, *Paul Was Not a Christian: The Original Message of a Misunderstood Apostle* (New York: HarperOne, 2009), and Reimund Bieringer and Didier Pollefeyt, *Paul and Judaism: Crosscurrents in Pauline Exegesis and the Study of Jewish-Christian Relations* (London and New York: T & T Clark, 2012).

VI

SPIRITUALITY:
SPIRITUAL PRACTICE
AND MYSTICISM

14

Toward a Theology of Empathy[1]

Arthur Green

INTRODUCTION

I write these words as a teacher, a teacher of teachers. I have devoted much of my life to the education of rabbis, having served as president of one seminary and then as founder of another. I firmly believe that Judaism, one of the world's great religious traditions, still has much to offer, both to its own adherents and to the universal community of seekers. The Torah in its broadest sense is a Tree of Life (Prov 3:18) to those who hold fast to it, indeed who *strengthen* it, by the energy of ever-fresh interpretation. The wisdom discovered in that process of Torah-study and constant reinterpretation is the inner light hidden within our Torah. It needs to be sought out in each generation, updated, and rendered accessible by newly trained rabbis, as it has been throughout time. This process demands much knowledge, but also love, faithful commitment, and openheartedness. Conveying this to future rabbis is the work in which I am engaged.

I do this work from a particular point of view. Although I do not belong to any of the well-known denominations within Judaism, I think of myself as a neo-Hasidic Jew. This means that I study and am inspired by the teachings of Hasidism, our great movement of popular piety that began in Eastern Europe, founded by disciples of the Ba'al Shem Tov, Rabbi Israel Master of the Good Name, who passed into eternity two hundred and fifty years ago.

Hasidism teaches a radically simplified version of Kabbalah, the Jewish mystical tradition. It emphasizes that "the whole earth is filled with God's glory" (Isa 6:3), that God can be found in each place and in every moment. "There is no place devoid of God" is a Hasidic watchword, as is "Know Him in all your ways" (Prov 3:6).[2] The pur-

149

pose of tradition, prayer, and ritual is to help us open our hearts to that presence. When we do so, we are able to uplift and redeem fallen sparks of divine light that are within us and all around us, restoring them to their source in the One. There need be nothing esoteric or otherworldly about this teaching; it is simplicity itself.

Neo-Hasidism differs from classical Hasidism, which still thrives, in two important ways. We do not share the Hasidic disdain for modernity, especially for modern education and science. We accept the legitimacy of scientific and historical investigation and believe that faith must be updated in response to it. We also do not believe that the insights of Hasidism should apply only to Jews. Its teachings are about God and the human spirit, expressed in many different languages across our vast human community. We seek a Judaism that recognizes its place within that wondrous and colorful spectrum, not one that proposes to stand outside or above it.[3]

We modern rabbis minister to people who are fairly secular in their daily lives. They do not spend much time either talking to God or talking about God. Yet there is about them a quality of deep search for meaning, even if they cannot articulate this in theological language. They want to understand their lives as having some higher purpose. They have a strong sense that we are supposed to help make the world a better place, to lessen human suffering, and increase goodness among people. It is not accidental that names of Jews are found among nearly every Western group that defends human rights and works to reduce human suffering; we still remember that we were slaves in Egypt. This memory, reinforced by more recent ones, causes us—including the secularized—to care for the oppressed and suffering, wherever they may be. The sense of family and intergenerational connection also remains very strong. Jews, even those of seemingly little faith or Jewish knowledge, believe that we have a valuable legacy that we have been given by our ancestors and that we must pass on to our children's children. Many struggle to understand what this legacy is, but they still seek to pass it onward.

EMPATHY'S CHALLENGE

It is especially around the life cycle and this sense of legacy that Jews find themselves turning to rabbis and synagogue communities.

The birth of a child, education in the tradition, celebration of life's milestones, tragic losses of life or misfortune, the ageing and illness of parents, death and mourning—all of these bring Jews back from their secular pursuits to seek out wisdom and consolation from their tradition, and the personal support and affection of rabbis and other clergy.

Rabbis are expected to meet Jews in such moments with empathy, drawing on a deep well of caring, having an ability to give and to be present to people with whom they otherwise may have little relationship. At such times, the traditional phrases of piety do not suffice, nor does the attempt at purely intellectual teaching. The rabbi has to be seen, above all, as genuine, truly caring, and not merely professional. As many readers of this volume know well, this ability to be present can only come out of one's own spiritual life. To live a life of giving to others, one needs to be nourished by God's presence in one's own life. To *hold* people, in their pain as well as in their joy, rabbis—or any pastoral workers—have to manifest their own strength, which is really not theirs at all, but God's, in which they are rooted by their own faith.

So teaching students to become rabbis, to help each one grow into his or her own rabbinate, as we like to say it, includes instructing them on how to cultivate their own inner garden. This includes prayer, both communal and personal. Spiritual direction and counseling also have a place in our program. But in our tradition, the inner life is also very much nurtured by study of the sources, taught and discussed in openhearted ways, so that each rabbi's spiritual life is rooted directly in the text and language of the ages. Remember that, in our tradition, the Word that was with God from the beginning did not become flesh, but remains Word, manifest in Torah, which includes the ongoing process of teaching, learning, and the constant creativity of new interpretations. The *beit midrash* or study hall, where students sit in pairs or small groups and discuss texts among themselves, lies at the heart of rabbinic education and of our sacred process altogether.

THE "WORD THAT REMAINS WORD"

The "word that remains Word" means that we know God best through careful listening. Ours is largely an aural/oral culture, one in which the heard and spoken word plays a decisive role. Judaism begins nowhere other than with *Shema' Yisra'el*, "Hear, O Israel, Y-H-W-H

our God, Y-H-W-H is one" (Deut 6:4). This biblical verse stands as
our watchword of faith, recited by the pious twice each day, "when
you lie down and when you rise up."

The best-known of all Jewish prayers, *Shema' Yisra'el*, is in fact
not technically a prayer at all. Prayer is an act in which the human
being turns toward God. Its essence lies in an opening of the heart;
prayer is indeed called by the early rabbis "worship within the
heart."[4] It usually, but by no means always, has a verbal component,
addressed to the Almighty. The most characteristic Jewish prayers are
called *berakhot* or "blessings," opening with the phrase "Blessed are
You, O Y-H-W-H...." But this line is rather addressed to the community, rather than to God. Now, I will translate more fully: "Hear, O
Israel"—"Listen, my fellow-Jews! Being is our God; Being is one!"

I am going to return later to the word *Israel* in this line, because
that is an essential part of our conversation. But let me begin here
with the functional question, the big question when it comes to reality: What difference does monotheism make? One god, ten gods, a
thousand, so what? Jews (we are most like Muslims in this regard)
insist on the absolute oneness of God and take pride in the "purity"
of our monotheism. But why should we? What is monotheism worth?

The only value of monotheism is to make one realize that all of
being, including every creature—and that means the rock and the
blade of grass in one's garden, as well as one's pet lizard and the some-
times-difficult human neighbor next door—are all one in origin. We
come from the same place. We are created in the same great act of
love. God takes delight in each form that emerges and bestows God's
own grace upon it.[5] Therefore—and this is the "payoff" line, the only
one that really counts—*Treat them that way!* They are all God's crea-
tures; they exist only because of the divine presence, the same divine
presence that makes us exist. This realization calls upon us to *get to
know them! Get to love them!* Discover the unique divine gift within
each of them! Live in amazement at the divine light strewn throughout the world. That is what it means to be a religious human being.

Within the human community, that love also means respect for
difference and for boundaries. The mystical spirit that seeks to overcome all distance and separation between God's children cannot
become an excuse for ignoring boundaries. Respecting otherness is
easy to forget in a religious context, where we want to allow ourselves to be overwhelmed by the oneness of being. It sometimes hap-

pens to good and well-meaning people that they are so overpowered by the love within them that they lose control. Love and self-restraint, the right and left hands of God, need to be properly balanced, within the cosmos as within the self. The Jewish mystical tradition calls this self-restraint *tsimtsum*, finding it in God's love for the world as well as in human behavior. God, as it were, has to pour forth the bounty of divine grace in measured ways in order for diverse beings to feel that they each exist in the world as distinct and individual selves.[6]

GOD'S NAME IS "BEING"

Now I return to the controversial part of my translation. The mystical tradition within Judaism, out of which I speak, insists on translating God's name as "Being." That is Y-H-W-H, the Hebrew name for God, the one we look at on the page but don't dare to pronounce. Scripture tells us that this is God's own name (Exod 6:2–3). But it is not really a name at all, not even fully a noun. Y-H-W-H is an impossible conflation of all the tenses of the verb "to be" in Hebrew: HYH, meaning "was"; HWH, indicating the present; and YHYH, "will be." They are all put together here in an impossible form. Probably it should best be translated as "Was-Is-Will Be." But since that is a little awkward to say each time, "Being" is the best we can do, though we must understand that "Being" as transcending time as well as space.

The meaning here is profound. "God" and existence are not separable from one another. God is not some fellow over there who created a separate, distinct entity called "world," over here. There are not two; there is only one. The mystics insist on carrying monotheism one step farther than some others do. There is not just one God; there is only One.

To say we believe in one God, but then depict that God as an old fellow with a beard seated on a throne—or in any other single way, taken literally—is just a concentrated form of idolatry. It is like that old story every Jewish child learns, in which Abraham's father, Terah, is the owner of an idol workshop. Once he needed to go out and asked his son to mind the store. Abraham smashed all the idols but the biggest one, then, put an axe in the large idol's hand. When Terah returned, he looked around and said, quite in shock, "What happened to all my gods?" Abraham answered: "The largest idol smashed them all." "Don't be silly," said Terah, "they're just idols." "Aha!" said Abraham, and that "Aha!" is supposed to be the beginning of monotheism.

But what if there is something important being said beneath the surface here? How do we know that our one God is not just the biggest idol? If monotheism is just about numbers, all we have left is a single big idol. Far too many people leave it at that. The real change has to be in the way we see existence itself. In fact, the way we say "existence" in Hebrew is HWYH, pronounced *havvayah*, the four letters of God's secret name, just rearranged. To see "God" when we look at existence is a rearranging of the molecules, as it were. Seeing the BIG picture instead of the many smaller ones. God is Being when we see Being as one, when we see the whole picture. Of course, we can't ever really see *all* of that big picture. The sum is infinitely more than the totality of its parts. Transcendent mystery remains, even in my very immanentist theology. But for me, transcendence resides *within* immanence. Transcendence does not refer to a God who dwells "out there" somewhere, on the far side of the universe (which has no sides, the astronomers assure us!). Transcendence means that God is *here*, present in this very moment, but in a way so intense and profound that we could never fathom it. *That* is the mystery.

This is the secret truth. Listen to one of the great sages, a Hasidic master who revealed it in a letter he wrote to his children and grandchildren. Here I quote the famous *Sefat Emet*, the rabbi of Ger or Gora Kalwarya[7] in Poland:

> The proclamation that we declare each day in saying *Shema' Yisra'el* needs to be understood as it truly is…the meaning of "Y-H-W-H is one" is not that He is the only God, negating other gods (though that too is true), but the meaning is deeper than that. There is no being other than Him….Everything that exists in the world, spiritual and physical, is God Himself….Because of this, every person can attach himself to God wherever he is, through the holiness that exists within every single thing, even corporeal things. You only have to be negated in the spark of holiness….
>
> This is the foundation of all the mystical teachings in the world.[8]

Of course, that is not as easy as it sounds. To "be negated in the spark of holiness," in order to make room for God's Self to enter, is a life-long labor. To do this inner work in a healthy and wholesome way is a goal toward which we all struggle.

WHO IS "ISRAEL"?

But now I have to turn back to the beginning of our non-prayer, "Hear, O Israel." Who is "Israel" in this phrase? Remember where the word comes from. Our ancestor Jacob once had an all-night wrestling match with an angel (Gen 32:23–33).[9] A tough fellow, that Jacob. Even an angel could not best him. When dawn came, the angel said, "Let me go! Time to sing God's praises!" "Uh-uh," Jacob said, "Not until you bless me." So Jacob came out of that encounter with a new name: Israel, meaning "Struggler with God."

I believe that name belongs to all strugglers, not just to Jews and not just to Christians. Everyone who wrestles with angels, who strug-gles to make sense out of life, is part of some broader community called "Israel." *Shema' Yisra'el, Y-H-W-H Elohenu, Y-H-W-H ehad* then means: "Listen, all you who struggle, all you who wrestle with life's meaning! Being is our God, Being is one!" Do not look beyond the stars. No need to stretch your neck. God is not "out there" some-where. God is right here, filling all of existence with endless bounty. Open your eyes. Turn that wrestling match into an embrace. Find God's presence in the unified, transforming vision of all that is, and in one another.

"Hear, O Israel" is followed immediately by "You shall love Y-H-W-H your God with all your heart, with all your soul, and with all your might" (Deut 6:5). This is one of the two great statements of love in the Torah that Jesus has told Christians constitutes the essence of its teachings.[10] Our sages have struggled for many centuries over the question of how it is possible to command love, if this is indeed a commandment. Does love not require spontaneity? Does it not spring up voluntarily from the heart? But when the *shema'* is recited in the context of our daily liturgy, it is always preceded by a declara-tion of God's love for us. In our daily morning prayers, we say, "How greatly have You loved us, pouring upon us the bountiful flow of Your compassion," and in the evening we say, "With eternal love have You loved the House of Israel, Your people." We are thus first reminded of God's love for us, and then call out the oneness of all being. At that point, we no longer need to be "commanded" to love. The love wells up from within us as response, as natural and essential to us as breathing or as speech itself. In this case, the proper translation into English is no longer "You *shall* love Y-H-W-H your God..." but rather "You *will* love...," a statement of fact rather than commandment.

Can the same apply to that other love prescribed by the Torah: "Love your neighbor as yourself" (Lev 19:18)? Can that love, too, become so natural that we no longer need to experience it as "commanded," but as welling up from within? For a Jewish response to this question, we have to turn to a famous debate between two of the early rabbis, who lived about a century after Jesus: Rabbi Akiva, also a martyr to the Romans, and his friend Ben Azzai. The Talmud[11] records that they struggled over the question: "What is the most basic principle of Torah?" What is the teaching for the sake of which all the rest of Judaism exists? Akiva had a ready answer: "Love your neighbor as yourself" (Lev 19:18). Akiva was Judaism's greatest advocate for the path of love, though perhaps I should say that he shares this honor with Jesus of Nazareth. Akiva was the one who insisted that the Song of Songs was indeed to be included in Sacred Scripture, calling it the "Holy of Holies," spoken by God and Israel at Mount Sinai.[12] The tale of Rabbi Akiva and his wife's love is one of the few truly romantic tales within rabbinic literature.[13] So too the account of Akiva's death: when he was being tortured by the Romans, he supposedly said, "Now I understand the commandment to love God with all your soul—even if He takes your soul, you shall love Him."[14] Thus, it is no surprise that Akiva is depicted as seeing love to be the most basic rule of Torah.

But Ben Azzai disagreed. He said, I have a greater principle than yours. He quoted Genesis 5:1–2: "On the day when God made human beings, they were made in the likeness of God; male and female God created them." That, he said, is Torah's most basic principle. *Every* human being is God's image, Ben Azzai says to Akiva. Some are easier to love, some are harder. Some days we can love them, some days we cannot. But you still have to recognize and treat them all as the image of God. Love is too shaky a pedestal on which to stand the entire Torah. It is too dangerous to base the world on the commandment to love. Perhaps Ben Azzai also saw that Akiva's principle might be narrowed, conceived only in terms of our own community. "Your *neighbor*," after all, might refer just to our fellow Jew. Or your fellow Catholic. Or our fellow in piety, in good behavior. How about the stranger? The sinner? How about our enemy? Ben Azzai's principle leaves no room for exceptions, since it goes back to Creation itself. It's not just "our kind of people" who were created in God's image, but everyone.[15]

Once we have a basic principle, or even a set of basic principles, we have a standard by which to evaluate all other rules and practices, teachings, and theological ideas. Does this particular idea or teaching lead us closer to seeing the Divine in every person? Might this interpretation of our Scripture be an obstacle toward doing so? Could we interpret it differently, in a way more in line with our basic principle? Here lies an inner Jewish basis for raising some important questions, one that should be more in use among those who shape our *halakhah* and your canon law for our day. I take the *kelal gadol*, the basic principle, to mean "that for which all the rest exists," the animating principle behind our entire religious life. In that case, any Judaism that veers from the ongoing work of helping us allow every human being to become and be seen as God's image in the fullest way possible is a distortion of our religion. That ongoing challenge requires us in each generation *to widen the circle* of those seen by us as fully human, as bearing God's image, as we seek to expand the bounds of the holy. *As we find God's image in ever more of humanity, we open ourselves to ever more of God's presence.* To find God in every human being is no small task. We could spend a lifetime at it and still not perfect this art, but I call upon you to join me in it.

THE CREATOR'S IMAGE AND EMPATHY

Judaism's moral voice begins with Creation. Our most essential teaching, that for the sake of which Judaism still needs to exist, is our insistence that each human being is the unique image of God. "Why was Adam created singly?" asks the Mishnah. "So that no person might say, 'My father was greater than yours.' How great is the Creator! A human king has coins stamped out in a press and each one looks alike. But God stamps us all out in the imprint of Adam, and no two human beings are the same!"[16] Each of us humans is needed as God's image and can be replaced by no other. It is as simple as that.

"Why are graven images forbidden by the Torah?" I once heard my teacher Abraham Joshua Heschel ask. Why is the Torah so concerned with idolatry? You might think (with the Maimonidians) that it is because God has no image, and any image of God is, therefore, a distortion. But Heschel read the commandment differently. "No," he said, "it is precisely because God *has* an image that idols are forbidden. *You* are the image of God. But the only way you can shape that image is by using the medium of your entire life. To take anything less than a full, living, breathing human being and try to create God's image out of it—that diminishes the Divine and is considered idolatry." We cannot *make* God's image; we can only *be* God's image.

Now I return to the question of empathy. To undergird empathy, I offer a theology where otherness is not quite absolute. Ultimately, we are all of the One, embodiments of the same divine presence. Behind the mask of the other lies the oneness of the Maker reflected in the deed. Empathy means both embracing each of us in our diversity and seeing through to our oneness.[17]

Christians have a great language for this in their tradition, that of "the Body of Christ." In the Jewish tradition (especially that of the mystics), we speak of the image, or even the body, of the cosmic Adam that embraces us all. But some confusion arises around these concepts. Does the language of "the Body of Christ" include only those inside the Church or does it embrace the entire human community, indeed the entire world? Of course, that is a question for Christian theologians to answer, not for me. But we have a different version of the same problem, one that we seldom confront, especially "in mixed company."

We Jews remain a distinct people, an ethnic entity, as well as a community of faith. We insist that we can be both at once. Our faith in the divine image is universal, going back to Adam and Eve. Of course, it must be all human souls that are contained within the soul of *Adam Kadmon*, the primal Adam. Yet the sources do not always see it that way. They sometimes speak of cosmic Adam as present in all the holy souls of Israel, seemingly ignoring the rest of humanity. How is this hardly accidental "error" related to the linking of universal religion and ethnic separateness? Does separateness automatically imply exclusivity? Our prayers are filled with appeals to God to bless us "and the whole people Israel." More universalist prayers do exist within the tradition, but they are the exception rather than the rule. What about the rest of humanity? If we recognize ourselves as part of a single human community, do we pray for them as well?

THE CIRCLE OF EMPATHY

This is the great struggle within Judaism today. How wide is our circle of empathy, of compassion? Can we open the doors of our hearts widely enough to include the whole human family, even the larger family of natural beings, within it, without losing our distinctive sense of history and ethnic identity? We have a tradition of *ahavat yisra'el*, a special love we are to have for fellow Jews, members of our own extended family. Can the special love I have for members of my own community be a love that encourages me to embrace ever wider circles in love? Or does it necessarily close me off from others, creating a circle of exclusiveness, to which most of humanity remains outsiders?

Surely our long history as a persecuted minority has much to do with this legacy. For nearly two millennia, we saw ourselves as struggling for survival amid hostile surroundings. The pressures of supersessionism were constant. Since Christianity (or Islam) is triumphant in the world, is it not clear that God has abandoned (the old) Israel and made another choice? Why not come along with what is obviously God's will? This psychological and theological pressure, reinforced by periodic rounds of active persecution, led us to see ourselves as ever struggling for survival, and that meant caring and praying primarily for "our own." Eventually, that led to a certain set of blinders, an inner toughening that said we would not recognize the divine soul in those others until they were willing to see it in us, accepting our legitimacy as a people of faith.

For many centuries, Judaism has not been an evangelical tradition. In large part because of Christianity's success, and the fact that Christian and Islamic regimes forbade conversion to Judaism, we have not worked to bring our tradition to others but have concentrated on our own survival. Yet our *essential* concerns remain universal. We want all humanity, not to embrace Judaism, but to live by our most basic truths: the oneness of God and the faith that each of us, every person on earth, bears God's image. This is our message for human-ity, the very essence of our redemptive vision.

We Jews and Christians are spiritual descendants of Israel's prophets, who were religious revolutionaries. They needed to stand up firmly for the uniqueness of their message. The God in whose name they spoke was *entirely different* from anything worshipped in the pagan world. The prophets mocked the gods of the heathen. "Eyes have they, but they see not; ears have they, but they hear not....Like them are those who make them and all those who trust in them. Israel, trust in Y-H-W-H" (Ps 115:5, 8–9). The nations of the ancient world each had their own gods. Thus, they saw themselves as separate from one another, each group or tribe concentrated solely on its own wel-fare, having little concern for the outsider. In proclaiming one God, the prophets also spoke for one world and one human family. That demanded true concern for the other, who is not entirely "other" after all. Witness the message of the Book of Jonah. The prophet has to be taught that God's caring is universal, embracing even wicked Ninevites who after all "do not know their right hand from their left," as well as "much cattle" (Jonah 4:11).

Like all revolutions, this one created a complex legacy. It claimed that we alone stood for the truth. "Israel," in the psalm quoted, are those who trust in Y-H-W-H, and no one else. When the Church inherited this mantle, becoming a "new Israel," it also inher-ited this shadow-side of exclusivism. Yes, Christianity broke down the ethnic walls; all peoples were welcomed into the new Church. But it replaced the ethnic walls with theological or ritual walls; Christendom became the community of the baptized or those who shared a specifically defined faith.

CONCLUSION: TO HEAL THE WORLD

We both need to struggle with that legacy of exclusivism. You may blame ancient Israel and its prophets for having started it, but the Church inherited it and raised the stakes, until we Jews too were seen as outsiders to a community that called itself "Israel." But it is too late now for all this. The world has become too small. We all live side by side with one another, and the outcry of the needy is in all of our ears; it is too urgent to ignore by busying ourselves with ancient wounds and rivalries. We need to work side by side in facing the great challenges before us. These include the degradation of the human spirit in our profane modern culture, the endless lure of creature comfort and materialism, fostered by unchecked capitalism and the great injustices it engenders, and the very preservation of our planet as a sustainable home for higher forms of life. All these are the real work of religious people and communities, and we must be united in facing them. To do this, we need to go back to "Y-H-W-H is one" and the demand for universal love that it implies. This represents the teaching of both of our traditions at its best. When I showed these words to my own sister, who is deeply engaged in this work, she reminded me that Mother Teresa once said, "The problem with the world is that we draw our family circle too small."

For us Jews, the struggle over exclusivism touches another matter that lies close to our hearts. I speak to you in the decade when the last survivors of our terrible Holocaust are about to end their time here on earth, the moment when their tortured memory of suffering will turn into "mere" history. We struggle daily with the question of the Holocaust's legacy, the murder of one third of our people, and the destruction of so many cultural and spiritual resources. What are we to learn from that terrible event? We do not believe that God visited it upon us; we believe it was the doing of human evil. Still, we must learn from it, we must seek God's message, there as everywhere. Many Jews feel that the message is clear. "Never again!" means that Jewish blood is not cheap. We will defend ourselves, take preemptory action against our enemies, and never allow Jews to be victims. But the best among the survivors, including both Heschel and (may he be blessed with long life!) Elie Wiesel, have understood "Never again!" to mean that never again will we permit genocide *anywhere* in our single human family, that we, as genocide's survivors, will stand up for humanity wherever such horrific deeds are perpetrated or threatened.

Many Christian Churches, including the Roman Catholic Church, have made great strides forward over the past half-century, partly in response to those same terrible events. The spirit of Vatican II, and especially the words of *Nostra Aetate*, gave us all much hope that the truest catholicity or universality of that faith was being given full expression. Many of us, including myself, have learned from and been inspired by the Catholic Church's ability to repent, to grow, and to change, while remaining faithful to its own identity. I hope with my whole heart that the Church will continue in the path of that growth, not compromising it in hearts or in teachings.

I can promise Christians moving in this direction that I, along with a host of my colleagues and students, present and future rabbis, struggle alongside you to read our own tradition also as one of universal human embrace. We need each other, we people of faith, to do the work of healing and repair that our communities, each in its own way, so desperately need. Let us help and support one another in this work. Let us not be divided by the burden of too much history or ancient claims of exclusive access to God's kingdom. That kingdom includes all of being, with all our differences, embracing us all. Let us work together to bring its day near.

NOTES

1. The first version of this article was presented at the Plenary Meeting of the International Union of Superiors General in Rome, May 9, 2010.

2. All translations of biblical and rabbinic texts are my own.

3. Among the key Jewish theological figures associated with neo-Hasidism (although none of them used this term) are Martin Buber, Abraham Joshua Heschel, and Hillel Zeitlin. Regarding Heschel and his drawing on his own Hasidic heritage, see my article "Abraham Joshua Heschel: Recasting Hasidism for Moderns" in *Modern Judaism* 29 (2009): 62–79. See my recent edition of a volume of Zeitlin's writings, *Hasidic Spirituality for a New Era*, Classics of Western Spirituality (New York and Mahwah, NJ: Paulist Press, 2012).

4 BTa`an. 2b.

5. My own unpacking of what this Creation language means in a contemporary post-Darwinian context is found in the opening chapter of my *Radical Judaism: Rethinking God and Tradition* (New Haven, CT: Yale, 2010).

6. I once heard a Hasidic rabbi use this understanding to explain why God did not allow manna to fall on the Sabbath (Exod 16:22–30). On the Sabbath, God's love for the world knows no limits. The divine wisdom was afraid, therefore, that if manna fell on the Sabbath, God would not have been able to withhold it, and "the world would have drowned in manna." Even God has to know when to hold back.

7. This makes him the "Calvary Hill" rabbi in Polish, a bit like being chief rabbi of Corpus Christi, Texas. Exile has put us in some strange situations....

8. Rabbi Judah Leib Alter of Gur, *Otsar Mikhtavim u-Ma'amarim* (Jerusalem: Makhon Gahaley Esh, 1968), 75; quoted more fully in my *The Language of Truth: The Torah Commentary of the Sefat Emet, Rabbi Yehudah Leib Alter of Ger*, trans. and interpreted by Arthur Green, Hebrew texts prepared by Shai Gluskin (Philadelphia: Jewish Publication Society, 1998), xxxvi–xxxvii.

9. Although I dare to guess that wrestling match was a bit like the one depicted in the film version of D. H. Lawrence's *Sons and Lovers*, where the boundary between wrestling and love-making is less than fully clear.

10. Mark 12:28–34; Matthew 22:34–40; Luke 10:35–38.

11. *Y. Ned.* 9:5.:5.

12. *M. Yad.* 3:5. The Canticle was one of the last books to be included in the Jewish canon, thanks to Akiva's insistence. Note that it is not yet quoted as Scripture in the New Testament books, authored slightly before this time.

13. *B. Ned.* 50a.

14. *B. Ber.* 54a.

15. A full discussion of this debate is found in Yair Lorberbaum, *Tselem Elohim* (Jerusalem: Schocken, 2004). This Hebrew study is soon to appear in English translation.

16. *M. Sanh.* 4:5.

17. The theology proposed here is intended to stand in contrast to the positions of both Buber and Levinas, who place recognition of otherness as central to their understanding of the human condition. My sympathies have always lain with the early Buber, prior to his abandonment of mystical thinking in favor of the dialogic. For the past several years, I have been immersed in the thought of Hillel Zeitlin (1871–1942), the leading theoretician of early neo-Hasidism, whose work I suggest as a Hasidic antidote to Levinas' *mitnaggedic* ("anti-Hasidic") origins and viewpoint. There is a dialogue that needs to happen here between two absolutes that only seemingly stand in contradiction: the uniqueness of each person and the oneness of all being. It would be especially worthwhile to bring some perspectives from Eastern religious thought into this all-too-Western conversation.

15

The Turn to the Self

Spirituality across Religious Borders

Michael Barnes

Kendal is a small market-town in the north of England, nestling in the Cumbrian mountains on the edge of the Lake District. At the beginning of the last decade, it was the focus for a sociological study on shifts in religious practice. In their report, published as *The Spiritual Revolution*, Paul Heelas and Linda Woodhead focused on the "massive subjective turn in modern culture."[1] Distinguishing between what they call "life-as" (living in tune with particular social roles and expectations) and "subjective life" (living in connection with one's own unique and deepest experiences), they examine the individual search for meaning as an illustration of wider shifts in the contemporary "sacred landscape." Their conclusion is that, in a culture that privileges the value of "subjective life," the religious forms and practices most likely to flourish will be those that prioritize interior experiences or "spirituality" over the associational activities of "religion."

Jews and Christians, and members of traditional "religions," can be forgiven for feeling a little uncomfortable with a dichotomy that raises as many questions as it answers. No doubt, there are plenty of people for whom the pursuit of a personal experience that communal practice has failed to provide is precisely the reason why they take to Yoga, Zen, Reiki, neo-paganism, and other forms of "spirituality" often associated with the New Age. It is, however, too easy to set the one against the other, as if "religion" were merely some sort of collective residue left over from the firsthand personal experience of mystics and other elite individuals. Sociologists of religion such as Grace Davie and theologians of mysticism like Mark McIntosh have

164

been working with versions of the spirituality/religion dichotomy for years.[2] In their different ways, they show that the relationship between interiority and religious practice is complex and contested, and bound up with broader shifts in society and culture. Some, perhaps most, forms of pre-modern religion were indeed accountable only to ecclesial authority. With the Enlightenment, the only acceptable form of religious belief became that which fitted the canons of reasoned critique; religion found itself tolerated as a matter of private conviction—but nothing more. The onset of an eclectic postmodernity has loosened up both forms of practice and their justification. The focus may remain fixed on inner experience, but it does not follow that we are dealing with yet another example of the foundational Cartesian subject. Indeed, the good people of Kendal seem less concerned with a sense of interior certainty than with a more *holistic* form of religious experience, one which, so far from seeking to isolate indubitable inner truth, is concerned to put the mental back in touch with the bodily, intellectual abstractions with the broader context of culture, language, and symbol out of which the sense of self is formed. To that extent, their instinct bears out what movements as diverse as feminism, liberation theology, and interreligious dialogue have discerned, namely, that theory and doctrine cannot be isolated from the total horizon of faith and practice, which constitutes a person's existence in the world.

Let's set the issue in slightly broader terms. The contemporary fascination with "spirituality" and the comprehensive visions of a harmonious spiritual universe to which it aspires go hand in hand with another dimension of today's "sacred landscape," namely, the growth of interest in all manner of human religiosity—including, it has to be said, the collective.[3] Not just spiritual technologies, such as Yoga and T'ai Chi, but religious texts, from the Christian desert fathers to Sufi poets and Tibetan lamas, are all available at the click of a mouse. So is a vast amount of information, both about the mainstream "world religions" and much more esoteric cults and new developments on every continent. In a rollicking grand tour of contemporary religious revival, John Micklethwait and Adrian Wooldridge argue that a combination of consumerism and globalization has led to an explosion of new religious forms, from house churches in China to Pentecostals in Sao Paolo.[4] Subtitled *How the Global Rise of Faith Is Changing the World*, the book *God Is Back* investigates the political impact of religion, particularly how an American model of the separation of church and state has created conditions in which religion can flourish. At times, the book reads like a macro-version of the "spiritual revolution"; there are plenty of examples of individuals and communities seeking personal authenticity in their religious practice. But much more prominent than personalized spirituality is the moral force of traditional religion, its capacity for building effective bulwarks against the most destructive incursions of modernity. Religion's power to construct ethical and political frameworks for living cannot be separated from a less familiar phenomenon, its extraordinary capacity to reinvent itself.

Heelas and Woodhead concede that *The Spiritual Revolution* is really a series of "mini-revolutions." Quite probably it has always been the case that "religion" (or "life-as") is dying and "spirituality" (or "subjective life") is growing. But maybe that is the point: faith is nothing if not a refusal to give in to the temptation of meaning lessness. The search or authenticity is never-ending. Thus, in his epic account of religion and modernity, *A Secular Age*, Charles Taylor shows how religion is forever growing and changing as people come up with new ways of speaking of themselves and their relationship with whatever they take to have supreme value in their lives.[5] In these terms, the "spiritual revolution" is less about the rejection of religion in favor of something else (what Taylor refers to as the "subtraction theory") than a recovery of what religions have always neglected at their peril—the formative power of prayer, meditation, and worship. Without this creative matrix the great religious traditions would be reduced to mere systems of thought, complexes of essentially comparable "religious" ideas, sets of concepts and symbols rather than unique configurations of the spirit of a people or, more exactly, "schools of faith"—to use Nicholas Lash's evocative term.[6] What keeps schools alive and active is not the instinct for self-preservation but a certain learned capacity to continue reformulating *and living them out* in face of what I have called elsewhere the "context of otherness"—the limitations which the other, human or divine, places on what can be known and what can be said.[7] Schools are nothing if not committed to developing the skills of communication, but they are also concerned with nurturing that practical wisdom, which knows when to replace the spoken word with a healthy reticence.

Such wisdom, with its own canons of critical rationality, cannot be separated from the formal and informal structures of communal living that give it a flesh and blood reality. The traditional structures of "religion"—from the ritual round of church and synagogue to practices of spiritual reading and Talmudic study—form the conditions within which holistic and comprehensive accounts of the world can be developed. In a perceptive essay on ecclesial spirituality, David Lonsdale turns a sharp theological eye on the distinction between the introverted spirituality of the religious market place and a more traditional form that "points to the experience and life of a community as it is ordered by its fundamental beliefs."[8] The latter prioritizes not discrete inner spiritual experiences but the supporting context of social relationships that provides the cultural space within which human beings can flourish. It is this complex interweaving of religious and nonreligious, which, Lonsdale argues, makes the "subjective turn" more than a homogenizing of all forms of religious practice under the heading of spiritual technology. Against an account of a sacred landscape that is understood in broader terms than alternative therapies for spiritual searchers, Lonsdale reminds us that even the most postmodern of subjective turns does not take place in a cultural and political vacuum. It is all too easy in today's fragmented world to leave tradition and institution out of account, to divide "the spiritual" from "the political," and to come up with a sense of holistic harmony that turns the otherwise admirable search for personal authenticity into a solipsistic culture of self-regard.

At stake here is a question about how spiritual practice, the individual *and* the communal, leads to and motivates engagement with "the world" at large. That question, I suggest, is what the schools of faith that are the great religious traditions of the world are expert in exploring. In what follows, I focus on one example, the Jewish-Christian relationship. Both traditions, at their best, are concerned with ethical questions about how the pursuit of spiritual integrity is transformative not just of the individual but also of wider society. In exploring this question of the relationship between "interiority" and "exteriority," I turn to the work of two Jewish thinkers, Emmanuel Levinas and Abraham Heschel, to map out an account of our contemporary sacred landscape that brings "spirituality" and "religion" back together. As a Christian, I have found in their writing profound examples of how lively debates within one school of faith can enhance learning and deepen spirituality within another. This, I want to argue, opens up the possibility of a "school of schools" in which Jewish and Christian learning and spiritual practice reinforce, challenge, and transform each other.

LEARNING FROM THE DIALOGUE OF RELIGIONS

There is no need to rehearse here the changes that have taken place in Jewish-Christian relations since the Second Vatican Council faced up to the destructive heritage of anti-Semitism, which issued in the Shoah.[9] That extraordinary moment in the history of the Catholic Church did not take place in a theological vacuum. Nor was it completed by the few short paragraphs in which *Nostra Aetate* retrieved something of Paul's ambivalent conviction that God does not forget his promises.[10] Since then, the Council of the Catholic Church has gone on to speak more positively of Judaism as a "living tradition" that is no longer to be patronized as a relic of the Old Testament in total ignorance of the post-biblical developments of rabbinical and Talmudic practice. The Council laid down the principles that have underpinned interreligious dialogue over the past fifty years, but perhaps more importantly it gave the impetus to a different style of theology in which critical defensiveness gave way to the demands of communication across previously impermeable frontiers. If the Council retrieved a sense of the intrinsically Jewish matrix for all Christian theology, meaning that Christianity can only be understood in terms of the history, culture, and language that it inherits from Judaism, it also returned the Church to a sense of its identity as a "school of faith." Conversation and learning from and with a variety of dialogue-partners—from "the world" itself to people of other faith traditions—becomes the hermeneutical key for understanding and living out the myriad demands of Christian discipleship.

To open up a sensitive and positive conversation with Judaism does not demand that Christians engage directly in Talmudic commentary—though the Scriptural Reasoning movement shows what is possible when people of different faiths exercise a theological hospitality, which generously seeks to share the insights of canonical and commentarial texts.[11] At the very least, it means reading the Hebrew Scriptures as the First, rather than the Old, Testament—texts without which the Church cannot understand itself, but which also, and more importantly, describe and promote the way of life of another "school of faith." That school depends, of course, on the tradition of Talmud, but it has also inspired forms of Jewish philosophy, from Maimonides to Martin Buber, which have left an indelible impression not just on contemporary philosophical thought but on the study of the Bible as well. As Walter Brueggemann notes, there is no single essence, scheme, or set of ideas in the First Testament. Rather the texts in all their variety record the divine-human "I-Thou" interactions in which God calls and God's partners in dialogue respond. "The defining category for faith in the Old Testament," he says, "is *dialogue*, where by all parties—including God—are engaged in a dialogical exchange that is potentially transformative for all parties...including God....The Old Testament is an invitation to re-imagine our life and our faith as an on-going dialogical transaction in which all parties are variously summoned to risk and change."[12] Rather than project back into the text the static categories of Hellenistic metaphysics, Brueggemann grapples with a line of dialogical reasoning, which he describes as "characteristically Jewish."

There is something here of Levinas's unremitting call to take responsibility for the other, but also of Heschel's account of prophecy as expressive not just of the action but of the very nature of a God who is concerned for the covenant relationship and affected by a history of engagement with his people. Heschel is clearly highly critical of what Levinas would call "Greek" philosophy, which depersonalizes God and dehumanizes humanity. As Brueggemann puts it, the God of Israel displays a "dialogical character" by engaging with four different but equally important partners: Israel, the human person, the nations, and creation itself. None of these four relationships is unproblematic, of course; any talk of the pathos of God raises difficult questions about the nature of God as personal, and how God as utterly transcendent can be said to relate to a changing world. In language that at times stresses the personal to the point of the anthropomorphic, Heschel says that "the fundamental experience of the prophet is a fellowship with the feelings of God, a *sympathy with the divine pathos*, a communion with the divine consciousness which comes about through the prophet's reflection of, or participation in, the divine pathos."[13]

This concept of the God who makes difficult demands on human beings would have been familiar to Emmanuel Levinas for whom the other takes priority in any account of human and divine relationality. Levinas, however, eschews any talk of a communion that would compromise the "height" or transcendence of the other. He is clearly not keen on any form of religion or spirituality that gets too close to God—or allows God to get too close to human beings. If we are to be genuinely free and responsible, then God too has to be free to remain distant, precisely not to come so close that our humanity is swamped by feelings of the spiritual, the numinous, or the sacred. Unlike Martin Buber, whose philosophy of the "I-Thou" relation has to be seen against the background of his deep interest in the Hasidic mysticism of his native Galicia, Levinas comes from the intellectualist tradition of the *mitnagdim* of Lithuania.[14] Brought up in the phenomenological tradition of Husserl, and increasingly at odds with Husserl's most influential protégé Heidegger, Levinas is determined to bring something of his own Jewish religious sensibility back into the mainstream of Western philosophy—to translate "Hebrew" into "Greek" thought. What has been left out of account is a type of non-intentional or pre-reflective consciousness where sense data are not objectified but have, in his terms, an "anarchic" quality to be characterized as pure passivity.

Something "other" is always mysteriously at work disturbing the familiarity and comfort of self-presence. In a dense discussion of the experience of wakefulness and awakening, for example, Levinas invokes the "obsolete language" of "the spirituality of the soul" to speak of how the subject is "sobered up, out of its being." Obsolete or not, the image of the soul trapped between the need to sleep and the desire to be awake and vigilant catches something of the complex interplay of same and other with which Levinas is always struggling.[15] He wants to show how human beings come to a sense of self not through isolating some interior consciousness that gathers all experience into a Totality but through acknowledging that which is strictly beyond or other than the self—what, to invoke the title of his most important philosophical work, is to be discerned in the drawing of God's Infinity.[16] For Levinas, the religious experience of the faithful Torah-observant Jew is precisely *not* vested in any sort of mystical awareness; it is, rather, to be found in the conviction of being commanded *despite* any such "inner" assurance. God can be said to be present to human beings—but only in the paradoxical form of an "absent" or veiled presence. Clearly, what Levinas wants to avoid is the tendency to make God the object of experience or to anchor the "glory of God" in what he calls "the said," some formula of words. Buber's "I-Thou" relationship subordinates God to the dialogical relationship of persons. For Levinas, Judaism is a much more uncomfortable religion and there is something about this discomfort that our world badly needs. The most he will say is that God is "illeity"—standing outside and quite beyond the I-Thou relationship but present as a "trace." In an interview he says:

> I am going to tell you a peculiar feature of Jewish mysticism. In certain very old prayers, fixed by ancient authorities, the faithful one begins by saying to God "Thou" and finishes the proposition thus begun by saying "He," as if in the course of this approach of the "Thou" its transcendence into "He" supervened. It is what in my descriptions I have called the "illeity" of the Infinite. Thus, in the "Here I am!" of the approach of the Other, the Infinite does not show itself. How then does it take on meaning? I will say that the subject who says "Here I am!" testifies to the Infinite.[17]

Since Levinas is intensely suspicious of the charismatic, indeed of any thematized or conceptual revelation beyond what is revealed through the exteriority of the face of the other, it might seem that he would make a far less amenable dialogue partner for Christians than Heschel. In addition, it is true that he can at times be highly critical of a Christian sacramentality, which in his opinion tends toward the sentimental and infantilizing.[18] Nevertheless, he does open up a different dimension of an encounter that takes place against a postmodern background of shifting identities and eclectic spiritual practices. Levinas fits the mold of Heschel's deeply compassionate prophet, struck through by empathy for human suffering of all kinds, as much for the fractured ego of postmodernity as the murdered of the Shoah. Yet this is not an empathy born from a consciousness founded on the pathos of God but in a more austere act of responsibility to the distant God who calls ego-centered projects of all kinds radically into question. If, for Descartes "I think, therefore I am," for Levinas "I am called, therefore I am." The obsession with a self-centered certainty gives way to a disarming act of recognizing the priority of the Divine

Word. Levinas sounds an important word of warning about the tendency to focus so much on the cultivation of inner feelings that the ethical and political dimensions of the spiritual life are occluded.

For Levinas, therefore, the "spirituality of the soul" has very little to do with a self-constituting consciousness, still less with the gathering of mystical experience, and everything to do with what he calls a "liturgy of study."[19] Here we find an important formal link between the spiritual practice of the gathered community of faith and the personal act of appropriation. It is the constant repetition of the traditions of learning inscribed in Torah that underpin a life of obedient and prayerful meditation on the God whose traces are all too dimly perceived in the world of suffering humanity. Levinas the philosopher is always focused on the conditions that encourage the act of personal responsibility. Just occasionally, he focuses on the collective prayer that encapsulates the formative experience of the people of Israel. While God for Levinas is always the utterly transcendent and unchanging, just occasionally he hints at something of Heschel's conviction that God suffers for and with his people. Prayer is always for the people, especially the persecuted people of Israel, called to reveal the "glory of God." "It is God who suffers most in human suffering. The *I* who suffers prays for the suffering of God, who suffers by the sin of man and the painful expiation of sin. A kenosis of God!"[20]

Such moments of theological celebration are rare. For the most part, Levinas maintains a discerning language of critique and communication, which makes it clear that any talk about God emerges not from pure theory or indubitable personal experience but from the everyday reality of human relations in all their otherness. As Hilary Putnam notes in his absorbing guide to the thought of Buber, Rosenzweig, and Levinas, philosophy as the analysis of arguments and the use of logical techniques is always at the service of philosophy as a way of life, a way of transforming one's understanding of one's place in the larger scheme of things and in human community.[21] At this point, philosophy—what Levinas famously describes as the "wisdom of love at the service of love"[22]—comes close to the description given earlier of spirituality as the transformational practice that reconnects the sense of self with the context of otherness.

SELF "BUFFERED" YET TRANSFORMED

How might Levinas have responded to the "spiritual revolution"? Taylor's image of the "buffered self," which has found confidence in its own powers of ordering, is also the self that has forgotten
how to be vulnerable in face of the other.[23] Whatever the merits
implied in the autonomy of the former, it is the dangerous solipsism
of the latter that most excites Levinas. He is often portrayed as a postmodern philosopher—and in the sense that he has been an important
influence on the likes of Derrida, that is entirely true. His determina-
tion to avoid the sort of philosophical language that would tie up
human beings in "the Totality" makes his style of writing, likened by
Derrida to waves ceaselessly beating against the seashore, very postmodern.[24] There is, however, nothing postmodern about his antipathy
to Heidegger. The Western philosophy epitomized by Heidegger's
self-oriented "philosophy of communion" is dominated by an episte-
mology that seeks some sort of "universal knowledge" and ends up
subordinating human relations to a self-centered system. Marked by
the experience of the Shoah, and conscious of the violence that lurks
unregarded in the philosophy and culture of the West, Levinas
believes that the only way in which the darkside of human nature can
be countered, and the altruistic side promoted, is through a language
that is always pressing the limits of what can be said, forever post-
poning the finished and definitive "said." Otherwise we run the risk
of being dominated by our own selfish desires and forcing others into
a system or way of life over which we can maintain control.

At times Levinas reads more like a mystic than a prophet, in the
sense that he is both entranced by and suspicious of the power of language to constrain human and divine freedom. In truth, he is both. He
insists on the absolute demand for justice in the face of blind self-
absorption while at the same time tempering the self-righteousness of
the zealot with the humility and caution of one who has himself experienced the baleful effects of human violence. A deep sadness suf-
fuses all his work, a melancholy that seems appropriate to an age that
is all too conscious of human failure and the death of so many ideals
and aspirations. Yet hope remains; there is still something remarkable
about the human capacity for empathy and moral action. "A high-
mindedness that is the honor [sic] of a still uncertain, still vacillating
modernity, emerging at the end of a century of unutterable suffering,

but in which suffering, the suffering for the useless suffering of the other, the just suffering in me for the unjustifiable suffering of the other, opens suffering to the ethical perspective of the inter-human."[25]

I began by noting that today's spiritual searchers have their own response to the deconstructive turn of postmodernity. At its best, the subjective turn represents a search for a more holistic form of personalized spirituality in which the fragmentation of a once homogeneous culture and a multiplicity of forms of belonging have given way to an individual choice. The problem is that the insistence on the sovereignty of the "buffered self," the autonomous, invulnerable subject that sets out to be proof against the shifting "context of otherness" in contemporary culture, risks compounding the very problem it presumes to solve. Levinas's critique of a philosophical culture that seeks to return everything to the dominance of the same is nothing if not a warning that such a focus on the "I" can end up doing the opposite: fragmenting further the relations on which our world depends. Even the desire for a properly holistic form of religious experience would probably elicit from him a sharp rebuke that at work is yet another version of the totalizing culture of certainty and control. To that extent, it is not just Levinas who would find much to criticize about today's obsession with interiority. The mystical-prophetic writings of both Judaism and Christianity stand for much more than particular versions of some generalized "spiritual" account of reality. Both cultivate, not a holistic vision of the interconnectedness of things in which the self is at the center, but a moral vision of a universe in which personal desires and feelings are made subject to the other—to God. As David Burrell reminds us, such writers, from Augustine and Teresa of Avila to Edith Stein and Etty Hillesum, have always produced not explanatory frameworks but statements of *conviction*.[26] That is to say that their moral force comes, not from simply repeating the traditional creedal formulae of the Christian "school of faith," but from allowing the creative imagination to give voice to particular experiences of living out that set of beliefs in all their beauty and ambivalence.

Ironically, the distinction between "religion" and "spirituality" with which I began is premised on their relevance of precisely those funds of traditional wisdom—about the formation of persons in response to a narrative of God's engagement with his people—that are best able to cultivate the virtues of human living. This is not to say that the problems of our postmodern world would all be solved if we but went back to the obedient observance taught by the "schools of faith." Indeed, there are lessons to be learned from the sidelining of traditional religious practices in favor of cultivating more personally satisfactory forms of spiritual sensibility. I have argued, however, that something more important is at stake. Holistic, comprehensive visions need a broader *inter-personal* base than interiorized pursuits allow. If the dialogue between religions can open up new relationships and retrieve old ones in a spirit of respect and understanding, then the "subjective turn" can be put to better use: not manufacturing an inviolable interiority but finding a more coherent and less allergic sense of persons-in-community. Such a "school of schools" would be worth the struggle.

NOTES

1. Paul Heelas and Linda Woodhead, *The Spiritual Revolution: Why Religion Is Giving Way to Spirituality* (Oxford: Blackwell, 2005).

2. Grace Davie, *Religion in Britain since 1945: Believing without Belonging* (Oxford: Blackwell, 1994). Mark McIntosh subtitles his *Mystical Theology* (Oxford: Blackwell, 1998) "The Integrity of Spirituality and Theology" and begins his preface with a distinction that intrigues him: "It is a distinction that poses a contemporary challenge to theology—but perhaps it does so by opening new possibility. 'I'm really not religious, at least not in any institutional sense,' students often say to me. Then they add, with varying degrees of urgency, 'But I have a strong commitment to spirituality.' And they are not alone."

3. It is notable, for instance, that while the "congregational domain" listed in the appendices consists mainly of the mainstream Christian Churches, plus spiritualist, Pentecostal, and various independent churches, the "holistic milieu activities" contain an extraordinary variety, from "acupressure" to "Yoga groups." Apart from forty-three persons given as participating in "Buddhist groups," none of the major religions is present. The subject of the survey, in other words, is the relationship between Christianity and alternative practices and personal therapies.

4. John Micklethwait and Adrian Wooldridge, *God Is Back* (London: Penguin, 2010).

5. Taylor begins by raising this question: "Why was it virtually impossible not to believe in God in, say, 1500 in our Western society, while

in 2000 many of us find this not only easy, but even inescapable?" *A Secular Age* (Cambridge, MA: Harvard University Press, 2007), 25.

6. Nicholas Lash, *The Beginning and the End of "Religion"* (Cambridge: Cambridge University Press, 1996).

7. Michael Barnes, *Theology and the Dialogue of Religions* (Cambridge: Cambridge University Press, 2002). See especially chap. 1.

8. David Lonsdale, "The Church as Context for Christian Spirituality," in *The Blackwell Companion to Christian Spirituality*, ed. Arthur Holder (Oxford: Blackwell, 2005), 239–53.

9. For a formidably detailed chronicle of the development of *Nostra Aetate*, the main document of Vatican II on interreligious relations, see Herbert Vorgrimler, ed., *Commentary on the Documents of Vatican II*, vol. 3 (New York: Herder and Herder, 1967), 1–154. The various versions of the text are unraveled in Miika Ruokanen, *The Catholic Doctrine of Non-Christian Religions* (Leiden: Brill, 1992).

10. For an attempt to situate the document within the retrieval of the "Jewish background" to Christian theology, see Barnes, *Theology and the Dialogue of Religions*, 29–64. For key documents in the development of the official dialogue between Catholics with the Jews, see "The Evolution of a Tradition: From *Nostra Aetate* to the 'Notes,'" in *Fifteen Years of Catholic-Jewish Dialogue, 1970–1985*, ed. Eugene Fisher (Libreria Editrice Vaticana, 1988).

11. For a theological overview and introduction to the practice of Scriptural Reasoning, see David Ford, "An Interfaith Wisdom: Scriptural Reasoning between Jews, Christians and Muslims," *Modern Theology* 22 (2006): 345–66. See also the online *Journal of Scriptural Reasoning* at www.virginia.edu/journals/ssr.

12. Walter Brueggemann, *An Unsettling God: The Heart of the Hebrew Bible* (Minneapolis: Fortress Press, 2009), xii.

13. Abraham Joseph Heschel, *The Prophets* (New York: Harper and Row, 1962), 26.

14. For this background to Levinas, see Salomon Malka, *Emmanuel Levinas: His Life and Legacy* (Pittsburgh: Duquesne University Press, 2006), esp. 8–19.

15. Emmanuel Levinas, "God and Philosophy," in *Collected Philosophical Papers*, trans. Alphonso Lingis (Dordrecht, Netherlands: Martinus Nijhoff, 1987), 156.

16. Emmanuel Levinas, *Totality and Infinity: An Essay in Exteriority*, trans. Alphonso Lingis (Pittsburgh: Duquesne University Press, 1969).

17. Emmanuel Levinas, *Ethics and Infinity: Conversations with Philippe Nemo*, trans. Richard A. Cohen (Pittsburgh: Duquesne University Press, 1985), 106.

18. See "On Loving the Torah More than God," in *Difficult Freedom: Essays on Judaism*, trans. Seán Hand (Baltimore: The Johns Hopkins University Press, 1990), esp. 142–45. For both text and a thoroughly absorbing Christian theological commentary, see F. J. van Beeck, *Loving the Torah More than God? Towards a Catholic Appreciation of Judaism* (Chicago: Loyola University Press, 1989).

19. See, for example, Emmanuel Levinas, *In the Time of the Nations*, trans. Michael B. Smith (Bloomington: Indiana University Press, 1994), 59.

20. Emmanuel Levinas, *Alterity and Transcendence*, trans. Michael B. Smith (London: The Athlone Press, 1999), 181–82.

21. Hilary Putnam, *Jewish Philosophy as a Guide to Life* (Bloomington: Indiana University Press, 2008).

22. Emmanuel Levinas, *Otherwise than Being or Beyond Essence*, trans. Alphonso Lingis (Dordrecht, Netherlands: Kluwer, 1991), 162.

23. *A Secular Age*, 27, 37–42.

24. In his review of Levinas's *Totality and Infinity*: "Return and repetition, always, of the same wave against the same shore, in which, however, as each return recapitulates itself, it also infinitely renews and enriches itself. Because of all these challenges to the commentator and the critic, *Totality and Infinity* is a work of art, and not a treatise"; *Violence and Metaphysics* (Chicago: Chicago University Press, 1978), 312.

25. Emmanuel Levinas, *Entre Nous: Essays on Thinking-of-The-Other*, trans. Michael B. Smith and Barbara Harshav (London: Athlone Press, 1998), 90.

26. David Burrell, "Assessing Statements of Faith: Augustine and Etty Hillesum," in *Faith and Freedom: An Interfaith Perspective* (Oxford: Blackwell, 2004), 245.

VII
NEW FRONTIERS

16

Latinos/as and Catholic-Jewish Relations in the United States

Hillel Cohn

INTRODUCTION

In 1965, Bob Dylan wrote and performed a song that became an anthem for frustrated youth. The refrain of that song, which became one of Dylan's early hits, was "For the times they are a-changin'." This truth is validated in many ways but especially as one looks at the past and present of Catholic-Jewish relations in America.

There were times, not all that long ago, when Jewish children in Europe and the United States were cautioned by their parents not to walk on the sidewalk in front of a Catholic Church or to have any contact with a *gallach*.[1] In 2006, Fr. John Pawlikowski and Rabbi David Sandmel jointly delivered The Joseph Cardinal Bernardin Jerusalem Lecture in Chicago. Rabbi Sandmel related the story of his own grandfather who had come to visit his family in Cincinnati. Rabbi Sandmel's father, the eminent biblical scholar Rabbi Samuel Sandmel, greeted his father and said, "I've got some tickets to see a production of *Tevya and His Daughters*; would you like to go?" Since the elder Sandmel was a great fan of Sholem Aleichem, author of Yiddish short stories, he told his son, "Sure, I would love to go." What Rabbi Samuel Sandmel neglected to tell his father was that the play was being produced at Edgecliff College, a small Roman Catholic women's college in Cincinnati that was renowned for its drama program. When the father and son arrived at the theater on the campus, the elder Sandmel looked around "and saw all of these men in collars and women in habits—priests and nuns—and his instinctive reaction was fear." He said to his son, "What did you bring me here for? Let's go." The younger Sandmel concluded his memory of that event by saying, "Before they could leave, of course, a number of these priests and nuns came up and greeted my father warmly. My grandfather ended up staying and enjoying the production immensely. But that shows you the significant difference between his experience of Christianity and my father's experience of it."[2]

The Sandmel account is relevant to our reflection on Latino/a Catholic-Jewish relations. While not all Latinos/as in the United States are Roman Catholics, certainly the largest percentage are. A recent study estimates that over 75 percent of Latinos/as in the United States are Catholic.[3] Other statistics suggest that the number of Mexicans, Central, and South Americans who are Roman Catholic is a little over 70 percent.[4] Latinos/as constitute 35 percent of the Catholic population in the United States. However, among young people, this percentage climbs to 50 percent.[5] Thus, an examination of Latinos/as Catholic-Jewish relations must begin with an examination of Catholic-Jewish relations in America in general.

Rabbi David Sandmel's story suggests the traditionally strained relationships between Jews and Catholics. In 1989, the Introduction to *A Resource Manual for Catholic-Jewish Dialogue*, developed in Los Angeles, observed:

> As early as the 1920s, friendships had developed between leaders of the two communities. In the 1950s and 1960s, Loyola University (now Loyola Marymount University) became a meeting place where, with the assistance of the American Jewish Committee, a rich program of intercultural education was developed....However, during this period, Catholic-Jewish relations were largely limited to especially motivated individuals.[6]

A new era in Catholic-Jewish relations opened up with the promulgation in 1965 of *Nostra Aetate* (The Declaration on the Relation of the Church to Non-Christian Religions).[7] The work of such Catholic leaders as Dr. Eugene Fisher, Father John Pawlikowski, Sr. Rose Thering, Father Royale M. Vadakin, and Dr. Eva Fleischner, and the work of such Jewish leaders as Rabbi Marc Tanenbaum, Rabbi Arthur Gilbert, Judy Banki, Rabbi A. James Rudin, Annette Daum, and Rabbi León Klenicki have done much to advance Jewish-

Catholic dialogue. Yet it is only quite recently that the efforts at creating more constructive relationships between Jews and Catholics have extended to the Hispanic community.

LATINO/A CATHOLICS AND JEWS:
THE NEED FOR COMMUNICATION

There are at least four reasons why Catholic-Jewish dialogue in the United States has not sufficiently included relations between Jews and Latino/a Catholics. First, there have been and continue to be language barriers that have made communication between newly arrived Latinos/as and Jews difficult and sometimes impossible. These barriers are not only evident among newly arrived Latinos/as. They continue among those who have been in the United States for relatively long periods of time. English remains a "second language" for many and their preference is to worship at Masses conducted in Spanish. Language barriers have even made communication between Spanish-speaking Catholics and non-Spanish-speaking Catholics difficult. As long as English remains a second language for Latinos/as and their day-to-day language is Spanish, communication with non-Spanish speakers can be problematic.

Second, there were and are marked differences between the cultures of Jews and Latinos/as. That would include such things as preferences in food, music, film, and other aspects of culture. In so many ways, Jews and Latinos/as are not just members of religious or faith communities. They are members of ethnic groups and those ethnicities are quite different.[8]

Third, for the most part, Jews and Latinos/as in the United States are at markedly different places on the socioeconomic ladder. There are certainly Latinos/as who are middle- and upper-class and there are certainly Jews who are middle and lower-class. Nonetheless, there are often striking socioeconomic disparities between Jews and Latinos/as, which makes the first necessary component of dialogue—realization of the need—difficult. The National Jewish Population Survey done in 2000 to 2001 concluded that the Jewish population in the United States totals 5.2 million people, consisting of an estimated 4.1 million adults and 1 million children. If one adds to that number those who are not Jewish but live with Jews, the total population increases to 6.7 million people. The study also concluded that, relative to the total U.S. population, "Jews are more highly educated, have more prestigious jobs and earn higher household incomes."[9] An estimated 353,000 people, including 272,000 adults and 81,000 children, live in poor Jewish households. Inasmuch as that study was done more than a decade ago, one would need to extrapolate current statistics by taking into account changes in the general economy.

Recent statistics published by *La Raza* suggest a very different reality for Latinos/as in the United States. It confirms the observation that Jews and Latinos/as are at markedly different places on the socioeconomic ladder.

> The Hispanic population is represented in a wide variety of occupations. For instance, in 2009 there were 57,000 Hispanic physicians and surgeons; 202,000 middle school teachers; 74,000 chief executives of businesses; 30,000 lawyers; and 284,000 fire fighters. In 2010, only about one in five (19%) Hispanics worked in management and professional occupations. However, Hispanics are disproportionately employed in service and support occupations. More than one in four (26%) work in service occupations; 21% in sales and office jobs; 16% in natural resources, construction, and maintenance jobs; and 17% in production, transportation, and material-moving occupations.

The study also showed that

> Latino median household income was $38,039 in 2009, which was similar to its 2008 level. In comparison, the median household income for White families was $54,461, and among Black families it was $32,584. The Latino poverty rate increased from 23.2% in 2008 to 25.3% in 2009. The poverty rate among all Americans increased from 13.2% in 2008 to 14.3% in 2009. Twelve million Latinos were counted as poor in 2009, representing an increase of 1.4 million since 2008. In 2009, a four-person family was considered poor if its income fell below $21,954.[10]

Fourth, the need and desire for dialogue and interaction often flows out of common neighborhood experiences. It is a fact of life that, with the exception of Los Angeles and New York City, in most urban centers in the United States, Jews and Latinos/as do not usually share the same neighborhoods. Both groups essentially have lived in isolation from one another and too often continue to do so.[11] Language and cultural barriers, socioeconomic disparities, and geographical isolation have all contributed to situations in which Jews have not been on the "radar" of Latinos/as, and Latinos/as have not been on the "radar" of Jews.

In 2001, the Foundation for Ethnic Understanding conducted a study of Latino-Jewish relations. One of the questions asked in that study was "How would you describe the relationship today between Hispanics and Jews in the United States today?" Interestingly, 44.6% of Latinos responding felt that the relationship was "fair"; 39.6% of Jewish respondents felt it was "fair." Only a little more than 1% of both groups felt that the relationships were excellent; 16.1% of Latinos and 17.7% of Jews were "not sure." When asked whether they thought there is anti-Semitism in the Latino community, 35.3% of Latinos felt there was and 21.8% were "not sure." Finally, when asked whether they thought there was anti-Latino sentiment in the Jewish community, 36.1% of Latinos responded affirmatively while 53.3% of Jews responded negatively.[12]

NEW DEVELOPMENTS

The factors that traditionally precluded any real attempts at dialogue between the two groups are diminishing slowly but surely, at least partly because of the ever-increasing impact of Latino/a cultures on U.S. film, music, food, literature, and more.[13] Second and third generation American Latinos/as are becoming predominantly English speakers and many English speakers are learning Spanish. As various kinds of interchange take place, cultural differences become less of a barrier. In some communities, the disparity in socioeconomic levels is less and less pronounced. And there is more and more day-to-day interaction between these two communities.

In addition, the general climate of positive Jewish-Christian, and specifically positive Jewish-Catholic, dialogue has influenced ways in which Jews and Latinos/as relate to one another in many places. The easing of historical Catholic-Jewish tensions has compelled both groups to address themselves to the need for meaningful conversation and provided dialogical space in which that might occur.

Another reason for an awakening of some interest in Latino/a–Catholic-Jewish dialogue is in the more recent awareness of the Jewish ancestry of some Latinos/as as observed at length by Professor Jacqueline Hernandez in her article in this volume. In some parts of the United States (especially New Mexico) and in Latin America, people who have discovered their *converso* roots have provided some impetus for dialogue and new relationships.[14] Other Latinos/as of Jewish descent are pursuing ways to reclaim their identity and take their place in the Jewish community.[15]

PLACES OF ENCOUNTER: THE ACADEMIC WORLD

The desire to create new relationships between the Jewish and Latino/a communities is reflected on some college campuses. In 2011, a new organization and a new word, *KenSI*, came into being. *KenSI* is an outgrowth of "Building Latino-Jewish Bridges on Campus," a program developed in 2011 to "develop sustained relationships between Jews and Latinos during their formative years on university and college campuses." A trip to Israel for Jewish and Latina women college students was organized jointly by the David Project, the National Hispana Leadership Institute, and the American Jewish Committee. At Boston University, students who had participated in the trip created a new organization called *KenSI*, a word that combined the Hebrew word *Ken*, and the Spanish word *Sí*, both meaning "yes."[16] Indeed, "the times they are a-changin'."

In reporting on the "Building Latino-Jewish Bridges on Campus" trip to Israel, Courtney Kravitz writes:

> Perhaps the trip's most memorable day was our visit to Yad Vashem, Israel's national Holocaust museum. Together we were able to share the raw feelings the museum evokes. Listening to many of the Jewish girls share stories of their grandparents being in the Holocaust made further impressions on the entire group. Those moments truly bonded all

of us to one another, deepening the Latinas' appreciation for
the many tragedies of Jewish history and the importance of
Israel to the Jewish people. That day truly built bridges
between us, and we began to believe in the importance of
supporting each other's respective communities.[17]

At the University of Texas at Austin, students who had participated in the "Building Latino-Jewish Bridges" trip hosted a large dinner for both Jews and Latinos/as, and students from Brandeis
University organized a dinner that included a "fishbowl" exercise
designed to give Jews and Latinos/as the chance to peek in on the
other's respective culture. These efforts led to the creation of a
"Jewtina" cookbook, a collection of recipes from all the girls, combining Jewish and Latina recipes.

Other programs reaching graduate students, seminarians, and
adult non-degree learners, include *"Comunidades y Convivencia*: A
Seminar on Catholic-Jewish Relations for Latino and Latina
Catholics in Ministry," cosponsored by the American Jewish
Committee and the Cardinal Joseph Bernardin Center of Catholic
Theological Union (Chicago) in June of 2007. There is also the ongo-
ing programming offered by the Center for Catholic-Jewish Studies
at Saint Leo University (St. Leo, Florida). Courses, individual lec-
tures, and other events reach a broad spectrum of the Jewish and
Catholic communities, including large numbers of Latinos/as.

Finally, the work of scholars like Carmen Nanko-Fernandez,
Jacqueline Hernandez, and Jean-Pierre Ruiz, all contributors to this
volume, carries the concerns for new relations between Jews and
Catholic Latinos/as to their own institutions. Their influence con-
tributes to broader conversations as professors, and their students bring
their insights to various communities in the United States and abroad
through publications and professional organizations such as the
American Academy of Religion, the Academy of Catholic Hispanic
Theologians of the United States, and the Society of Biblical Literature.

PLACES OF ENCOUNTER: POLITICAL ACTION

Attempts to establish new forms of relationships are, however,
not restricted to academic environments. Latinos/as and Jews have

joined in the work of social justice through such efforts as "Fighting Poverty With Faith"[18] and the "Poverty Campaign."[19] The Anti-Defamation League and the American Jewish Committee partner with Latino/a communities, both locally and nationally, in the struggle for comprehensive immigration reform and in combating anti-immigrant xenophobia.[20]

Political action, whether for immigration reform or for local questions, brings Jews together with Christians of many denominations, including Latinos/as and other Catholics as well as Muslims to work on health care, immigration reform—including the Dream Act—housing, and other issues through Brooklyn Congregations United.[21] In 1991, in San Bernardino and Riverside counties of Southern California, the Inland Congregations United for Change, an affiliate of PICO, was established. It was perhaps the first time that clergy and laity of the Roman Catholic Church, both mainline as well as evangelical Protestants, and Jews came together to work cooperatively on social issues. One of the many positive benefits of this inter-religious cooperation was the coming together of Jews and Latino/a Catholics. The author was one of the co-founders of ICUC and can well remember the initial meetings held at Our Lady of Guadalupe Church in San Bernardino, a primarily Hispanic church, where the words of the rabbi were translated into Spanish and where the rabbi became more knowledgeable about Hispanic religious practice and culture.[22] Such coalitions are significant because they impact the lives of thousands in ways that allow people who might otherwise distrust one another, or simply be ignorant of one another, to join in partnership with those of different faiths to pursue justice.

CULTURAL ENCOUNTERS

Local projects in a variety of settings include cultural events that bring people together. The efforts in Chicago are indicative of what can be done in more and more communities. In 1994, the Alliance of Latinos and Jews was

...created to build relationships between the two communities by building relationships between people. Participants have included individuals from the Chicago area's largest corporations and most successful small businesses, elected and appointed officials, volunteer and professional leaders from some of Chicago's most prestigious non-profit organizations....[23]

The report of this effort recognizes that when it started in 1994, very few relationships existed between the Latino/a and Jewish communities in the Chicago area.

Among some of the more interesting programs that have taken place in Chicago are a trip of 24 Latinos/as and Jews to the United States Holocaust Memorial Museum, an evening at the Chicago Latino Film Festival with dinner and discussion following the movie *Un amor en Mosesville*, evenings at the Israel Film Festival, and a Passover Sephardic Model Seder done in the style of Jews who were expelled from Spain and Portugal in the fifteenth and sixteenth centuries. These sorts of programs bode well for the future of Latino/a and Jewish dialogue and, since the vast majority of Latinos/as are Catholic, it can be assumed that the dialogue will also be a Jewish-Catholic dialogue.

While there is much to which one can point on a national level or in large urban centers, the interaction of Catholics and Jews in smaller communities is also worth noting. As a rabbi of a mid-size community, Congregation Emanu El in San Bernardino (now relocated to Redlands), this author has, over the course of a ministry of close to 50 years, had many interesting opportunities to be involved in dialogic relationships with Catholics and, in recent years, with Latino/a Catholics as well. One such opportunity is worth sharing.

For over thirty years, this writer has often been invited to lead Passover Seders for Christian churches but most especially for Catholic parishes. At these Seders, generally held during or close to Holy Week, the attendees are invited to consider themselves as part of a Jewish household for the duration of the Seder, and they are led through the many rites and practices of the Seder including the festive meal. It is, thus, not just a "Seder meal." It is an actual complete Seder. These celebrations enable Christian participants to become more knowledgeable about the practices that may have been observed by Jesus and his disciples, something which is of particular interest during Holy Week. The Seder also enables them to learn more about some of the fundamental values of Judaism, especially the Jewish commitment to freedom. The story of the Exodus itself, which is at the heart of the Seder experience, resonates with these immigrants and children of immigrants who have experienced their own kind of liberation from slavery as newcomers to the United States, as well as with those who still experience forms of oppression as farmworkers.

In recent years, I have been called on to lead such Seders at parishes that are predominantly Hispanic.[24] Major portions of the Passover Haggadah are repeated in Spanish. For many of those attending such Seders, it is their first real contact with anything Jewish. There are, of course, exceptions. In preparing for a recent Seder at a parish that is 80% to 90% Latino/a, the parish planning committee turned to one of its members to make the *Charoset*,[25] since she has been at Seders for years as a domestic working in numerous Jewish households. A memorable blending of traditions took place a number of years ago when, despite the instructions provided by the writer for the foods that needed to be provided for the Seder at a pre-dominately Latino/a church, the committee neglected to buy the horseradish that is traditionally eaten at a Seder as a reminder of the bitterness of being enslaved. The pastor of the church quickly came to the rescue as he brought a healthy portion of salsa from his rectory to be distributed to all those attending to serve as the bitter herb.

COMPLEXITY AND CHALLENGE

The creation of Jewish-Catholic dialogue groups around the country, especially with Latino/a Catholics, is a welcome development. In those groups, there is an honest and frank interchange of experiences and concerns. There is a greater awareness of the commonality of the immigrant experience. There is a breakdown of negative stereotyping that has existed for too long. Prejudices are exposed and confronted and, hopefully, eradicated.

However, closer study reveals far more complicated and challenging realities. As we contemplate the future of relations between Jews and Latino/a Catholics we cannot help but be concerned that anti-Semitism, according to some, still exists to a disturbing degree among Latinos/as. A study commissioned by the Foundation for Ethnic Understanding in 2011 found that nearly half of all Latinos believe that the United States is too supportive of Israel. Commenting on that finding, Rabbi Marc Schneier said:

> These findings are a wake-up call to both communities....We need to understand how real anti-Semitism is within the Latino community and how we can encounter it as well as find more effective ways to communicate the value of Israel to bolster Latino empathy for the Jewish state. This is truer than ever as Latinos now number more than 50 million in the U.S. One out of every six Americans is Latino. It therefore behooves the Jewish community to reach out and foster an alliance with this significant ethnic group.[26]

While one can debate whether non-support for Israel is actually anti-Semitism, one cannot dispute the fact that there is a disturbing amount of ignorance on the part of Latinos/as about Jews and Judaism and Jewish interests. Nor can one deny that, conversely, there is a disturbing amount of ignorance on the part of Jews about Christianity in general, Catholicism in particular, and especially Hispanic ethnicity. All of this is further complicated by the reality that in too many situations, Jews and Latinos/as meet one another in situations of disparate power relations, with Jews as landlords and/or employers and Latinos/as as domestic workers, gardeners, construction workers, and shop assistants.

One thinks of corresponding realities in New York City, when relations between Jews and African Americans appeared to have become strained despite the conspicuous role that Jews had played in leading the struggle for racial justice in the United States. It was observed that among the five authority figures that an African American might encounter in a large urban center such as New York City, four were likely to be Jewish: the school teacher, welfare worker, landlord, and shopkeeper. The only one of these five people that was generally not Jewish was the police officer. When African Americans' experiences with people in these roles were negative, they were presumed to be Jews and, thus, the negative feelings toward people in these roles became negative feelings about Jews and were directed to the whole Jewish community.[27] One wonders whether similar power dynamics pertain in Jewish-Latino/a relations and whether this con-

192 TOWARD THE FUTURE

tributes to negative images of Jews present among some in Latino/a communities. In these circumstances, engagement in meaningful dialogue is all the more difficult and all the more important.

As this writer was preparing this essay, he was made aware (incidentally by a Catholic priest who was stunned by the report) of an event that took place in a Mexican town as part of its Easter celebration. The report said:

> The world is full of charming Easter traditions, but this isn't one of them. A newspaper in Mexico is detailing Sunday's "burning of the Jews," an annual tradition in Coita, a small town in the state of Chiapas. As part of the custom, locals spend the middle of their Holy Week making Jewish effigies—a reference to Judas Iscariot, the disciple who betrayed Jesus before his crucifixion. The fake Jews are then displayed for three days in different parts of the town, serving as an example of poor conduct.
>
> They're ultimately paraded through the streets on Easter Sunday, with local children assigned to stand in front of them and collect money for flammable materials.
>
> The article notes that the tradition differs in Coita, where locals set fire to the effigies on Easter itself, rather than the day before, as in other towns. The burning is followed by a dance, where locals eat a corn treat made with cocoa. The article says the custom "strengthens" the culture of the Zoque, an indigenous people in southern Mexico who were converted to Catholicism.
>
> The *Chiapas Herald* takes an uncritical view of the ritual, reporting that it "fosters unity and respect" and "purifies the soul."[28]

Nostra Aetate and the revisions of Catholic liturgy in 1970, especially traditional Lenten and Good Friday liturgies, eliminated reference to the "perfidious Jews." Nonetheless, there remain vestiges of age-old anti-Jewish attitudes enacted in the celebration described in this article. Passion plays, dramatizations of the last days of Jesus' life and the events surrounding his death, are common in many Latino/a U.S. Catholic communities, as well as in parts of Mexico, Central America and South America. These rituals reflect traditions introduced by European missionaries during the colonial era, as well as indigenous realities, both ritual and historical.[29] One cannot help but wonder about the degree to which some Latino/a Catholics' attitudes toward Jews are influenced by the images of the Jews and the figure of Judas represented in the passion plays. Additionally, the influx of priests from other countries whose knowledge of Jews is limited or even nonexistent and who are called to lead parishes in the United States because of the shortage of American-born and trained priests holds out the possibility of these misconceptions about Jews being preserved rather than eroded.

TOWARD THE FUTURE: A PRAYER OF
BLESSING AND THE WORK AHEAD

In keeping with the central theme of this volume, *Toward the Future*, one can only hope, pray, and work so that the opportunities for meaningful dialogue between Jews and Latino/a Catholics will be nurtured on an international and national level but also on a local level.

In 1987, a collection of prayers and blessings for various occasions, composed by two Brazilians, a Catholic priest and a Jewish community leader, who had been active in interfaith dialogue, included a "Prayer for Religious Dialogue." It says, in part:

Being of all beings, Lord of all lords,
you are the blessed and supreme light
of all the peoples of the world.

I bless you and thank you
for the new atmosphere of dialogue
that you have encouraged among the world's
religions and cultures.

Through our common defense of universal values,
you fostered in us a sincere and conscious search
for the things that unite us.

We now see that our motives are capable of uniting
all people of good will and faith
in a common effort toward peace....

Favor us with providential and effective means
to overcome aggressive confrontation
and the spirit of opposition.

Grant us the willingness to abandon
polemic positions and obsessive fanaticisms,
which destroy dignity, nobility, and human togetherness....

Guide and help the work of religious leaders
who try, with clear minds and generous hearts,
to find a constructive and healthy path
to sincere dialogue —
the path of dialogue among people
of all creeds, cultures and traditions.
Amen.[30]

It is noteworthy that two forewords were written for that book —
one by Dr. Eugene J. Fisher and the other by Rabbi León Klenicki, a
Latino immigrant to the United States. May the immediate future find
that the Jewish and Catholic communities — and particularly Latino/a
Catholics — are guided by that prayer and work more cooperatively to
engage in the kind of dialogue that the prayer envisions.

NOTES

1. This is the Yiddish word for "priest."
2. Rabbi David Sandmel, The Joseph Cardinal Bernardin Jerusalem
Lecture (lecture, Chicago, February 28, 2006), 10–11.
3. Bruce Murray, "Latino Religion in the U.S.: Demographic Shifts
and Trend," June 3, 2012, www.nhclc.org: "The association between Latin
Americans and Catholicism is so strong that it belies a surprising fact:
Almost one quarter of all Latinos in the United States are Protestants." A
recent study by the Pew Hispanic Center indicates that in the overall
Latino/a population, 62 percent identify themselves as Roman Catholic. See
http://www.pewhispanic.org/2012/04/04/v-politics-values-and-religion/.
Murray, "Latino Religion," http://www.nhclc.org/es/news/latino-religion-
us-demographic-shifts-and-trend (accessed September 6, 2012): "Of the
41.3 million Latinos in the United States in 2004, about 23 percent (9.5 million) identify themselves as Protestants or other Christians (including
Jehovah's Witnesses and Mormons). Moreover, 37 percent (14.2 million) of

all Latino Protestants and Catholics say they have been born again or are evangelical"; see Gastón Espinosa, Virgilio Elizondo, and Jesse Miranda, eds., *Latino Religions and Civic Activism in the United States* (New York: Oxford University Press, 2005).

4. See http://www.catholicnews.com/data/stories/cns/0503707.htm.

5. See http://www.uscbb.org/news/2011/11-188.cfm.

6. Alfred Wolf and Royale M. Vadakin, eds., *A Journey of Discovery: A Resource Manual for Catholic-Jewish Dialogue*, Skirball Institute on American Values of the American Jewish Committee and the Office of Ecumenical and Interreligious Activities of the Archdiocese of Los Angeles (Valencia, CA: Tabor Publishing, 1989), 1.

7. In English, http://www.vatican.va/archive/hist_councils/ii_vatican _council/documents/vatii_decl_19651028_nostra-aetate_en.html. In Spanish, http://www.vatican.va/archive/hist_councilsii_vatican_council/documents/ vat-ii_decl_196551028_nistra-aetate_sp.html.

8. See, for example, Abraham D. Lavender, "A History of Jewish-Hispanic Interaction in Miami-Dade County, Florida," in *Latinos and Jews: Old Luggage, New Itineraries*, ed. Stephen Steinlight with contribution by David A. Harris (New York: The American Jewish Committee, 2002), 94.

9. National Jewish Population Survey 2000–2001, p. 6. "More than half of all Jewish adults (55%) have received a college degree, and a quarter (25%) have earned a graduate degree. The comparable figures for the total U.S. population are 29% and 6%. Jewish men are more likely than Jewish women to have college degrees (61% vs. 50%) and graduate degrees (29% vs. 21%). Proportionally, slightly fewer adult Jews are currently employed (61%) than in the total U.S. population (65%), reflecting the older Jewish population. More than 60% of all employed Jews are in one of the three highest status job categories: professional/technical (41%), management and executive (13%), and business and finance (7%). In contrast, 46% of all Americans work in these three high status areas, including 29% in professional/technical jobs, 12% in management and executive positions, and 5% in business and finance.

"The distribution of household income among Jews, especially at the high end of the income scale, reflects their relatively high education levels and high status jobs. More than one-third of Jewish households (36%) report income over $75,000, compared to 18% of all U.S. households. Proportionally fewer Jewish households (22%) than total U.S. households (28%) report household income under $25,000. The current median income of Jewish households is $54,000, 29% higher than the median U.S. household income of $42,000. In 1990, the median income of Jewish households was $39,000, 34% higher than the median income of $29,000 for all U.S. households."

10. The National Council of *La Raza* circulated U20 FAQS about Hispanics. See http://www.nclr.org/index.php/about_us/faqs/most_frequent ly_asked_questions_about_hispanics_in_the_us/ (accessed July 5, 2012).

11. See Roberto Suro, "Two People on a Journey," in *Latinos and Jews*, 26–27.

12. See www.jewishvirtuallibrary.org/jsource/US-Israel/latinosurvey .html (accessed June 1, 2012).

13. See http://news.bbc.co.uk/2/hi/Americas/3238523.stm.

14. One thinks of the work of Rabbi Manny Vinas and the Centro de Estudios Judio in New York City: http://www.centrojudio.org/.

15. An anecdotal support of this observation is from the author's own experience. He occasionally attends Shabbat morning services at a Temple Sholom in Ontario, CA. The congregation is affiliated with the conservative movement. Close to 50% of the regular worshippers on a Shabbat morning are Hispanic converts to Judaism.

16. Reported in *The Jewish Journal* 27, June 1–7, 2012, 12, 29.

17. Ibid.

18. Among the endorsing organizations of "Fighting Poverty with Faith" are The Apostolic Catholic Church, AVODAH: The Jewish Service Corps, B'nai B'rith Youth Organization, Catholic Charities USA, Jewish Community Center Association, Jewish Council for Public Affairs, Jewish Labor Committee, Jewish Reconstructionist Federation, Jewish Women International, The Jewish Federations of North America, MAZON: A Jewish Response to Hunger, The National Advocacy Center of the Sisters of the Good Shepherd, National Council of Jewish Women, National Hispanic Christian Leadership Conference, National Latino Evangelical Coalition, NETWORK: A National Catholic Social Justice Lobby, Sisters of Mercy of the Americas, and Uri L'Tzedek, http://fightingpovertywithfaith.com/f2/ actiontoolkits/.

19. See http://engage.jewishpublicaffairs.org/t/1686/p/salsa/web/ common/public/content?content_item_KEY=1527.

20. See http://www.adl.org/civil_rights/immigration.asp and http:// www.ajc.org/site/c.ijIT12PHKoG/b.6447551/k.95B1/Immigration.htm.

21. See http://www.brooklyncongregationsunited.org/about.

22. ICUC, Inland Congregations United for Change, was founded by Bishop Philip Straling of the Diocese of San Bernardino and Riverside, Rabbi Hillel Cohn of Congregation Emanu El, the Rev. Dr. Kendall Baker of First Congregational United Church of Christ, and laity from various churches.

23. See www.latinosandjews.org.History.html/ (accessed June 3, 2012).

24. In 1969, the Department of Interreligious Affairs of the Union of American Hebrew Congregations published *An Interreligious Guide to*

Passover and Easter by Rabbi Balfour Brickner. It provided a supplement to the *Union Haggadah*, relating various elements of the Seder to early Christian practice, and included quotations from the New Testament; see Balfour Brickner, *An Interreligious Guide to Passover and Easter, Experimental Edition*, 2nd ed. (New York: Union of American Hebrew Congregations, 1976), 19–32. These additions to the Seder have been used as part of the hundreds of interfaith Seders that the author of this essay has led over the years. León Klenicki also recognized the importance of such events, as evident in the 1980 publication of León Klenicki, ed., *The Passover Celebration: A Haggadah for the Seder*, Introduction by Gabe Huck (New York: The Anti-Defamation League of B'nai B'rith and the Liturgy Training Program for the Archdiocese of Chicago, 1980); León Klenicki, *Celebración de la Pascua* (Buenos Aires, Argentina: Ediciones Paulinas, 1984). Subsequently, a new edition of Klenicki's guide for a Seder has been published. "The service provided in this booklet is completely faithful to the Jewish tradition and provides background on the Seder meal, instruction and commentary." It is *The Passover Celebration* prepared by Rabbi León Klenicki and Myra Cohen Klenicki (Chicago: Liturgy Training Publications, 2007).

25. A mixture of apples, nuts, wine, and cinnamon used at the Seder whose color is a reminder of the mortar used by the Hebrew slaves to build storehouses for the Pharaoh and whose sweetness is a reminder of the sweetness of the freedom attained by the Hebrews.

26. See www.ynetnews.com/articles/o.7340,L-4049880.00.html. Poll: Anti-Semitism among U.S. Latinos (accessed May 25, 2012).

27. The author is unable to ascertain the origin of this observation but knows it was made repeatedly during the height of the tensions between Jews and African Americans. One African American who had a regular program on television in Southern California, Louis Lomax, referred to this observation.

28. See http://www.timesofisrael.com/mexican-town-celebrates-easter-with-burning-of-the-jews/. Quoted in an e-mail received by Fr. Alexei Smith from William Keevers, April 10, 2012.

29. See, for example, Thomas J. Steele, SJ, "The Spanish Passion Play in New Mexico and Colorado," *New Mexico Historical Review* 53 (1978): 239–59; Mark Clatterbuck, "Friars Lurking behind Burkhart's Nahuas: Conflicting Agendas at Play in the Production of Holy Wednesday," *Latin American Indian Literatures Journal* 22 (2006): 1–21; June Nash, "The Passion Play in Maya Indian Communities," *Comparative Studies in Society and History* 10 (1968): 218–327.

30. Hugo Schlesinger, Humberto Porto, *Prayers of Blessing and Praise for All Occasions* (Mystic, CT: Twenty-Third Publications, 1987).

17

Latinas/os and Catholic-Jewish Relations in the Americas

Jacqueline M. Hidalgo

In his book on Latina/o Muslims, Hjamil Martínez-Vásquez describes how his ninth-grade religion teacher claimed that non-Catholics were somehow "less" Puerto Rican. This teacher presumed that Roman Catholicism performed "a primary role in the construction of identity among Latin Americans."[1] In writing a book on U.S. Latina/o Muslims, Martínez-Vázquez hopes to push past this assumption, and he reconsiders Latina/o identities, or *latinidades*, as inclusive of many different religious identities. Martínez-Vázquez's work demonstrates that Latinas/os have always and already reflect a plurality of religious identification and practice in their own daily lives and at the levels of cultural memory.

In order to contemplate the future of Latina/o Catholic-Jewish relations in the Americas, I wish to pick up on Martínez-Vázquez's challenges to the religious components of *latinidad*. First, I wish to engage in cultural remembering and retrieval. A more multi-vocal historical excavation grounds itself in the reality of daily experiences of *mezcolanza* and *otredad* ("mixture and otherness"),[2] the reality that many Latinas/os have inherited plural religious identities. Such investigation will suggest that Latina/o identities depend upon a shared history that includes indigenous traditions, African traditions, Buddhist traditions, as well as Judaism, Christianity, and Islam. Latina/o Catholics and Jews share a fraught and challenging history, but the reality of this shared history, one that includes an emphasis on *otredad*/otherness, forms a significant basis for future conversations.

Such a practice of historical remembering cannot and must not be entered upon naively or simplistically. The history of Latina/o

Catholic-Jewish relations is a non-innocent history.[3] Therefore, Roman Catholics should examine this *mezcolanza* and *otredad* with the cautious recognition that this shared history is also a fraught and ongoing history; it is not an opening for cultural supersessionism. The perception that Judaism has been important to the history of Latin American Catholics should not open the door to static, universalist, or unitary claims on Latin American and Latina/o religious history. Roman Catholics must wrestle with the non-innocent, often violent and genocidal manner by which much of Latin America became Roman Catholic even while recognizing and affirming that their faith is the product of mixture, albeit violent and unequal. Yet remembering this shared history can provide us with a basis in cultural memory from which to perceive that Latina/o Catholics and Jews have already worked together and impacted each other in ways that can open the door to a better future.

Three different moments can serve as foci for thinking about Latina/o Roman Catholic and Jewish shared histories in the Americas. First, we turn to Spain, colonial Latin America, and the relationships between Roman Catholics and *anusim*/*conversos*/crypto-Jews.[4] Second, we consider the mixture created in post-colonial Latin America. Finally, as Latina/o Catholics living in the United States have also shared and continue to share spaces, resources, and connections with Jewish colleagues, neighbors, friends, and family, such interactions have shaped U.S. *latinidad*, and such interactions will likely become more numerous and varied in the current century. Given the importance of the knowledge and experience of Latina/o cultural identities to Latina/o theologies, recognition of Latina/o Catholic and Jewish historical relations should no doubt inform Latina/o theologies of Catholic-Jewish relations.

U.S. LATINA/O THEOLOGIES, *LO COTIDIANO*, *MEZCOLANZA*, AND MEMORY

Within the context of U.S. Latina/o Roman Catholic theology, community and daily life are especially important. Latina/o theologians regularly emphasize their work as a process of *teología de y en conjunto*, working with and from particular communities, especially in daily life.[5] Mujerista theologian Ada María Isasi-Díaz values *lo cotidiano* (the everyday) as a source of knowledge about the world that must be fruitfully engaged as part of scholarly reflection. At the same time, daily life cannot be overly romanticized or presumed to always be right and better; rather, it should be a critical source of dialogical reflection.[6] This emphasis on critical dialogue with daily life also opens up the importance of a critical retrieval of history.

Isasi-Díaz additionally elevates *mestizaje* and *mulatez/mulataje*, the racial mixtures of Africans, Amerindians, and Europeans, as the proper *locus theologicus* of mujerista theology.[7] Here, I employ Fernando F. Segovia's term *mezcolanza* in order to emphasize plurality and differences that include more than "race." At the same time, as Néstor Medina's recent work elucidates, though *mestizaje* and *mezcolanza* are important loci for Latina/o identities and Latina/o religious thought, mixture must be critically remembered. *Mestizaje* has too often been employed to preserve the dominance of white cultures and Roman Catholic religion atop a racialized hierarchy that silences still-surviving Amerindians, Africans, Muslims, Jews, and peoples who have mixed Amerindian, African, Jewish, or Muslim ancestry. Any appropriation of *mestizaje* must recognize that people of differing ethnic, racial, and religious traditions have been and still are part of Latin American and U.S. *latinidades*. At the same time, the pluralities in the mixture, including Roman Catholicism, were transformed in the process.[8]

In addition to mixture, Segovia also elevates a sense of *otredad*, rooting *mezcolanza* in an experience of otherness before another cultural world, an experience of being able to navigate different worlds even while not feeling at home in any of them.[9] However diversely valenced, mixture and otherness are, working from them necessitates attention to the historical realities of both internal theological and experiential diversity within the Roman Catholic tradition, as well as attention to and conversation with other religious traditions that continue to be part of U.S. Latina/o daily life. As María Pilar Aquino outlines, recognizing theological diversity demands attention to the "historicity" of all theological assumptions.[10] Aquino's own theological method depends upon "intercultural dialogue," which values the rationality of different peoples as embedded in particular cultures and historical moments, hence the particularities of historical remembering matter.[11]

In addition to intercultural dialogue, the employment and reworking of cultural memory are also important tools of Latina/o theologies that can serve as bases for Latina/o Catholic-Jewish work. Drawing on the work of Jeanette Rodríguez and Ted Fortier, Martínez-Vázquez highlights the importance of cultural memory to the daily processes of identity negotiation among Latina/o Muslims.[12] Latina/o identities are not static or unitary. Different religious experiences may lead to different cultural memories, but also cultural memory is informed by pluralistic religious experiences. As Martínez-Vázquez highlights, some practices of cultural memory can be a "subversive activity" when "people dis-cover their histories" that have been ignored in dominant historical narratives.[13] To remember the fraught but shared history of Latina/o Catholics and Jews may necessitate that, to some extent, dominant narratives of Latina/o history are subverted and altered, and, hence, dominant narratives of *latinidad* are also changed. As the stories below demonstrate, such remembering additionally entails a reorganization of self-perception.

As Aquino reminds us, all intercultural dialogue must reflect seriously upon "the asymmetric character of social power relations at all levels" that informs "the plural fabric of reality and of knowledge."[14] Hence, taking up intercultural dialogue as a tool of theology also attends to and recognizes that a shared cultural history was created amid imbalances of social power; in the case of Latin American Roman Catholicism, such history was often created in a relationship of dominance over other religious groups, including Judaism.

Although this essay is only an introductory foray into Latinas/os and Catholic-Jewish relations, I have sought to include three brief narratives drawn from border spaces of religious mixture and cultural memory in daily life. For this essay, I have interviewed three individuals whose identity narratives speak to three different aspects of Latina/o Catholic-Jewish interactions in three different historical moments. I have changed each individual's name in order to keep his identity confidential. All three narratives signal the importance of work done to retrieve and renegotiate historical memory so that Latina/o Catholics and Jews can learn from each other's distinct histories while recognizing that these histories are also shared. These memories can only be retrieved with critical recognition of the tensions of colonialism, racism, and violence that surround their creation and narration.

A SHARED HISTORY UNDER COLONIALISM:
CRYPTO-JEWISH PASTS AND *LO COTIDIANO*

As a child, Manuel felt his home was structured around a "guarded secrecy," but he never understood what the secrets were and why they needed to be protected. Over the course of years, Manuel traced his ancestors through colonial Mexico and back to Spain. Eventually, his research confirmed his own suspicions: he was, in part, descended from *conversos*. He began to perceive how certain Jewish practices survived, such as lighting candles on Friday nights. For Manuel, Latin America and the U.S. Latina/o diaspora is uniquely marked by this history of layered traditions and "submerged" memories.[15] In raising his children, Manuel has hoped to cultivate a greater consciousness of these forgotten histories.

Manuel is not alone. Studies suggest that other descendants of *conversos* and crypto-Jews also remained in varying parts of Latin America and the U.S. Southwest. Cuban American Rabbi Rigoberto Emmanuel Vinas works with Latinas/os who were born and raised Jewish, as well as with Latinas/os who were raised Roman Catholic but who felt drawn to Judaism because of self-perception as "crypto-Jews."[16] Vinas's experience hints at the plural religious experiences that frame the cultural memories of Latina/o Catholics and Jews.

Such plurality goes back centuries, to an Iberia before Columbus. Often, medieval Spain, especially under Muslim rule, is held up as an era of remarkable openness and fluidity between religious groups, especially when compared to the rest of Europe at that time. While the history of medieval *convivencia* (roughly translated as "living together") in Spain can be an important site of historical retrieval for dialogue, it can also be overly romanticized and ignore legacies of violence and domination. In the earliest Spanish conceptions of the term *convivencia*, it was employed for nationalist purposes, in an attempt to explain a supposedly unique "Spanish civilization."[17] Jonathan Ray's analysis provides a useful lens with which to think about medieval Spain as "a product of a variety of contending identities and social, cultural, and religious tensions."[18] Hence, it is important both to recall the history of Iberian religious *mezcolanza* and *otredad* that precedes the Spanish conquest of the New World, even while remembering that *convivencia* was as much about tension, competition, conflict, and contestation as it was about conversation.

In addition, the era of *convivencia* ended in the forced eradication, through expulsion or conversion, of the Jews and Muslims who remained in Iberia. The historical tensions that fall out from that moment have shaped many of the struggles over cultural memory that persists today. We cannot know how many Jews and Muslims were converted, how many kept a secret faith, and how many came to the Iberian Americas. Spanish treatment of *conversos* involved laws that excluded them from the Spanish Indies, though a significant minority of colonial settlers in New Spain may have been *conversos*.[19] Anti-Jewish rhetoric persisted as an aspect of the Spanish conquest of the Americas, even in areas where there were certainly no Jewish settlers. In fact, anti-Jewish invective was all too frequently a part of the catechesis of new Amerindian converts to Roman Catholicism during the conquest of the Americas.[20]

Spanish legal exclusions of *conversos* revealed the slippage between "religion" and "race" as concepts in colonial Latin America.[21] The Spanish often used the religious difference, or otherness, of Jews to think about the racial difference, or otherness, of Amerindians.[22] This problem also appeared in frequent orthographic slips where *Iudio* (the modern Spanish is *judío*) and *Indio* were mistakenly exchanged.[23] At the same time, Santiago E. Slabodsky has examined texts from the sixteenth and seventeenth centuries in which some colonial Jewish figures and some Andean peoples affirm camaraderie as tribes of Israel. As Slabodsky discusses, these stories may demonstrate a shared history of subversion in which these two groups of colonized "others" tentatively aligned in opposition to a dominating empire.[24]

The Inquisition also operated in the Americas, impacting indigenous peoples and *conversos*. Perhaps this history is a source of Manuel's sense of "guarded secrecy" in his family home. As Seth Kunin argues, the Inquisition's pursuit of potentially non-Catholic religious practices both "narrow[ed] the range and complexity of [crypto-Jewish] religious practice" while also cultivating a "need for secrecy."[25] The colonial arm of the Inquisition may have led to some crypto-Jews settling in present-day New Mexico in order to reside distant from colonial centers where inquisitorial power was strongest.[26] Manuel's story demonstrates exactly these tensions. His own family lived as Roman Catholics while they kept hidden traditions. They had almost forgotten their Jewish ancestry or even why they led lives devoted to secrecy.

Yet Manuel's story also points to the enduring impact of medieval Spain and crypto-Jewish life on some Latina/o religious identities. Kunin chronicles a process of "identity juggling" through which crypto-Jewish individuals came to weave together Jewish and Catholic ritual practices.[27] For instance, Kunin describes a few families in New Mexico who light candles on Friday nights at sunset, and women also recite the rosary as they light candles. As Kunin portrays this practice, these families have brought together both traditions in a way that constructs something distinct from either tradition.[28] Hence, for certain Latina/o communities, Jewish and Roman Catholic histories have significantly blended together to form a hybrid historical identity that impacts both Roman Catholic and Jewish lives and identities. Still, Roman Catholics cannot ignore the role of rhetorical, cultural, and physical violence that required a scarring secrecy for crypto-Jewish survival.

SHARING HISTORY AFTER COLONIALISM: EUROPEAN JEWISH IMMIGRATION TO LATIN AMERICA AND *MEZCOLANZA*

Crypto-Jewish pasts are not the only sites of shared Latina/o Catholic and Jewish histories. Another interlocutor, Michael, has spent much of his adult life exploring and wrestling with plural religious identities and traditions in his own spirituality and cultural identity. Partially of Argentine descent and raised as a Christian, Michael grew up in a largely Jewish neighborhood outside Dallas. His maternal grandparents had been Jewish Argentines who had converted to Roman Catholicism and ultimately to Protestant fundamentalism. He belonged to a multi-faith family, noting that some relatives were rabbis and some were nuns and priests. Remembering his childhood, he reflected upon mixed religious rituals, such as celebrating Christmas but also receiving Hanukkah gelt.[29]

As an adult, Michael explored a plurality of Christian traditions, a journey he describes as marked by "ambivalence." Ultimately, Michael converted to Judaism, recognizing it not only as a religious home, but also as a cultural home. He learned that while some of his family remained Jewish, much of his family had emigrated from Argentina and/or converted from Judaism in response to "a big turn in a tide of anti-Semitism that took root…both under right-wing and under left-wing governments in Latin America."[30] At present, most of Michael's family resides outside of Argentina. Michael's story, hence, highlights another moment in this ongoing, shared history between Latina/o Roman Catholics, a shared and ambivalent history that is again marked by mixture and otherness, but also by violence and domination.

Following independence from Iberian rule throughout the nineteenth century, Latin American nations accepted more diverse immigrants from Europe, though this acceptance was not without tensions as Roman Catholicism was the sanctioned state religion in many Latin American nations.[31] Only a few thousand Jews lived in Latin America by 1889, and the largest influx of Jewish immigrants to Latin America occurred between 1889 and World War I.[32] While the immigrants were predominantly Eastern European Jews, Sephardic Jews immigrated as well.[33] Although Jewish communities exist throughout Latin America, the largest, and most studied, Latin American Jewish population is that of Argentina.[34]

Anti-Jewish rhetoric and practices have appeared among Latin American Roman Catholics across the political spectrum, right and left. For instance, some members of the Chilean right wing from 1970 to 1973 attacked Salvador Allende Gossens "as the pawn of Jewish Bolsheviks" because of the participation of Jewish leftists in his administration.[35] Though fewer than 1 percent of Argentina's population was Jewish, 13 percent of the "disappeared" Argentines in the era from 1976 to 1983 were Jewish.[36] At the same time, leftist Latin American groups also attacked Jewish Latin Americans as connected to Israel and, by extension, "imperialist powers" such as the United States and Great Britain.[37]

Despite this fraught history, at times, Roman Catholics and Jews already worked together for political purposes and social change. León Klenicki observed that, from 1880 to 1914, many Latin American union leaders were Jewish immigrants, and Jewish workers and Jewish thought had a significant impact on Latin American social justice and social consciousness.[38] Since the 1980s, Jewish individuals have come to hold more diverse roles of political prominence in many Latin American countries.[39] Yet even this history of shared struggles for social justice is not without its problems. In the post–Vatican II era, when some members of the Roman Catholic Church experienced "a reckoning of the soul concerning Jews and Judaism," Klenicki observed that such a reckoning was barely on the radar of early liberation theology. Attention to Jews and Judaism, after 70 CE, was largely absent from the Medellín Document (1968), and barely a footnote in the Puebla Document (1979).[40] Klenicki feared that liberation theology, in its critique of capitalism and U.S. dominance also fed too easily accusations of Latin American Jews as "agents of Wall Street and American imperialism."[41]

Michael perceives himself to be an ambivalent and ambiguous product of the confluence of this history of mixture and otherness, of domination and fear, though this confluence ultimately led him to choose conversion to Judaism. The tensions that surround historical and cultural memory are especially poignant in Michael's perception of his family's struggles with religious mixture. Even among those who converted to Catholicism, he finds that Judaism became a "history, that you have no control over, and yet at the same time [you are] never... able to get rid of it. Both interestingly because others won't allow you to, but also because part of yourself will not allow yourself to."[42] Choosing to return to Judaism and retrieve that part of his family's history gave Michael "more sense of purpose and belonging than it ever did to say 'I'm going to go to church.'"[43] Even while recognizing his place in the midst of a mixed and shared history, Michael still found a way of affirming and standing within an identity.

MEMORY, IDENTITY, *OTREDAD*, AND LATINA/O CATHOLIC AND JEWISH NEIGHBORS IN U.S. CITIES

In addition to the importance of shared histories between Roman Catholics and Jews in Latin America, Latina/o Roman Catholic and Jewish communities have interacted in the United States, especially in major urban areas, such as Los Angeles, Miami, and New York.[44] Jewish Latinas/os are an important part of the U.S. Latina/o community. A shared history has also grown between Catholic Latinas/os and their non-Latina/o Jewish neighbors.

One of my interlocutors for this essay speaks to this interaction in the United States. Daniel lived most of his life perceiving himself as a Chicano and a Catholic. Born in East Los Angeles, he never knew his maternal grandfather, and it was only as an adult, during an argument with his mother, that he learned his grandfather was Jewish. This revelation caused Daniel to research his grandmother's neighborhood, and he learned that Boyle Heights was once a diverse neighborhood where a Mexican American Catholic cemetery might rest across the street from a Jewish cemetery.[45]

Socioeconomic factors often prevent Latina/o Catholics and non-Latina/o Jews from living in the same neighborhoods.[46] In addition, negative stereotypes about each other can prevent both communities from engaging in equal interactions.[47] Although educational work and dialogue must address and challenge these negative perceptions, such work and dialogue may also remind both communities of a shared history. Daniel's story exposes how, in the early part of the twentieth century, Latina/o Catholics and Jewish Americans already lived together and worked together in the United States. Boyle Heights is just one such place where multiple ethnicities shared a neighborhood.

While such a history is not without conflict, it also reflects that different communities have come together before, especially through the experience of otherness vis-à-vis a dominant U.S. culture. As Ruiz has stated earlier, grassroots efforts that engage members of both groups, and not just top scholars and clerical leaders, are necessary steps in creating real dialogue and relationships.[48] We know from history that such grassroots efforts have already transpired; we now need to work more at making them known more widely.

The knowledge of a shared history can have a transformational impact on individual lives. Daniel also felt that this knowledge of his ancestry and a lost cultural memory made sense of some of his adult experiences. Knowledge of the religious and cultural mixture in his own family background has sparked "a digression of remembering," one that is especially connected to meditation on otherness.[49] Learning more about his Jewish grandfather and the history of Boyle Heights has had an impact on Daniel's "sense of self."[50] After reading a *Los Angeles Times* article that tells the story of Eddie Goldstein, an elderly Jewish man who married a Mexican American woman and continues to live in Boyle Heights, Daniel felt a sense of awe because "I'm not a novelty; I'm part of two cultural traditions that blended together for a while. And I just never anticipated that."[51] A change in

Daniel's own familial memory has caused a shift in his understanding of the relationships between his Mexican American Catholic background and Jewish culture. He is now more aware of the shared history and connections between these two groups in Los Angeles.

SHARED AND FRAUGHT HISTORIES

This essay has sought to provide a brief critical retrieval of a shared history as a basis of future dialogue between Latina/o Catholics and Jews. On the one hand, drawing on the three different stories of Manuel, Michael, and Daniel, we already have witnesses to preexisting, "on-the-ground," daily lived histories and realities in which Roman Catholic Latina/o and Jewish individuals have interacted, albeit in complex ways. A critical retrieval of this history can challenge and reshape dominant cultural memory even while such a critical retrieval acknowledges the fraught and painful aspects of this past. This brief exercise in critical, cultural remembering cracks open only slivers of shared history. Hopefully such histories can complement a theological openness to a different future as a basis for dialogue.

NOTES

1. Hjamil A. Martínez-Vázquez, *Latina/o y Musulmán: The Construction of Latina/o Identity among Latina/o Muslims in the United States* (Eugene, OR: Pickwick Publications, 2010), 1–2.

2. I draw this pair of terms from Fernando F. Segovia, "Two Places and No Place on which to Stand: Mixture and Otherness in Hispanic American Theology," *Listening* 27 (1992): 33–34.

3. I take the term *non-innocent history* from Justo L. González and Jean-Pierre Ruiz. González critiques perceptions of U.S. history as "innocent" because such narratives ignore genocidal conquest, violence, slavery, and "theft." Latinas/os have had to recognize that they are the products of "a non-innocent history," of conqueror, conquered, enslaved, and persecuted peoples, all of whom were capable of both heroism and grievous crimes. See Justo L. González, *Mañana: Christian Theology from a Hispanic Perspective* (Nashville: Abingdon Press, 1990), 39–40. Jean-Pierre Ruiz specifically takes this "non-innocent history" as a complex, painful hybridity that can serve as the starting point for reading the Bible. Jean-Pierre Ruiz, "The Bible and U.S. Hispanic American Theological Discourse: Lessons from a Non-

Innocent History," in *From the Heart of Our People: Latino/a Explorations in Catholic Systematic Theology*, ed. Orlando O. Espín and Miguel H. Díaz (Maryknoll, NY: Orbis Books, 1999), 101–2.

4. Many different terms exist for "a range of communities whose members outwardly profess one cultural identity as well as having some aspect of a hidden Jewish identity—sometimes religious, cultural, or even historical." These terms include *marrano, converso*, crypto-Jew, secret Jew, *anús* (plural *anusim*), which Kunin suggests may become the preferred term among community members who seek "to maintain some aspect of identity separate from that of mainstream Jews." Such naming has to do with the particular connections being drawn between "past and present," or in other words, perhaps, the particular cultural memories being activated and employed. See Seth D. Kunin, *Juggling Identities: Identity and Authenticity among the Crypto-Jews* (New York: Columbia University Press, 2009), 1–3.

5. Neomi DeAnda and Néstor Medina, "Convivencias: What Have We Learned? Toward a Latino/a Ecumenical Theology," in *Building Bridges, Doing Justice: Constructing a Latino/a Ecumenical Theology*, ed. Orlando O. Espín (Maryknoll, NY: Orbis Books, 2009), 185.

6. Ada-María Isasi-Díaz, *Mujerista Theology: A Theology for the Twenty-First Century* (Maryknoll, NY: Orbis Books, 2001 [1996]), 69.

7. Ibid., 64.

8. Néstor Medina, *Mestizaje: (Re)Mapping Race, Culture, and Faith in Latina/o Catholicism* (Maryknoll, NY: Orbis Books, 2009), passim, esp. 137–43.

9. Segovia, "Two Places," 33–34.

10. María Pilar Aquino, "Theological Method in U.S. Latino/a Theology: Toward an Intercultural Theology for the Third Millennium," in *From the Heart of Our People*, 9.

11. Ibid., 11.

12. Martínez-Vázquez, *Latina/o y Mulsulmán*, 5.

13. Ibid., 85.

14. Aquino, "Theological Method," 36.

15. Interview with Manuel, Skype, July 12, 2010.

16. Jennifer Medina, "Shades of Gray: A Conservative Cuban Rabbi Takes on Race Issues That Could Have Powerful Implications for Jews and Latinos," *ColorLines Magazine* 8 (2005): 20.

17. Jonathan Ray, "Beyond Tolerance and Persecution: Reassessing Our Approach to Medieval *Convivencia*," *Jewish Social Studies* 11 (2005): 2.

18. Ibid., 13.

19. Kunin, *Juggling Identities*, 7.

20. Judith Laikin Elkin, "Imagining Idolatry: Missionaries, Indians, and Jews," in *Religion and the Authority of the Past*, ed. Tobin Siebers,

75–99, RATIO: Institute for the Humanities (Ann Arbor: University of Michigan, 1993), 75. Her article examines the ways and reasons that images of Jews were connected to idolatry as part of the catechism of new converts.

21. Ibid., 79.

22. Ibid., 80.

23. Ibid., 81.

24. Santiago E. Slabodsky, "De-colonial Jewish Thought and the Americas," in *Postcolonial Philosophy of Religion*, ed. Purushottama Bilimoria and Andrew B. Irvine (London: Springer, 2009), 263.

25. Kunin, *Juggling Identities*, 5, 19, 45–81. Some researchers have doubted whether New Mexico's crypto-Jews really are the descendants of *conversos*, but Kunin disputes their arguments. See Kunin, 81.

26. Ibid., 7. Stanley Hordes argues that many *conversos* took part in Juan de Oñate's 1595 settlement of New Mexico. See Stanley M. Hordes, *To the End of the Earth: A History of the Crypto-Jews of New Mexico* (New York: Columbia University Press, 2005), 72–93.

27. Ibid., 151.

28. Ibid., 153.

29. Interview with Michael, Los Angeles, CA, May 18, 2010. I wish to offer a special note of gratitude to Michael, who conversed with me at length about this essay. Of course, all the flaws in this essay are my responsibility.

30. Ibid.

31. Judith Laikin Elkin, *The Jews of Latin America*, rev. ed. (New York: Holmes & Meier, 1998), 25–26.

32. Ibid., 47 and 51. As Laikin Elkin points out, some Latin American nations opened their doors to European immigrants in part because they wanted to "whiten" their population away from mestizo, indigenous, and African populations (26–27).

33. Ibid., 33–34.

34. Ibid., 252.

35. Ibid., 268.

36. Slabodsky, "De-colonial Jewish Thought," 257.

37. Laikin Elkin, *Jews of Latin America*, 256.

38. León Klenicki, "The Theology of Liberation: A Latin American Jewish Exploration," *American Jewish Archives Journal* 35 (1983): 27.

39. Laikin Elkin, *Jews of Latin America*, 271.

40. Klenicki, "The Theology of Liberation," 36.

41. Ibid., 35–36.

42. Interview with Michael.

43. Ibid.

44. Hector Avalos, *Strangers in Our Own Land: Religion and U.S. Latina/o Literature* (Nashville: Abingdon Press, 2005), 119.

45. Interview with Daniel, Los Angeles, CA, May 18, 2010.

46. The AJC volume, *Latinos and Jews: Old Luggage, New Itineraries* noted this socioeconomic disparity in several cases. Yet such differences, whether in income, status, neighborhood, or certain political orientations, are not always perceived as prohibitive of dialogue. See, for example, Charles Kamasaki, "Divergent Understandings or Conflicting Interests? Latino and Jewish Policy Differences," in *Latinos and Jews: Old Luggage, New Itineraries*, 54.

47. Roberto Suro, "Two Peoples on a Journey," in *Latinos and Jews: Old Luggage, New Itineraries*, 13. Suro's essay does not speak much about the reality that some Latinas/os are also Jewish. One problem noted in different essays in the *Latinos and Jews* volume focused on U.S. Latina/o stereotypes of Jewish wealth and power combined with a lack of knowledge about the Shoah and its impact on Jewish American life. See, for example, the discussion in Abraham D. Lavender, "A History of Jewish and Hispanic Interaction in Miami-Dade County, Florida," in *Latinos and Jews: Old Luggage, New Itineraries*, 96. Hector Avalos also cites different surveys that point out anti-Jewish "propensities" in a rather high proportion of Latin American immigrants and U.S.-born Latinas/os. See Avalos, *Strangers in Our Own Land*, 119.

48. Jean-Pierre Ruiz, "Sharing History and Hopes: Latinos and Jews in the United States," in *Latinos and Jews: Old Luggage, New Itineraries*, 42.

49. Interview with Daniel.

50. Ibid.

51. Ibid. The article is Hector Becerra, "One of a Kind in Boyle Heights," *Los Angeles Times*, December 9, 2009, A1.

VIII
CONCLUSIONS

18

Catholics and Jews

Looking Ahead

David M. Gordis and Peter C. Phan

This concluding essay is somewhat unusual in that it is written by a rabbi and a Roman Catholic theologian in collaboration. Each read the other's text and suggested changes and additions, which were incorporated into the final version. Such a collaborative work would have been unimaginable without the dialogical spirit animating Jewish-Catholic relations in the last several decades, to which Rabbi León Klenicki, the man whose life and work are celebrated in this book, made an enormous contribution.

WHERE WE HAVE BEEN

The question before us—What's next in Jewish-Catholic relations?—appears on the face of it quite straightforward inasmuch as it may be taken to simply entail an enumeration of "things to be done," as in a to-do list. Yet it is extremely complex since each of its key terms is fraught, for, it may be asked, what counts as a Jew or Judaism, what is the identity of a Catholic or the nature of the Catholic Church, and what kind of relations is possible and desirable between them today? As we engage these questions about the road ahead of Catholic-Jewish relations for the twenty-first century, we can and should reflect on the extraordinary years of the twentieth, which brought with them remarkable achievements in science and technology, significant political transformations and accomplishments, as well as unspeakable horrors such as the Shoah, which dwarfed earlier perpetrations of wickedness in scope and impact. Relations between Catholics and Jews during the

215

twentieth century mirrored events in the larger world and have evolved in recent years in dramatically positive ways, promising new possibilities and challenges for the twenty-first century.

Reactions to the horrors of the Shoah generated a good deal of soul-searching and self-examination, not only in the worlds of Catholics and Jews, but among all thinking and responsible people who were challenged to understand how human beings could have descended to such depths of bestial cruelty. Religious people of every faith faced in the most dramatic way conceivable the anguished issue of theodicy, the intertwining of atrocious evil, divine omnipotence, and divine infinite love: How could an infinitely powerful and loving God permit such an abomination? And within the Christian world, there began a coming to terms with the role of the Christian *adversus Judaeos* (against Jews) tradition and history in creating at least the preconditions for the horrors of the Shoah.

Undoubtedly, the initiatives of Pope John XXIII and Vatican II were profoundly transformative in Catholic-Jewish relations. Seeking to overcome its anti-Jewish tradition once and for all, Vatican II initiated a new understanding of Jews and Judaism in its groundbreaking Declaration on the Church's Relation to Non-Christian Religions (*Nostra Aetate*). The Church acknowledged that "the beginnings of its faith and election are to be found already among the patriarchs, Moses, and the prophets" (4). The Council affirmed the continuing validity of covenantal relationship between God and the Jewish people. Furthermore, it rejected the deicide charge against Jews. Finally, it "deplores feelings of hatred, persecutions and demonstrations of anti-Semitism directed against the Jews at whatever time and by whomsoever"(4).[1] While some conservatives in the Church have backtracked on this, the reference to "unbelieving" or "perfidious" Jews was removed from the liturgy, a further expression of the desire to heal and overcome a tragic and pernicious history. The establishment of the Commission of the Holy See for Religious Relations with Jews in 1974 signaled a new era of mutual goodwill and theological enrichment, and the numerous documents issued by the Commission since then eloquently testify to the importance the Catholic Church attaches to its relations to the Jews.

There is no doubt that in the post-conciliar period, from the end of the Second Vatican Council (1965) to the death of Pope John Paul II (2005), the amity between Catholics and Jews as well as the Catholic theology of Judaism reached unparalleled heights, thanks principally to the activities of the Polish pope who counted many Jews among his closest friends. In the real world of human interactions and relationships, Jews and Catholics have achieved new levels of understanding and fellowship. Interrelationships thrive among clergy, laypersons, and academics in an atmosphere of civility and mutual respect. As we reflect on how far we have come, it's natural to ponder where we can hope to go from here, what is possible, and what might be aspired to, even adopting a visionary or prophetic perspective.

Unfortunately, in the last years, certain gestures from the Vatican seem to have put a damper on Jewish-Catholic relations. Chief among these are Pope Benedict's permission for a wider use of the so-called Tridentine Mass with its Good Friday prayer for the conversion of the Jews and the lifting of excommunication of the schismatic Holocaust-denying bishop Richard Williamson.[2] Of course, these and many other events can be (and have been) given a benign interpretation,[3] but the offence that many Jews have taken at them and their impassioned critique of the implied theology are fully understandable. For those committed to improving Catholic-Jewish dialogue, however, these unfortunate events can serve as powerful incentives to renew and deepen the mutual understanding and love that have already existed among Jews and Christians.

THE ROAD AHEAD

On the current agenda, efforts should be made to strengthen and broaden initiatives that have begun. Interreligious relationships have been somewhat limited to "elite" and leadership groups. While these should continue, including efforts to train future priests and rabbis in interreligious leadership skills and enhancing their knowledge of religious traditions and cultures other than their own, broader community involvement in interreligious activities is essential for enhancing the way we deal with "otherness," a critical need in building a compassionate and responsive pluralist society. Our religious communities should overcome suspicion and antipathy toward the other, including Catholics and Jews, by learning about and experiencing the living realities of each other's traditions, beliefs, rituals, and institutions.

Interreligious dialogue should not, of course, be limited to discovering areas of convergence in the different religious traditions.

Perhaps the most significant explorations involve open and honest consideration of areas of divergence. For example, while there are widespread differences among individuals within both communities, Jews and Catholics generally take divergent approaches to many moral issues, such as abortion and homosexuality. This is true, not only in relation to individual positions, but particularly in the context of the developments of traditions and teaching. Genuine interreligious relationship should allow for understanding and even learning from positions differing from one's own, without the overwhelming impulse to attempt to persuade the other of the rightness of one's own position. The ability to hear and appreciate, though not necessarily to adopt, alternative narratives, in whole or in part, may in fact be the best indicator of a genuinely valuable and enhancing interrelationship. This goes well beyond politeness and civility, certainly important advances over hostility and violence; rather, it suggests that the other, in his or her "otherness" and speaking from a different religious tradition, is a human being of value with something to say that is worth listening to and learning from, even if very different from one's own intellectual and religious positions.

Words and policies have the power to inspire and ennoble, but also to inflame and ignite. This suggests that on the future agenda of Catholic-Jewish relations, we should both separately and together look at how language and policy decisions function in the real world. With regard to language, both traditions have to deal with the challenge of troubling texts that have historically contributed to poisoning the relationships between them. These are not simply texts that are part of the respective religious cultures; they are canonized and privileged, playing a liturgical role, claiming authority and truth. Religious leaders in each of our communities have begun to develop strategies for navigating these texts. A good deal of work remains to be done in this area and the results must then be translated into the life of our respective lay communities, which are often limited to literalist readings and are negatively impacted by them.

Concerning policy decisions, they must no longer be made unilaterally and with an exclusive eye on what they mean or may appear to mean internally. Their impact upon other religious communities, in our case, Jewish and Catholic, must also be considered. For example, the decisions to permit a wider use of the Tridentine Mass or to lift the excommunication of a Holocaust-denying schismatic bishop should not have been done simply with the view to reconcile right-wing schismatics with the Church, without considering how these decisions may affect the relations between Catholics and Jews.[4]

Beyond the language of privileged texts and canonical decisions, we need to pay more attention to the use of language in common discourse. Both of us are of the view that less separates Catholics and Jews on many ethical and moral issues than at first glance. For instance, in the matter of abortion, there is less difference than sometimes appears. By and large, Jews and Catholics, though differing on issues such as the moment when a fully human life begins and ensoulment takes place, share the sense that abortion is a tragedy and that reducing its incidence is a sacred obligation. But constructive conversation between Catholics and Jews is made more difficult when one side characterizes its position as "pro-life," implying that those who view the issues differently are anti-life. Words are the instrument of communication, but careless appropriation of words can preclude communication as well.

This leads to the more visionary dimensions of our aspirations for the future of Jewish-Catholic relations. These are rooted in our conviction that, for all the blessed progress we have made in relating to each other, our religious traditions, be it Judaism, Christianity, or Islam, to cite the three Abrahamic religions, still fall far short in playing a significant role in healing a world torn by hatred and violence. Our traditions have brought great enhancements to human experience but, at the same time, have contributed to engendering hatred and oppression. This has often been the product of our assertion of exclusive access to truth and salvation. Both traditions have affirmed that they are not only unique but superior to all others. We use a special language to describe ourselves as being "chosen," and to relegate the "other" to the position of subaltern. And even when we adopt an attitude of outward civility toward the other, we assume the superiority of our own tradition and the deficiency of the other. This attitude often leads to a pernicious and destructive stance, which can undermine civility and lead to hatred and violence. Whatever the formulation, whether "We were at Sinai and you were not," or *extra ecclesiam nulla sallus* ("outside the Church, there is no salvation"), this stance easily engenders condescension toward the other, or worse.

At this point, in response to the question of what lies ahead in the dialogue between Jews and Catholics, it may be tempting to list a few urgent items for the agenda. Different dialogue partners will no doubt select a particular set of issues, depending on their political and theological perspectives. Some of these are as old as the dialogue itself, such as the permanent validity of God's covenant with the Jews, the interpretation of Scripture, preaching to and conversion of Jews, and the universality of Jesus as savior. Our volume in honor of Rabbi León Klenicki has dealt with some of these key issues ranging from the Bible to religious identity, Christology, spirituality, and Latino/a theology. Despite their near-intractable complexity, thanks to decades of serious dialogue, much clarity, albeit not a consensus, has been achieved on at least the meaning and limitations of these faith claims.

Writing in 2007, Cardinal Walter Kasper, then President of the Pontifical Council for Promoting Christian Unity and of the Pontifical Commission for Religious Relations with the Jews, suggested three "future tasks and challenges" for Christian-Jewish dialogue: "all the historical problems that relate to our common, often difficult, history"; "the theological relationship between Judaism and Christianity"; and "our practical cooperation."[5] The cardinal acknowledges that much progress has been made in these three areas. However, in the context of recent events in the Catholic Church mentioned above, they have reemerged with greater urgency.[6] From the Catholic perspective, it seems that its theological language, especially in Christology and ecclesiology, is still wedded to expressions such as *universality, uniqueness, absolute necessity,* and *exclusivity,* which, born in the context of controversies and imperialism, are highly liable to misunderstanding today.

Moreover, weighty as these theological issues are, they cannot be fully discussed apart from the political situation in the Middle East, and more specifically, the conflict between the State of Israel and the Palestinians. Consequently, the "dialogue" between Catholics (and Christians in general) and Jews must become a "trialogue" among Jews, Christians, and Muslims. Here, once again, the questions we raised at the beginning of our essay raise their troublesome heads: Which Jews, which Christians, and which Muslims? The Catholic Church, with the Vatican City State and all its diplomatic resources, is arguably better equipped to deal with these political issues than any Jewish or Muslim group, but this historical advantage puts a particular onus on the Catholic Church as it tries to improve relations with Jews.

This wider context of the Catholic-Jewish dialogue leads us to articulate what may certainly be viewed as a utopian hope for the future of the relationship between these two religious communities. We need to radically transform the way we talk about ourselves and the way we talk about each other. This new mode of religious discourse that we are urging is rooted, not in our conviction about all that we know, but rather in the conviction that there is much that we do not and cannot know. We seek to understand more about ourselves and our world than we can possibly comprehend. Our reach exceeds our grasp. Our religious traditions and cultures are best understood not as repositories of truth but rather as instruments that have been developed by our respective religious communities to accompany us on the universal human journey to try to make sense out of the mystery of what human life is all about. Our questions are consistently deeper than our answers. And since no one tradition has all the answers or even the best formulations of the questions, the rationale for interreligious relationship, including Catholic-Jewish relationship, becomes clear. Our journey can be enhanced by visiting the home of the other, literally and figuratively, and learning about and from the other, who is also embarking on a journey like our own.

We must learn to not be threatened by the "otherness" of the other. Our identities may be shaped in no small measure by defining our own cultures and traditions and placing ourselves within them, but we must find a way of overcoming invidious comparison with and defining ourselves over against the other as the key to shaping our own religious identities. I can learn from other traditions without compromising who I am within my own. I can participate in the rituals and observances of my tradition comfortably and at peace, while at the same time understanding that others who participate in other traditions and observe other rituals are engaged in an enterprise analogous to my own and are no less comfortable with who they are and where they place themselves within their religious traditions.

This will require a radical transformation in discourse and practice. Our religious language often communicates a pretentiousness and arrogance in describing our respective doctrines and institutions. We need to replace this with a language of humility and "epistemological modesty." We should certainly teach our respective doctrines and beliefs, but we should do so with the awareness that these can make no claim to having represented the truth definitively and absolutely the truth. Only God is divine; humans are only (and all too) human. All of us are "chosen," and none of us is exclusively. The notion of "one and only true Church" not only precludes genuine interrelationships but strains credulity in view of the Church's human character. It is all very well for religious authorities to assert that such claims to exclusivity indicate neither intellectual nor moral arrogance but rather deep humility and faithful obedience to God's revelation, and that failure to claim absolute truth would be falling victim to the "dictatorship of relativism." Whether such assertion is convincing, we leave to the judgment of readers. We simply note that recent scandals in the Church, from clerical sexual abuse to criminal attempts at concealment and obstruction of justice, even by the higher ecclesiastical echelons, to financial shenanigans in our religious communities make claims about the Church being the only repository of truth and goodness ring hollow. Consequently, what is being demanded of us is a posture of modesty in our words and in our practice.

If, in fact, we continue to find in religious traditions the strength and the power to contribute to the healing and repair of a torn and fragmented world, we need to be able to work together across religious lines to effect this repair. To do so, Catholics, Jews, and followers of other traditions must approach each other and the world, which we confront together with modesty, humility, and faith. Together, Jews and Christians have come a long way, as León Klenicki has amply shown, and let his life and work be gratefully celebrated, but the journey remains arduous and unfinished—until the *eschaton*, when God is in all and all is in God.

NOTES

1. The English translation of *Nostra Aetate* is taken from *Decrees of the Ecumenical Councils,* vol. 2, *Trent to Vatican II*, trans. Norman P. Tanner (Washington, DC: Sheed & Ward and Georgetown University Press, 1990), 971.

2. From the editors: On October 24, 2012, the Society of St. Pius X announced that it had expelled Bishop Williamson. See http://www.catholic news.com/data/stories/cns/1204487.htm.

3. Pope Benedict XVI altered the text of the prayer in question; http://www.ccjr.us/dialogika-resources/themes-in-todays-dialogue/good-

friday-prayer/440-b1608feb5. See Cardinal Walter Kasper's response to Rabbi David Rosen; http://www.ccjr.us/dialogika-resources/themes-in-todays-dialogue/good-friday-prayer/457-kasper08feb13.

4. From the editors: The declaration by the Society of St. Pius X on June 30, 2013, appears to preclude further negotiation with the Vatican. See http://sspx.org/en/sspxs-bishops-declaration-25th-anniversary.

5. "Paths Taken and Enduring Questions in Jewish-Christian Relations Today: Thirty Years of the Commission for Religious Relations with the Jews," in *The Catholic Church and the Jewish People: Recent Reflections from Rome*, ed. Phillip A. Cunningham, Norbert J. Hoffmann, Joseph Sievers (New York: Fordham University Press, 2007), 9–10. Cardinal Kasper has summarized in six points his own theology of Judaism and Christianity in Philip A. Cunningham et al., eds., *Christ Jesus and the Jewish People Today: New Explorations of Theological Interrelationships* (Grand Rapids, MI: Eerdmans, 2011), x–xviii. Kasper's theses are as follows: (1) Israel's election by and covenant with God remains eternally valid and has never been revoked; (2) we must consider not only the relationship between the Old and the New covenants but also the relationship between post-biblical rabbinic and Talmudic Judaism and the Church; (3) both the rabbinic and the Christian interpretations of the Hebrew Scriptures are valid; (4) post-biblical Judaism and the Church are not two covenant peoples but one covenant people; (5) there is no institutionally sponsored mission to the Jews, though Christians must bear witness to Jesus; and (6) Jews and Christians must engage in common work for a better world. Even though Kasper's positions cannot be considered as the "official" teachings of the Roman Catholic Church on the subject, nevertheless, given his hierarchical status and his tenure as President of the Pontifical Commission for Religious Relations with the Jews (2001–2010), his statements no doubt represent basic positions currently supported by the Vatican, as indicated by the fact that they can be found in official documents issued by the Pontifical Commission for Religious Relations with the Jews in 1974, 1985, and 1998, and by the Pontifical Biblical Commission in 2001. Going beyond these positions would represent individual theological speculation. These documents may be found at http://www.vatican.va/roman_curia/pontifical_coun cils/chrstuni/relations-jews-docs/rc_pc_chrstuni_doc_19741201_nostra-aetate_en.html;http://www.vatican.va/roman_curia/pontifical_councils/chrs tuni/relations-jews-docs/rc_pc_chrstuni_doc_19820306_jews-judaism_ en.html; http://www.vatican.va/roman_curia/pontifical_councils/chrstuni/ documents/rc_pc_chrstuni_doc_16031998_shoah_en.html; and http://www. vatican.va/roman_curia/congregations/cfaith/pcb_documents/rc_con_cfaith _doc_20020212_popolo-ebraico_en.html.

6. For a recent and influential discussion of these issues, see the articles in Cunningham, *The Catholic Church and the Jewish People*.

Epilogue

Toward the Future

Celia M. Deutsch

Is there a future for Catholic-Jewish relations? Such was the question that preoccupied León Klenicki at the end of his long life and prompted this project. With him, the authors of this collection respond "yes." Decades of hard work have brought us to the point of standing together before God, in recognition of each other and of the Other, in mutual respect and openness, each giving and receiving. The degree to which the experience of dialogue would be mutually transforming was perhaps unforeseen during the years of crafting *Nostra Aetate*. To be sure, the Council's declaration was the result of the experience of the Shoah and of Catholics beginning to confront its harsh reality. It was also the result of Jews' willingness to risk the possibilities of new relationships. In addition, *Nostra Aetate* was the fruit of decades of biblical scholarship, and of the beginnings of Christian exploration of Jewish sources of the Second Temple and rabbinic periods, and Jews' exploration of the New Testament and early Christian sources. We had begun to know Jesus in a new way. Old assumptions about the Hebrew Scriptures, about early Judaism, and about Jesus' relation to his tradition were already changing, in some measure because of conversations between Christian and Jewish scholars. Transformation had already begun.[1]

The results of that transformative process are evident in the articles presented here. Jews and Catholics do not simply learn *about* each other, as important as that is. We turn to one another for resources in understanding *ourselves* and our traditions. New ways of relating to each other help us to understand differently the resources of the past, and to draw on them for further conversation. Eskenazi guides readers of both traditions to look to the sacred text of the Hebrew Bible for resources for dialogue. Nanko-Fernandez and Ruiz

224

enter into a dialogue with a medieval text that León loved, not only as a means of conversation with the text of the Hebrew Bible, but with Jews and Catholics of fifteenth-century Spain and today, including León himself. Henrix brings the traditional teaching of Chalcedon into conversation with Jewish thinkers Michael Wyschogrod and Emmanuel Levinas, thereby articulating fresh understandings for reflecting on the particularity of the Incarnation. And Gregerman turns to two Catholic theologians for insights into the nature of paradox that will offer new possibilities for considering the question of theodicy in the face of the Shoah.

Institutionally, the Catholic Church continues to pose the question of Christology for our reflection. As Cardinal Kurt Koch, President of the Pontifical Council for Promoting Christian Unity and the Commission for Religious Relations with the Jews, reminds us, there remains the "highly complex theological question how the Christian belief in the universal salvific significance of Jesus Christ can coherently be conceptually combined with the equally clear conviction of faith in the never-revoked covenant of God with Israel."[2] He refers to the project *Christ Jesus and the Jewish People Today*, initiated by the Commission for Religious Relations with the Jews. Cardinal Koch cites Cardinal Walter Kasper, his predecessor: "We are only standing at the threshold of a new beginning. Many exegetical, historical and systematical questions are still open and there will presumably always be such questions."[3] This reality is evident in official dialogues engaging questions, such as "Sources of Authority in Catholicism and Judaism" (May 24, 2011, USCCB and NCS),[4] and the presentation of Judaism and Christianity in one another's religious education materials and programs (January 19, 2012, USCCB and NCS).[5]

The opening words of section 4 of *Nostra Aetate* introduce the document's consideration of the Church's relationship to the Jewish people: "As the sacred synod searches into the mystery of the Church, it remembers the bond that spiritually ties the people of the New Covenant to Abraham's stock."[6] These words place Christian-Jewish relations at the heart of the Church's understanding of its own identity. *Nostra Aetate* speaks of that identity as "mystery," suggesting a never-ending quest for what is ultimately only revealed by God. As Gordis and Phan remind us, "We seek to understand more about ourselves and our world than we can possibly comprehend. Our reach exceeds our grasp."[7]

The search into mystery suggests that Catholic-Jewish relations —as is true of all forms of ecumenical, interfaith, and interreligious dialogue—is a matter of spiritual experience. The word *mystery* invites us into the contemplative depth of God, of our traditions, and the vast space opened up by the process of encounter and conversation. That contemplative depth is engaged in individual spiritual practices, as Barnes and Green tell us. But the experience of the Absolute is collective as well as personal, as they also suggest. It encompasses the transformative personal practices of prayer and meditation *and* listening to a Word revealed in our communities in the context of study and communal worship. Catholic-Jewish dialogue can model ways in which interiority and religious practice, personal and collective, take the practitioner beyond the community's established boundaries to engage others as partners in encounter with the Divine, in care of humankind and of the earth itself.

This "going beyond" is described in another context as the "third desert," suggesting a vast and difficult landscape, one filled with risk and possibility.[8] That landscape challenges previous modes of self-understanding, sometimes provoking internal as well as intergroup debate, as Lander observes in her discussion of Jewish identity and her analysis of the controversy surrounding the study document "Reflections on Covenant and Mission" and the subsequent documents by the USCCB.

The "third desert" of dialogue also requires that we examine previous understandings of liturgical practice. Liturgy presents a particular challenge because, in collective rituals, a community enacts and is transformed by that which it remembers. The tragic history of Holy Week practice indicates how liturgy can create ways of memorializing the past. However, the experience of *dialogue*, of encountering the religious other, has already begun to create new ways of remembering and interpreting our histories and traditions, as Langer demonstrates in her reflection on remembering and blotting out, and Cunningham suggests in his imagining a reinstatement of the Feast of the Circumcision of Jesus.

Today, at the beginning of the twenty-first century, the move toward the future in Catholic-Jewish relations opens onto a broad, non-European horizon, as some of our authors tell us (Hidalgo, Cohn,

Groppe, Gordis and Phan, Ruiz and Nanko-Fernandez). Recent decades—the decades since the promulgation of *Nostra Aetate*, the decades since León first began his work—have seen a dramatic shift in the demographics of the Roman Catholic Church, as of other Christian denominations. The majority of Christians, including Roman Catholics, now live in the global south and the east (Africa, Latin America, and Asia). And because of immigration, many of the Catholics in the global north are actually from the south and, to a lesser extent, the east. The Church is thus no longer predominantly a population dominated by Europeans or people of European descent. The global south is in the global north, and in some places east and west have converged.

Conversations between Jews and Catholics in official dialogue contexts, however, are often still dominated by Europeans and people of European descent. Perhaps one of the most difficult challenges facing Christian-Jewish dialogue is expanding the circle to include people from other contexts. Catholic-Jewish dialogue has a history in several Latin American countries, such as Argentina, Brazil, Uruguay, Costa Rica, and Mexico. Each of these countries gives its own particular character to Catholic-Jewish relations in its context. One thinks, for example, of El Salvador, where members of the tiny Jewish community work together for peace and justice with Roman Catholics, Protestants, Muslims, and others in *Religiones por la Paz*.[9] And Roman Catholics as well as Protestants collaborate with Jews and others in the Confraternidad Argentina Judeo Cristiana.[10]

Roman Catholicism is a majority religion in Mexico, and Central and South America. However, that is not the case in Asia and Africa. Each location brings its own character to a dialogue that is marginal to the consciousness of most, even among the theological elite. In 2006, the ILC (International Catholic-Jewish Liaison Committee) held a conference in Cape Town, South Africa, titled "Dignifying the Divine Image: Jewish and Catholic Perspectives on Health Care with Special Reference to the HIV/AIDS Pandemic."[11] This conversation brought together theologians and religious and political leaders from South Africa as well as from abroad.

In the twenty-first-century context, Catholic-Jewish dialogue will mean conversation *in* the global south with people living in countries where Jewish communities are either tiny or nonexistent.[12] It will also mean assuring a significant presence of partners from non-western and non-northern regions in the conversations of official international dialogues, such as those represented by the ILC.[13] It will require learning to engage in conversation with partners for whom the questions of the legacy of the Shoah and the survival of the State of Israel are secondary, and whose primary concerns are not those of Catholic-Jewish relations or interreligious dialogue, but of poverty and hunger, war and violence in their own lands.[14]

Catholic-Jewish dialogue will need to reach beyond the current bounds of Latin-Rite Catholicism to include Catholics of the Eastern Rites (Melkite, Maronite, Greek, Ukrainian, Coptic, Ethiopian, and so on), many of whom live in countries where interfaith and interreligious relations are sometimes tense and even hostile. The words of Melkite Archbishop Cyril Bustros at the Special Synod of Bishops for the Middle East and the ensuing controversy, suggest that *Nostra Aetate* and subsequent developments have not found a home in some quarters of those communities.[15] The parameters of the conversation will be transformed in the process of being extended in the new global context.

In the north, inclusion means immigrants from Latin America, as well as Africa and Asia. Latin American immigrants include indigenous people, in addition to those whose ancestors have actually been in the Americas since the fifteenth or sixteenth century, whether through Spanish and Portuguese colonialism or the slave trade, and others of whom are newly arrived. For new immigrants, as for those in the Churches of the global south, the questions of Christian-Jewish relations are simply not on the agenda. Rather, their immediate concerns often focus on matters of immigration status, employment, housing and food, and education of children. All of this is complicated by the fact that, while many recent immigrants have never met Jews before coming to the United States, they may carry with them traditional forms of theological anti-Judaism that are the legacy of a colonial past[16] or of more recent European influences.[17] Immigrants from Central and South America also bring with them the associations of "Israel" with both the United States and with the contemporary State of Israel, both of which played major roles in supporting dictatorships in many countries of those regions.[18]

There are also challenges in professional and theological circles. Many Latin American, Asian, and African theologians, as well as theologians from the north and west, use the tools of liberation theology to articulate their religious self-understanding. Liberation theologies provide effective tools of doing contextual theology. However, they sometimes use an inadequately understood "Judaism" as the "opponent" to Jesus who liberates people, particularly women, the poor, the oppressed, and those marginalized from oppressive religious and political structures. In so doing, these analyses can reinscribe colonial anti-Jewish categories.[19] In recent years, conversations have opened between Christian and Jewish scholars to address these challenges.

The agendas differ, providing challenges that require conversation partners to open themselves to the concerns of the other, and perhaps to understand their own assumptions, questions, and positions in new ways. The future of Jewish-Catholic relations will challenge participants to find ways to relate to broader populations than in the past. What will it mean, what will it "look like" to engage the theological questions, the questions of spirituality enriched by the collaboration of these new partners? It will bring further transformation in ways that are tentatively suggested by some of our authors, even as we continue to live dialogically, sensitive to the profound questions of language, whether that be the language of foundational texts or of ongoing conversations, as Gordis and Phan note. Continuing transformation will result in new levels of awareness for all involved. For those from the north and west, it will require learning the realities of living with hunger, war, dictatorship, and violence. It will imply that Jews and Christians learn to be present to ways of being in the world that do not interpret Judaism or Christian as central. For those from the east and global south, whether living in their countries or in the north and west, it will require acknowledging the ongoing trauma of the Shoah, and the sense of profound vulnerability Jews often experience in relation to Israel. It will also require learning new ways of interpreting the biblical texts, both the Hebrew Bible and the New Testament.[20]

This future has already begun. Indeed, in the more general context of Christian-Jewish dialogue, broadly based conversations have been taking place for some time, as is evident in the conferences held in Nairobi in 1986, Hong Kong in 1992, Cochin in 1993, Johannesburg in 1995, Yaoundé in 2001, and Buenos Aires in 2006.[21] Cohn's article notes the "Comunidades y Convivencia" conference at Catholic Theological Union in Chicago in 2007. And the Episcopal Divinity School (Cambridge, MA) recently sponsored a conference,

"What Would It Take to Move the Map: Abrahamic Traditions on the Silk Road."[22]

The global nature of these dialogues is at the same time daunting and exciting, filled with possibility and challenge. Why, one wonders, have important conferences in Asia, Africa, and Latin America gone so widely unnoted in the west and in the global north? We in the north and west assume that our insights and discoveries help to prompt the efforts of dialogue in the global south and east. But do we allow sufficiently these projects to inform *our* work in the north and west? Moreover, the ecumenical nature of such programs underscores the reality that, while we must acknowledge the particularities of relations between Jews and Roman Catholics, that relationship has its broader framework in the totality of the Christian communion.

This new global context for Jewish-Catholic relations expands the circle of conversation in intercultural, ecumenical, and interreligious ways. In the context of recent decades, we are impelled to consider this relationship as inseparable from a global interreligious dialogue, first in relation to Islam and then to Hinduism, Buddhism, Confucianism, and Daoism, as well as to local traditional religions. It is not simply that all of us inhabit the same planet. Globalization and mass migration have made us neighbors in the north and west. Certainly, relationships between these traditions have their own distinctive characteristics. However, in this twenty-first-century reality it would seem to be imperative that we engage in the smaller conversations always with a mind to the broader framework.

This is already happening, among specialists and in grassroots circles, as a glance at websites, such as that of *The Interfaith Observer* would suggest.[23] In recent years, the ICCJ has included the "Abrahamic Forum" for conversation between Christians, Jews, and Muslims, and its Young Leadership Council includes members of all three traditions. The Center for the Study of Jewish-Christian-Muslim Relations at Merrimack College (North Andover, MA)[24] and the Milstein Center for Interreligious Dialogue[25] represent new initiatives to broaden the conversation. The Interfaith Center of New York is a center of adult learning that serves the people of New York in the context of global religious traditions. The Elijah Institute focuses on spiritual practice, and has offices in Israel, Asia, North America, Europe, and Great Britain. It convenes gatherings of spiritual leaders of the world's religions. The Lassalle-Haus Bad Schönbrunn Center, a Catholic spirituality center in Switzerland, focuses on spiritual practice in the context of global religions, including Judaism.[26]

The Interfaith Youth Corps, founded in the United States is interreligious, bringing together youth in dialogue and service.[27] In a very different context, in the midst of ongoing conflict, the Interreligious Coordinating Council in Israel seeks to foster reconciliation through the religious traditions of the land of Israel, Judaism, Christianity, and Islam.[28] The Interfaith Encounter Association brings together Jews, Christians (Protestants, Catholics, Orthodox), and Muslims in dozens of small groups throughout Israel and the West Bank in ongoing exchange in the conviction that "religion can and should be a source of the solution for the conflicts that exist in the region and beyond."[29]

All of this would appear to have led us far from the focus on theology and spirituality that León asked be the focus of *Toward the Future*. This is not the case. Rather, we have turned to the expanding contexts that are becoming the new framework for Catholic-Jewish relations. These broader contexts, as do the articles in this volume, remind us that Catholic-Jewish relations, as well as ecumenical, interfaith, and interreligious dialogue develop in multiple forms.

Honoring León's wishes, this volume focuses on the "dialogue of theological exchange" and "the dialogue of religious experience," in the words of "Dialogue and Proclamation." However, our authors show that the realities of Catholic-Jewish relations cannot be confined to a single form or forms. Rather, these new forms of relationship converge and intersect, so that a Catholic theologian is led to reflect on the Church and the Jewish people as people of God even as her university's Jewish chaplain and Catholic colleagues worked together for "the redemption of the world" in bringing two Haitian children to a new family and in sending an interfaith group of students to Guatemala on a medical mission.

"Is there a future for Catholic-Jewish relations?" León Klenicki asked at the end of his life. We, his colleagues and friends, can say that there is indeed a future for more inclusive ways of relating and work that has only begun. We are convinced that we can walk together in the quest for the Absolute, caring for our planet and working to create a more just society. Our journey together will continue to bring all of us into a deeper relationship with our own traditions even as we encounter the ways of others.

NOTES

1. See John Connelly, *From Enemy to Brother: The Revolution in Catholic Teaching on the Jews, 1933–1965* (Cambridge, MA, and London, England: Harvard University Press, 2012), 210–38.

2. See http://www.ccjr.us/dialogika-resources/documents-and-statements/roman-catholic/kurt-cardinal-koch/1116-koch2012may16.

3. Walter Cardinal Kasper, "Foreword," in *Christ Jesus and the Jewish People Today: New Explorations of Theological Interrelationships*, ed. Philip A. Cunningham et al. (Grand Rapids, MI, and Cambridge, UK: William B. Eerdmans, 2011), xiv.

4. May 24, 2011, USCCB and NCS; http://old.usccb.org/comm/archives/2011/11-109.shtml.

5. "Jewish-Catholic Dialogue Studies How Religious Identities are Presented in Textbooks"; and NCS; http://www.ccjr.us/dialogika-resources/documents-and-statements/interreligious/bceia-ncs/1097-bceia-ncs2012jan19.

6. See http://www.ccjr.us/dialogika-resources/documents-and-statements/roman-catholic/second-vatican-council/293-nostra-aetate. The Latin text reads: *Mysterium Ecclesiae perscrutans, Sacra haec Synodus meminit vinculi, quo populus Novi Testamenti cum stirpe Abrahae spiritualiter coniunctus est.* See http://www.vatican.va/archive/hist_councils/ii_vatican_council/documents/vat-ii_decl_19651028_nostra-aetate_lt.html.

7. "Catholics and Jews: Looking Ahead."

8. Fabrice Blée, *The Third Desert: The Story of Monastic Interreligious Dialogue*, trans. William Skudlarek with Mary Grady (Collegeville, MN: Liturgical Press, 2004).

9. See http://www.webislam.com/noticias/51405-consejo_de_religiones_por_la_paz_cumple_dos_anos_en_el_salvador.html.

10. See http://confraternidadjc.blogspot.com/.

11. See http://www.bc.edu/dam/files/research_sites/cjl/texts/cjrelations/resources/documents/interreligious/ILC_joint_communique_06.htm.

12. See, for example, Hans Ucko, ed., *People of God, Peoples of God: A Jewish-Christian Conversation in Asia* (Geneva: WCC Publications, 1996); Jean Halpérin and Hans Ucko, eds., *Worlds of Memory and Wisdom; Encounters of Jews and African Christians* (Geneva: WCC Publications, 2006).

13. See http://www.reuters.com/article/2011/03/02/us-religion-dialogue-catholic-jewish-idUSTRE7216R120110302.

14. See the response of Musimbi Kanyoro to Amy-Jill Levine's article, "The Disease of Postcolonial New Testament Studies and the Hermeneutics of Healing," *Journal of Feminist Studies in Religion* 20

(2004): 91–99. Kanyoro's response can be found on pp. 106–11 in "Roundtable Discussion: Anti-Judaism and Postcolonial Biblical Interpretation," *JFSR* 20 (2004): 91–132.

15. See http://www.ccjr.us/dialogika-resources/themes-in-todays-dialogue/isrpal/896-bustros2010nov1.

16. See, for example, Richard C. Trexler, *Reliving Golgotha: The Passion Play of Iztapalapa* (Cambridge, MA, and London: Harvard University Press, 2003).

17. Jean-Pierre Ruiz, *Readings from the Edges: The Bible and People on the Move* (Maryknoll, NY: Orbis, 2011), 17–23.

18. See Judith Laikin Elkin, *The Jews of Latin America*, rev. ed. (Ann Arbor: University of Michigan Library, 2010), 230–50.

19. See a summary of the issues and bibliography in "Roundtable Discussion: Anti-Judaism and Postcolonial Biblical Interpretation," *Journal of Feminist Studies in Religion* 20 (2004): 91–132; also John T. Pawlikowski, *Christ in the Light of the Christian-Jewish Dialogue* (New York and Ramsey, NJ: Paulist Press, 1982); S. Heschel, "Anti-Judaism in Christian Feminist Theology," *Tikkun*, May/June, 1990, 25, 28, 95–97; Kwok Pui-Lan, "Jewish-Christian Dialogue in the Non-Western World," http://www.iccj.org/redaktion/upload_pdf/201207091629340.Kwok%20Pui%20Lan.pdf; *Postcolonial Imagination and Feminist Theology* (Louisvile, KY: Westminster John Knox Press, 2005), 92–99; Mary Boys, *Has God Only One Blessing? Judaism as a Source of Christian Self-Understanding* (New York and Mahwah, NJ: Stimulus Books/Paulist Press, 2000), 13–14, 135; Peter C. Phan, *Being Religious Interreligiously*, esp. chap. 10, "Jews and Judaism in Light of the *Catechism of the Catholic Church*: On the Way to Reconciliation," pp. 147–60, and chap. 11, "The Holocaust: Reflections from the Perspective of Asian Liberation Theology," 161–85.

20. Phan, *Being Religious*, chap. 11.

21. Kwok Pui-Lan, "Jewish-Christian Dialogue in the Non-Western World," ICCJ, Manchester UK, July 4, 2012, http://www.iccj.org/redaktion/upload_pdf/201207091629340.Kwok%20Pui%20Lan.pdf; https://www.bc.edu/dam/files/research_sites/cjl/texts/cjrelations/resources/documents/interreligious/Argentina_17May06.htm; Ucko, *Worlds of Memory and Wisdom*.

22. See http://99brattle.blogspot.com/2012/02/what-would-it-take-to-move-map.html (accessed September 1, 2012).

23. See http://theinterfaithobserver.org/.

24. See http://www.merrimack.edu/academics/jcr/jewish_christian_relations/.

25 See http://www.jtsa.edu/Academics/Registrar/Academic_Bulletin/AB_Milstein_Center_for_Interreligious_Dialogue.xml.

26. See http://www.lassalle-haus.org/.

27. See http://www.ifyc.org/. See also Eboo Patel and Patrice Brodeur, eds., *Building the Interfaith Youth Movement: Beyond Dialogue to Action* (Lanham, Boulder, New York, Toronto, Oxford: Rowman and Littlefield Publishers, Inc., 2006).

28. See http://www.icci.co.il/.

29. See http://interfaithencounter.wordpress.com/. These groups vary; there are women's groups, as well as groups for children, students, Arabic speakers, and so on. Particularly in the north, they include Druze.

Select Bibliography of the Work of León Klenicki

Eugene J. Fisher

León Klenicki en español

Klenicki, León. *Celebración de la Pascua*. Buenos Aires, Argentina: Ediciones Paulinas, 1984.

————. *Hagadá de Pesaj*. New York: Bloch Publishing Company, 1981.

————. *Haggadah de Pesaj*. Buenos Aires, Argentina: Congregacion Emanu-El, 1969.

————. *Libro de Oraciones*. Buenos Aires, Argentina: Congregación Emanu-El, 1973.

Klenicki, León, ed. *La Fe de Israel: Vivencias de Dios en el Judaismo*. Buenos Aires, Argentina: Olam Seguros, 1979.

Klenicki, León et al. *De Dios, el Hombre y la Vida, Comentarios de la Biblia Hebrea y del Nuevo Testamento*. Buenos Aires: Manrice Zago Ediciones, 1995.

Klenicki, León, and Eugene J. Fisher. *El Judaísmo Rabínico y los Comienzos del Cristianismo*. Medellín: Revista Medellín, 1988.

————. *Juan Pablo II y el Judaismo, Compilacion 1979–1987*. Buenos Aires, Argentina: Ediciones Paulinas, 1988.

Klenicki, León, and Roberto Graetz. *Mahsor: Libro de Oraciones para las Altas Fiestas*. Buenos Aires, Argentina: Congregación Emanu-El, 1969.

León Klenicki in English

Boadt, Lawrence, Helga Croner, and Rabbi León Klenicki, eds. *Biblical Studies: Meeting Ground of Jews and Christians*. New York: Paulist Press/A Stimulus Book, 1980.

Croner, Helga, and León Klenicki, eds. *Issues in the Jewish-Christian Dialogue: Jewish Perspectives on Covenant, Mission and Witness*. New York: Paulist Press/A Stimulus Book, 1979.

Dulles, Avery, León Klenicki, and Edward Idris Cassidy. *The Holocaust, Never to Be Forgotten: Reflections on the Holy See's Document*. New York and Mahwah, NJ: Paulist Press/A Stimulus Book, 2001.

Fisher, Eugene J., and León Klenicki. *A Challenge Long Delayed: The Diplomatic Exchange between the Holy See and the State of Israel*. New York: Anti-Defamation League (hereafter, ADL), 1996.

———. *On the Death of Jesus: Jewish and Christian Interpretations*. New York: ADL and United States Conference of Catholic Bishops, 2001.

Fisher, Eugene J., and León Klenicki, eds. *A New Millennium: From Dialogue to Reconciliation, Christian and Jewish Reflections*. New York: ADL, 1999.

———. *In Our Times: The Flowering of Jewish-Catholic Dialogue*. New York: Paulist Press/Stimulus Book, 1990.

———. *The Saint for Shalom: How Pope John Paul II Transformed Catholic-Jewish Relations: The Complete Texts 1979–2005*. A Publication of the Anti-Defamation League. New York: Crossroad Publishing Company, 2011.

———. *Spiritual Pilgrimage: Pope John Paul II, Texts on Jews and Judaism, 1979–1995*. New York: Crossroad Herder and ADL, 1995 (Winner of National Jewish Book Award).

Klenicki, León. "Dabru Emet: une appréciation personnelle." *Théologiques* 11 (2003): 171–86.

———. "Ecclesia et Synagoga: Judaism and Christianity: A Reflection toward the Future." *Central Conference of American Rabbis Journal* 52 (Spring 2005): 18–28.

———. *The New Oberammergau Passion Play's Script: The Year 2000 Presentation*. New York: ADL, 2000.

———. "The Theology of Liberation: A Latin American Jewish Experience." *American Jewish Archives Journal* 35 (1983): 27–39.

Klenicki, León, ed. *The Passover Celebration: A Haggadah for the Seder*. Introduction by Gabe Huck. New York: The Anti-Defamation League of B'nai B'rith and the Liturgy Training Program of the Archdiocese of Chicago, 1980.

———. *People of God, Peoples of God: A World Council of Churches' Consultation on the Church and the Jewish People, Budapest, October 15–21, 1994*. New York: ADL and The Consultation on the Church and the Jewish People, 1996.

———. *Toward a Theological Encounter: Jewish Understandings of Christianity*. New York: Paulist Press/A Stimulus Book, 1991.

Klenicki, León, and Myra Cohen, eds. *The Passover Celebration: A Haggadah for the Seder*. Chicago: Liturgy Training Publications and ADL, 2000.

Klenicki, León, and Eugene J. Fisher. *Root and Branches: Biblical Judaism, Rabbinic Judaism and Early Christianity*. Winona, MN: Saint Mary's Press, 1987.

Klenicki, León, and Gabe Huck, eds. *Spirituality and Prayer: Jewish and Christian Understandings*. New York: Paulist Press/A Stimulus Book, 1983.

Klenicki, León, and Dennis McManus. *Matthew 23:13–33. A Commentary by Rabbi Leon Klenicki and Professor Dennis McManus*. New York: ADL, 2000.

Klenicki, León, and Richard John Neuhaus. *Believing Today: Jew and Christian in Conversation*. Grand Rapids, MI: Eerdmans Publishing Co., 1989.

Klenicki, León, and Bruce Robbins. "Building New Bridges in Hope." in *A Commentary on the United Methodist Statement on Christian-Jewish Relations*. New York: ADL, 1999.

Klenicki, León, and Franklin Sherman. *Towards a New Day in Jewish-Lutheran Relations*. New York: ADL and Evangelical Lutheran Church in America, 1999.

Klenicki, León, and Geoffrey Wigoder, eds. *A Dictionary of the Jewish-Christian Dialogue*. New York and Mahwah, NJ: Paulist Press/A Stimulus Book, 1991.

Stravinskas, Peter, and León Klenicki. *A Catholic Jewish Encounter*. Huntington, IN: Our Sunday Visitor Publishing Division, 1994.

For Further Reading

Sacred Scripture

Abrami, Leo Michel. "Were All the Pharisees 'Hypocrites'?" *Journal of Ecumenical Studies* 47 (2012): 427–35.

Barnes, Michael. "Reading Other Texts: Intratextuality and the Logic of Scripture." *Journal of Ecumenical Studies* 46 (2011): 389–410.

Bishops' Committee for Ecumenical and Interreligious Affairs. *The Bible, the Jews and the Death of Jesus: A Collection of Catholic Documents*. U.S. Conference of Catholic Bishops, 2004.

Boadt, Lawrence. *Reading the Old Testament: An Introduction*. 2nd ed. New York and Mahwah, NJ: Paulist Press, 2012.

Boys, Mary. *Has God Only One Blessing? Judaism as a Source of Christian Self-Understanding*. New York and Mahwah, NJ: Paulist Press/ Stimulus Books, 2000.

Cook, Michael. *Modern Jews Engage the New Testament*. Woodstock, VT: Jewish Lights, 2008.

Ford, David F. "An Interfaith Wisdom: Scriptural Reasoning between Jews, Christians and Muslims." *Modern Theology* 22 (2006): 345–66.

Garber, Zev, ed. *The Jewish Jesus: Revelation, Reflection, Reclamation*. West Lafayette, IN: Purdue University Press, 2011.

Griffiths, Paul. *Religious Reading: The Place of Reading in the Practice of Religion*. New York: Oxford University, 1999.

Harrington, Daniel J., Alan J. Avery-Peck, and Jacob Neusner, eds. *When Judaism and Christianity Began: Essays in Memory of Anthony J. Saldarini*. Leiden and Boston: Brill, 2004.

Jenson, Robert, and Eugene Korn. *Covenant and Hope: Christian and Jewish Reflections*. Grand Rapids, MI: Eerdmans Publ., 2012.

Kasper, Walter. "The Relation of the Old and the New Covenant as One of the Central Issues in Jewish-Christian Dialogue," Cambridge, UK, December 6, 2004. See www.bc.edu/dam/files/research_sites/cjl/texts/ cjrelations/resources/articles/Kasper_Cambridge_6Dec04.htm.

Kepnes, Steven. "A Handbook for Scriptural Reasoning." *Modern Theology* 22 (2006): 367–83.

Knowles, Melody D., John T. Pawlikowski, Esther Menn, and Timothy J. Sandoval, eds. *Contesting Texts: Jews and Christians in Conversation about the Bible*. Minneapolis, MN: Fortress, 2007.

Levine, Amy-Jill, and Marc Zvi Brettler, eds. *The Jewish Annotated New Testament, New Revised Standard Version Bible Translation*. New York: Oxford University Press, 2011.

Madigan, Kevin, and Jon Levenson. *Resurrection: The Power of God for Christians and Jews*. New Haven, CT, and London: Yale University Press, 2008.

Ochs, Peter, ed. *The Return to Scripture in Judaism and Christianity: Essays in Post-Critical Interpretation*. New York and Mahwah, NJ: Paulist Press, 1993.

Oldenhage, Tania. *Parables for Our Time: Rereading New Testament Scholarship after the Holocaust*. Oxford: Oxford University Press, 2002.

Pontifical Biblical Commission. *The Jewish People and their Sacred Scriptures in the Christian Bible*. Vatican City, 2001. See http://www.vatican.va/roman_curia/congregations/cfaith/pcb_documents/rc_con_cfaith_doc_20020212_popolo-ebraico_en.html.

Reinhartz, Adele. *Befriending the Beloved Disciple: A Jewish Reading of the Gospel of John*. New York: Continuum, 2001.

Ruiz, Jean-Pierre. "The Bible and U.S. Hispanic American Theological Discourse: Lessons from a Non-Innocent History." In *From the Heart of Our People: Latino/a Explorations in Catholic Systematic Theology*. Edited by Orlando O. Espin and Miguel H. Diaz, 100–120. Maryknoll, NY: Orbis Books, 1999.

Vermes, Geza. *Christian Beginnings: From Nazareth to Nicaea (AD 30–325)*. New Haven, CT: Yale University Press, 2013.

Theology, Identity, and Dialogue

Baima, Thomas A., ed. *A Legacy of Catholic-Jewish Dialogue: The Joseph Cardinal Bernardin Lectures*. Chicago IL: Liturgy Training Publications, 2012.

Banki, Judith H., and John T. Pawlikowski. *Ethics in the Shadow of the Holocaust: Christian and Jewish Perspectives*. Franklin, WI, and Chicago: Sheed & Ward, 2002.

Barnes, Michael. *Theology and the Dialogue of Religions*. Esp. chapters 2 ("Remembering the Covenant," pp. 29–64) and 3 ("Facing the Other," pp. 65–96). Cambridge, UK: Cambridge University Press, 2002.

Batnitzky, Leora Faye. *How Judaism Became a Religion: An Introduction to Modern Jewish Thought*. Princeton, NJ: Princeton University Press, 2011.

Bayfield, Tony, Sidney Brichto, and Eugene Fisher. *He Kissed Him and They Wept: Towards a Theology of Jewish-Catholic Partnership*. London: SCM Press, 2012.

Bemporad, Jack, John Pawlikowski, and Joseph Sievers. *Good and Evil After Auschwitz: Ethical Implications for Today*. Hoboken, NJ: KTAV, 2001.

Braiterman, Zachary. *(God) After Auschwitz: Tradition and Change in Post-Holocaust Jewish Thought*. Princeton, NJ: Princeton University Press, 1998.

Brill, Alan. *Judaism and Other Religions: Models of Understanding*. New York: Palgrave-Macmillan, 2010.

Cohn-Sherbok, Dan, ed. *Holocaust Theology: A Reader*. New York: New York University Press, 2002.

Connelly, John. *From Enemy to Brother: The Revolution in Catholic Teaching on the Jews, 1933–1965*. Cambridge, MA: Harvard University Press, 2012.

Cunningham, Philip, Norbert Hofmann, and Joseph Sievers. *The Catholic Church and the Jewish People: Recent Reflections from Rome*. The Abrahamic Dialogue Series. New York: Fordham University Press, 2007.

Cunningham, Philip A., Joseph Sievers, Mary Boy, Hans Hermann Henrix, and Jesper Svartvik, eds. *Christ Jesus and the Jewish People Today: New Explorations of Theological Relationships*. Grand Rapids, MI, and London: William B. Eerdmans, 2011.

Feldman, Egal. *Catholics and Jews in Twentieth-Century America*. Urbana and Chicago, IL: University of Illinois Press, 2001.

Fisher, Eugene. *Memoria Futuri, Catholic-Jewish Dialogue Yesterday, Today and Tomorrow: Selected Texts and Addresses of Cardinal William H. Keeler*. New York and Mahwah, NJ: Paulist Press/Stimulus, 2012.

Fisher, Eugene, and León Klenicki, eds. *The Saint for Shalom: The Complete Texts and addresses of Pope John Paul II on Jews and Judaism, 1979–2005*. New York: Crossroad and Anti-Defamation League, 2011.

Fisher, Eugene, and Daniel Polish, eds. *Liturgical Foundations of Social Policy in the Catholic and Jewish Traditions*. Notre Dame, IN: University of Notre Dame Press, 1983.

Frederikson, Paula. *Augustine and the Jews: A Christian Defense of Jews and Judaism*. New Haven, CT: Yale University Press, 2010.

———. *Jesus of Nazareth King of the Jews*. New York: Random House/Vintage Books, 1999.

Frymer-Kensky, Tikva, David Novak, Peter Ochs, David Fox Sandmel, Michael A. Signer, eds. *Christianity in Jewish Terms*. Boulder, CO: Westview Press, 2000.

Goldstein, Phyllis. *A Convenient Hatred: The History of Antisemitism*. Brookline, MA: Facing History and Ourselves, 2012.

Greenberg, I. *For the Sake of Heaven and Earth: The New Encounter between Judaism and Christianity*. Philadelphia: Jewish Publication Society, 2004.

Grob, Leonard, and John K. Roth. *Encountering the Stranger: A Jewish-Christian-Muslim Trialogue*. Seattle, WA: University of Washington Press, 2012.

Halivni, David Weiss. *Breaking the Tablets: Jewish Theology after the Shoah*. Edited by Peter Ochs. Lanham, MD: Rowman and Littlefield, 2007.

Hoff, Gregor Maria. "A Realm of Differences: The Meaning of Jewish Monotheism for Christology and Trinitarian Theology." In *Christ Jesus and the Jewish People Today*, 202–20.

Katz, Steven T. *Post-Holocaust Dialogues: Critical Studies in Modern Jewish Thought*. New York and London: New York University Press, 1983.

Katz, Steven T., Shlomo Biderman, and Gershon Greenberg, eds. *Wrestling with God: Jewish Theological Responses during and after the Holocaust*. Oxford, UK and New York: Oxford University Press, 2006.

Kessler, Edward, and N. Wenbord, eds. *A Dictionary of Jewish-Christian Relations*. Cambridge, UK: Cambridge University Press, 2005.

———. *An Introduction to Jewish-Christian Relations*. Cambridge, UK: Cambridge University Press, 2010.

Kessler, E., J. K. Banki, and J. Pawlikowski, eds. *Jews and Christians in Conversation: Crossing Cultures and Generations*. Cambridge, UK: Orchard Academic, 2002.

Lamdan, Neville, and Alberto Melloni, eds. *Nostra Aetate: Origins, Promulgation, Impact on Jewish-Catholic Relations*. Berlin: LIT Verlag Dr. W. Hopf, 2007.

Levine, Amy-Jill. *The Misunderstood Jew: The Church and the Scandal of the Jewish Jesus*. San Francisco, CA: Harper, 2006.

Lux, Richard C. *The Jewish People, the Holy Land, and the State of Israel: A Catholic View*. New York and Mahwah, NJ: Paulist Press/Stimulus, 2010.

Merkle, John. *Faith Transformed: Christian Encounters with Jews and Judaism*. Collegeville, MN: Liturgical Press, 2003.

Phan, Peter C. *Being Religious Interreligiously: Asian Perspectives on Interfaith Dialogue*. Esp. chapters 10 ("Jews and Judaism in Light of the Catechism of the Catholic Church; on the Way to Reconciliation," pp. 147–60) and 11 ("The Holocaust: Reflections from the Perspective of Asian Liberation Theology," pp. 161–85). Maryknoll, NY: Orbis Books, 2004.

Ratzinger, Joseph. *Many Religions—One Covenant*. Translated by Graham Garrison. San Francisco: Ignatius Press, 1999.

Rittner, Carol. *Learn, Teach, Prevent: Holocaust Education in the 21st Century*. Greensburg, PA: Seton Hill University/National Catholic Center for Holocaust Education, 2010.

Rudin, James. *Christians and Jews: Faith to Faith, Tragic History, Promising Present, Fragile Future*. Woodstock, VT: Jewish Lights, 2011.

————. *Cushing, Spellman, O'Connor: The Surprising Story of How Three American Cardinals Transformed Catholic-Jewish Relations*. Grand Rapids, MI, and Cambridge, UK: William Eerdmans, 2012.

Saperstein, Marc. *Moments of Crisis in Jewish-Christian Relations*. Philadelphia: Trinity Press International, 1989.

Secretariat for Ecumenical and Interreligious Affairs, National Conference of Catholic Bishops. *Catholics Remember the Holocaust*. Washington, DC: U.S. Catholic Conference, 1998.

————. *Catholic Teaching on the Shoah: Implementing the Holy See's We Remember*. Washington, DC: United States Catholic Conference, 2001.

Sherman, Franklin, ed. *Bridges: Documents of the Christian-Jewish Dialogue; The Road to Reconciliation*. 2 vols. New York and Mahwah, NJ: Paulist Press/Stimulus, 2011, 2013.

Signer, Michael, and Hans-Peter Heinz, eds. *Coming Together for the Sake of God: Contributions to Jewish-Christian Dialogue from Post-Holocaust Germany*. Collegeville, MN: Liturgical Press, 2007.

Tilley, Terence. "Doing Theology in the Context of the Gift and the Promise of *Nostra Aetate*." *Studies in Christian-Jewish Relations* 6 (2011): 1–15.

Liturgy

Adams, William Seth. "Christian Liturgy, Scripture and the Jews: A Problematic in Jewish-Christian Relations." *Journal of Ecumenical Studies* 25 (1988): 39–55.

Bradshaw, Paul F., and Lawrence A. Hoffman, eds. *The Making of Jewish and Christian Worship*. Notre Dame, IN: University of Notre Dame, 1991.

Ferrone, Rita. "Anti-Jewish Elements in the Extraordinary Form." *Worship* 84 (2010): 498–513.

Fisher, Eugene, ed. *The Jewish Roots of Christian Liturgy*. New York: Paulist Press, 1990.

Gerdhards, Albert, and Clemens Leonhard, eds. *Jewish and Christian Liturgy and Worship: New Insights into Its History and Interaction*. Leiden and Boston: Brill, 2007.

Hoffman, Lawrence A., et al. *My People's Prayer Book: Traditional Prayers, Modern Commentaries*. 10 vols. Woodstock, VT: Jewish Lights, 1997–2007.

Katzoff, Binjamin. "'God of Our Fathers': Rabbinic Liturgy and Jewish-Christian Engagement." *Jewish Quarterly Review*, n.s. 3 (2009): 303–22.

Langer, Ruth. *Cursing the Christians? A History of the Birkat HaMinim*. Oxford UK: Oxford University Press, 2012.

———. "Liturgy in the Light of Jewish-Christian Dialogue." *Studies in Christian-Jewish Relations* 4 (2009). See http://ejournals.bc.edu/ojs/index.php/scjr/article/view/1541/.

———. "The Liturgical Parting(s) of the Ways: A Preliminary Foray." In *A Living Tradition: On the Intersection of Liturgical History and Pastoral Practice*. Edited by David A. Pitt, et al., 43–58. Collegeville MN: Liturgical Press, 2012.

Rashkover, Randi, and C. C. Pecknold, eds. *Liturgy, Time and the Politics of Redemption*. Grand Rapids, MI, and Cambridge, UK: William B. Eerdmans, 2006.

Saperstein, Marc. "Issues in Jewish Liturgy." In *Jews and Christians in Conversation*, 203–12.

Townsend, John T. *A Liturgical Interpretation in Narrative Form of the Passion of Jesus Christ*. New York: National Conference of Christians and Jews, 1985.

Tracey, Liam. "Adequate Words to Praise You: The Experience of Christian Worship at the Turn of the Millenium." In *Jews and Christians in Conversations*, 197–201.

Spirituality

Athans, Mary Christine. *The Jewish Mary: The Mother of Jesus in History, Theology and Spirituality*. Maryknoll, NY: Orbis Books, 2012.

Barnes, Michael, SJ. *Interreligious Learning: Dialogue, Spirituality and the Christian Imagination*. Cambridge, UK: Cambridge University Press, 2012.

Béthune, Pierre-François, OSB. *By Faith and Hospitality: The Monastic Tradition as a Model for Interreligious Encounter*. Translated by Dame Mary Groves, OSB. Leominster, UK: Gracewing, 2002.

Boys, Mary. "The Salutary Experience of Pushing Religious Boundaries: Abraham Joshua Heschel in Conversation with Michael Barnes." *Modern Judaism* 29 (2009): 16–26.

Klenicki, León, and Gabe Huck, eds. *Spirituality and Prayer: Jewish and Christian Understandings*. Stimulus: Studies in Judaism and Christianity. New York and Ramsey, NJ: Paulist Press, 1982.

Kushner, Lawrence. *Jewish Spirituality: A Brief Introduction for Christians*. Woodstock, NY: Jewish Lights, 2001.

Lourié, Basile, and Andrei A. Orlov, eds. *The Theophaneia School: Jewish Roots of Eastern Christian Mysticism*. Saint Petersburg: Byzantinorossica, 2007.

Moore, Donald, SJ. "An Ignatian Perspective on Contemporary Jewish Spirituality." In *Friends on the Way: Jesuits Encounter Contemporary Judaism*, 57–70. Edited by Thomas Michel, SJ. New York: Fordham University Press, 2007.

Rutishauser, Christian M. "The Goal of the Ignatian Exercises and Soloveitchik's Halakhic Spirituality," in *Friends on the Way*, 38–56.

Standaert, Benoît. *Sharing Sacred Space: Interreligious Dialogue as Spiritual Encounter*. Esp. chapter 1 ("Jesus and Judaism," pp. 1–37). Translated by William Skudlarek. Collegeville, MN: Liturgical Press, 2009.

Latino/a Catholic-Jewish Relations

Aquino, Maria Pilar, and Maria José Rosado-Nunes, eds. *Feminist Intercultural Theology: Latina Explorations for a Just World*. Maryknoll, NY: Orbis Books, 2007.

Fellous, Sonia. "Cultural Subversion: Text and Image in the Alba Bible, 1422–33." *Exemplaria* 12 (2000): 205–29.

———. "Les Rois et la Royauté dans la *biblia de Alba*." *Jewish History* 21 (2007): 69–95.

———. *Histoire de la Bible de Moïse Arragel, Tolède 1422–1433: quand un rabbin interprète la Bible pour les chrétiens*. Paris: Somogy, 2001.

Gutworth, Eleazar. "The Transmission of Rabbi Moses Arragel: Maqueda, Paris, London." *Sefarad* 63 (2003): 69–87.

Klenicki, León. "The Theology of Liberation: A Latin American Jewish Exploration." *American Jewish Archives Journal* 35 (1983): 27–39.

Kunin, Seth D. *Juggling Identities: Identity and Authenticity among the Crypto-Jews*. New York: Columbia University Press, 2009.

Laikin Elkins, Judith. *The Jews of Latin America*. Revised edition. New York: Homes and Meier, 2011.

Martínez-Vásquez, Hjamil A. *Latina/o y Musulmán: The Construction of Latina/o Identity among Latina/o Muslims in the United States*. Eugene, OR: Pickwick Publications, 2010.

Medina, Néstor. *Mestizaje: (Re)Mapping Race, Culture, and Faith in Latina/o Catholicism*. Studies in Latino/a Catholicism. Maryknoll, NY: Orbis Books, 2009.

Nanko-Fernandez, Carmen M. "Locating the Daily: *Lo cotidiano* as a Locus for Exploring Christian-Jewish Relations latinamente." *Apuntes* 29 (2009): 56–72.

————. *Theologizing en Espanglish: Context, Community and Ministry*. Maryknoll, NY: Orbis Books, 2007.

Rodríguez, Jeanette, and Ted Fortier. *Cultural Memory: Resistance, Faith, and Identity*. Austin, TX: University of Texas Press, 2007.

Ruiz, Jean-Pierre. "Beginning a Conversation: Unlikely *Hermanos*: Jews and Latino/as in the U.S." *Apuntes* 20 (2009): 44–55.

————. "From Disputation to Dialogue, Jews and Latino/as toward a New Convivencia." *New Theology Review* 22 (2009): 36–48.

Sainz de la Manza, Carlos. "Poder politico y poder doctrinal en la creación de la Biblia de Alba." *e-Spania* (June 3, 2007). See http://e-spania. revues.org/116.

Schonfield, Jeremy. "Biblia para la Concordia: La Biblia de Alba." *FMR* Edición española 4 (1992): 83–108.

Segovia, Fernando F. "Two Places and No Place on Which to Stand: Mixture and Otherness in Hispanic American Theology." *Listening* 27 (1992): 26–40.

Steinlight, Stephen, ed. *Latinos and Jews: Old Luggage, New Itineraries*. American Jewish Committee Publications, 2002. See http://www.pol icyarchive.org/handle/10207/bitstreams/12297.pdf.

Contributors

Judith Banki is Senior Advisor, Interreligious Affairs at the Tanenbaum Center for Interreligious Understanding in New York.

Rev. Michael Barnes, SJ, PhD, is Dean of Research Students and Professor of Interreligious Relations at Heythrop College, University of London, in Kensington.

Rabbi Hillel Cohn, DMin, is Rabbi Emeritus of Congregation Emanu El in San Bernardino, California.

Philip A. Cunningham, PhD, is Professor of Theology in the Department of Theology and Religious Studies and Director of the Institute for Jewish-Catholic Relations at St. Joseph University in Philadelphia.

Celia M. Deutsch, NDS, PhD, is Research Scholar in the Department of Religion at Barnard College/Columbia University in New York.

Tamara Cohn Eskenazi, PhD, is Professor of Bible at Hebrew Union College–Jewish Institute of Religion, in Los Angeles.

Eugene J. Fisher is Distinguished Professor of Catholic-Jewish Studies at Saint Leo University in Florida, and former Associate Director of the Secretariat for Ecumenical and Interreligious Affairs of the United States Conference of Catholic Bishops in Washington, DC.

Abraham H. Foxman is National Director of the Anti-Defamation League in New York.

Rabbi David Gordis, PhD, is Visiting Senior Scholar at the University at Albany of the State University of New York (SUNY), in Albany, New York, and President Emeritus of Hebrew College in Newton Centre, Massachusetts.

Rabbi Arthur Green, PhD, is Rector of the Rabbinical School and Professor of Philosophy and Religion at Hebrew College in Newton Centre, Massachusetts.

Rabbi Eric J. Greenberg is Director of Interreligious Affairs at the Anti-Defamation League in New York.

Adam Gregerman, PhD, is Assistant Professor in the Department of Theology and Religious Studies and Assistant Director of the Institute for Jewish-Catholic Relations at St. Joseph University in Philadelphia.

Elizabeth Groppe, PhD, is Associate Professor of Theology in the Department of Theology at Xavier University in Cincinnati, Ohio.

247

Hans Hermann Henrix, DPhil, is Honorary Professor of the University of Salzburg in the Centre for Intercultural Theology and the Study of Religion, and Director Emeritus of the Episcopal Academy of the Roman Catholic Diocese of Aachen, Germany.

Jacqueline Hidalgo, PhD, is Assistant Professor of Latina/o Studies and Religion at Williams College in Williamstown, Massachusetts.

William Cardinal Keeler, STL, is Archbishop Emeritus of Baltimore Maryland, and former moderator for Catholic-Jewish dialogue for the National Conference of Catholic Bishops and chairman of the Bishops' Committee for Ecumenical and Interreligious Affairs.

Rabbi Shira Lander, PhD, is the Anna Smith Fine Senior Lecturer of Jewish Studies at Rice University in Houston.

Rabbi Ruth Langer, PhD, is Professor of Jewish Studies and Associate Director of the Center for Christian-Jewish Learning in the Theology Department at Boston College in Chestnut Hill, Massachusetts.

Carmen M. Nanko-Fernández, DMin, is Associate Professor of Pastoral Ministry at the Catholic Theological Union in Chicago.

Rev. Peter C. Phan, STD, PhD, DD, is Professor of Catholic Social Thought in the Department of Theology at Georgetown University in Washington, DC.

Rabbi A. James Rudin is Senior Interreligious Advisor for The American Jewish Committee and Distinguished Visiting Professor of Religion and Judaica at Saint Leo University in Tampa, Florida.

Rev. Jean-Pierre Ruiz, PhD, is Associate Professor in the Department of Theology and Religious Studies at St. John's University in New York.

Rev. Peter Stravinskas, PhD, is Executive Director of the Catholic Education Foundation and serves on the faculties of Fordham University's School of Education in New York and the Maryvale Institute in Birmingham, England.

Index